THE EMPTY THRONE

THE EMPTY THRONE

AMERICA'S ABDICATION *of* GLOBAL LEADERSHIP

IVO H. DAALDER
&
JAMES M. LINDSAY

PUBLICAFFAIRS

NEW YORK

PublicAffairs
Hachette Book Group
1290 Avenue of the Americas, New York, NY 10104
www.publicaffairsbooks.com
@Public_Affairs

Printed in the United States of America

First Edition: October 2018

Published by PublicAffairs, an imprint of Perseus Books, LLC, a subsidiary of Hachette Book Group, Inc. The PublicAffairs name and logo is a trademark of the Hachette Book Group.

The Hachette Speakers Bureau provides a wide range of authors for speaking events. To find out more, go to www.hachettespeakersbureau.com or call (866) 376-6591.

The publisher is not responsible for websites (or their content) that are not owned by the publisher.

Print book interior design by Amnet Systems.

The Empty Throne

Library of Congress Cataloging in Publication Control Number: 2018028633

ISBNs: 978-1-5417-7385-1 (hardcover), 978-1-5417-7387-5 (ebook)

LSC-C

10 9 8 7 6 5 4 3 2 1

To our parents,
Hans Daalder and Annie Pauline Daalder–Neukircher
and
James H. Lindsay and Collette G. Lindsay, who witnessed the
cost of war and understood the value of American leadership.

One cannot rise to be in many ways the leading community in the civilized world without being involved in its problems, without being convulsed by its agonies and inspired by its causes. If this had been proved in the past as it had been, it will become indisputable in the future. The people in the United States cannot escape world responsibility.

Winston Churchill
September 1943

Contents

1

The Empty Throne

Room 2E924 in the outermost ring of the Pentagon was packed. Better known as "the Tank," it is one of the most secure facilities in the US government and the meeting place for the Joint Chiefs of Staff. On the morning of July 20, 2017, though, it hosted a special guest—the president of the United States. Gathered with Donald Trump in the small, windowless room was virtually everyone who was anyone dealing with foreign and national security policy: the vice president, cabinet secretaries, assorted White House advisers, and the chair and vice chair of the Joint Chiefs of Staff. They were there to provide Trump with a crash course on American global leadership.[1]

The long-scheduled visit was on the face of things unremarkable. Many presidents had traveled to the Tank to receive briefings and show their appreciation for America's service men and women. But Secretary of Defense James Mattis and Secretary of State Rex Tillerson had an ulterior motive in arranging Trump's trip that day. They believed that six months into his presidency he still had much to learn about the world and America's role in it. On the campaign trail he had repeatedly shown his ignorance about basic foreign policy issues, even as he castigated past administrations, Democratic and Republican alike, for what he called their catastrophic choices. Reaching the Oval Office hadn't miraculously given him a deeper grasp of global politics or a greater appreciation for the "lousy" deals and "stupid" commitments his predecessors had made. Instead, he resisted inconvenient facts, repeated urban legends, and contested the counsel his advisers offered. Perhaps a tutorial in the Tank on how and why the United States had pursued an outsized role around the world since World War II might persuade him that it was worth continuing to do so.

Mattis set the context for the meeting at the start. "The greatest thing the 'greatest generation' left us," the retired Marine four-star general said to open the briefing, "was the rules-based postwar international order."[2] The briefers then took Trump on a tour around the globe. Using maps, charts, and photos, they laid out America's far-flung overseas commitments. They reviewed alliances and trade deals, carefully explaining what challenges and opportunities the United States faced beyond its borders. To make their brief more compelling to a president who had made his fortune in real estate and who had committed his administration to bringing jobs back home, they stressed how America's global leadership benefitted US businesses and created jobs for Americans back home.

The student, though, eventually challenged his tutors. He wasn't impressed with the alliances and agreements they were praising. "This is exactly what I don't want," he objected.[3] He peppered them with questions. Why were US troops in South Korea? Why didn't America's free-trade agreements generate surpluses for the United States? Why didn't Europe pay its fair share for NATO? Why shouldn't the United States build up its nuclear stockpile? Some of the exchanges grew testy as the experts tried to persuade a president who thought he knew more than he did to adopt a worldview utterly foreign to his thinking. At several points Trump rebuked his briefers with a simple and direct rebuttal: "I don't agree!"[4]

When the meeting ended after two hours, Trump praised his briefers to the reporters waiting outside the Tank. The discussion had been "great" and the people at the Pentagon "tremendous," he said. "The job they do—absolutely incredible."[5] That didn't mean, however, that they had dented his deep skepticism about the value of America's military alliances and the benefits of its many trade agreements, let alone persuaded him to lead what he saw as ungrateful friends who laughed at America while stealing its jobs and wealth.

The July 20 meeting later gained fame for the pithy assessment Tillerson made of Trump's intelligence after the president left the Tank to return to the White House. He's a "fucking moron," the former Eagle Scout told a few colleagues. Tillerson's blunt assessment dominated Washington conversation when it leaked months later. But the more consequential assessment, even though it drew almost no attention, was the one Trump made in the Tank as the meeting ended: the rules-based world order that so captivated his briefers was "not working at all."[6]

The overriding question for America and the rest of the world was, would Trump try to fix it or walk away from it?

"I INHERITED A mess," Donald Trump complained repeatedly after becoming president.[7] The specific challenges he faced were easy to list. North Korea was gaining the capability to hit the United States with nuclear-armed missiles. A revanchist Russia was challenging American interests in the Middle East, sowing divisions in Europe, and interfering in US domestic politics. A rising China was looking to dominate Asia and rewrite the rules of global politics in its favor. An aggressive Iran was seeking regional hegemony in the Middle East. The Islamic State controlled parts of Iraq and Syria, inspiring jihadists around the globe. The list went on.

Underlying these problems, however, was a broader, more fundamental one: the world that the United States created in the aftermath of World War II and that Mattis and his colleagues explained to Trump in the Tank that July day was fracturing. Franklin Roosevelt and Harry Truman had wisely steered the United States away from repeating the grave error it had made in turning its back on Europe after World War I. Determined to chart a different course and confronted with a new mortal adversary in the Soviet Union, they defined America's interests globally and sought to lead other countries in creating a world that would be more conducive to US interests and values—and to countries that shared them. That world would be built on advancing collective security; opening free markets; and promoting democracy, human rights, and the rule of law.

It was a radical strategy. For millennia world politics had been driven by the logic of domination—"The strong do as they will; the weak suffer what they must," as the ancient Greeks put it. The United States could have done the same after 1945. It stood atop the world, towering over both its vanquished enemies and weary allies. But it didn't. It instead created a system based on the logic of cooperation—countries willing to follow America's lead would flourish, and as they did, so too would the United States. The country would do well by putting aside narrow nationalism and promoting a broader common good. "We could be the wealthiest and the most mighty nation," President Dwight Eisenhower later wrote, "and still lose the battle of the world if we do not help our world neighbors protect their freedom and advance their social and economic progress."[8]

The rules-based order never fully matched its founders' aspirations. Its reach was limited to the West throughout the Cold War. Large portions of the world lived under communist domination outside the order, and even more lived uneasily between the two. Cold War divisions, moreover, limited what the United Nations and other international institutions could do. The United States at times failed to live up to its lofty rhetoric as narrow interests trumped broader ones in its foreign policy choices. Human rights were often sacrificed to political expediency. And global leadership didn't guarantee good judgment, as the Bay of Pigs and the Vietnam War attested.

Yet even taking these failures into account, the American decision to lead the Free World after World War II was a historic success. Europe and Japan were rebuilt. The reach of democracy and human rights was extended. Most important, American leadership helped facilitate one of history's great geopolitical triumphs: the peaceful collapse of the Soviet Union. That in turn created the opportunity to extend the benefits of the American-led order well beyond the West. Washington believed it had discovered "the secret sauce" of national success and was eager to share it. Just as important, other capitals were eager to embrace Washington's guidance. Democracy was on the march. Global trade boomed. Hundreds of millions were lifted from abject poverty. For a moment it seemed that the world had reached the "end of history."[9]

But history didn't end. Even as the ambitions for what US foreign policy could achieve grew in the post–Cold War era and Americans became comfortable thinking of themselves as the "indispensable nation," the world they had created was unraveling. Great-power competition once thought dead began to revive. The rapid growth in the movement of goods, money, people, and ideas across borders—globalization, as it came to be called—produced more problems and at a faster rate than national governments could handle. International institutions seemed stuck in the Cold War, unable to grapple with these new transnational challenges. The Middle East was in turmoil, populism was rising, and terrorists were striking with seeming impunity around the globe. Two decades after the end of the Cold War, the optimism of a *Pax Americana* had given way, as Richard Haass aptly put it, to "a world in disarray."[10]

This disarray had multiple causes. Countries like Russia and Iran never accepted the premises of American global leadership or the world it sought to create, and they resented what they saw as the United States treading on their interests. They preferred traditional geopolitics, where they dominated their regional spheres of interest, and sought to return to it. Meanwhile, policy makers in Washington failed to see just how quickly their recipe of market economics and open trade would generate the "rise of the rest," as Fareed Zakaria described it, and didn't anticipate what it would mean for American leadership.[11] They hoped to get "responsible stakeholders" who would gradually take on more responsibilities while still deferring to Washington's lead.[12] They instead got countries that often preferred free riding on Washington's efforts or championing their own ideas for improvements to the rules-based order. Finally, Washington's own missteps and misjudgments undercut its leadership. The invasion of Iraq plunged the United States into an intractable Middle East maelstrom and sowed doubts about the wisdom of American leaders. The Great Recession of 2008–2009 threw into question Washington's recipe for success. Free markets and open trade suddenly looked to be the road to ruin rather than the path to success.

Saddled with the bitter harvest of the Iraq War and the Great Recession, Barack Obama came to office amid a growing realization within the foreign policy establishment that American global leadership needed to be adjusted and the rules-based order put on a more sustainable footing. Obama sought the answer in encouraging allies to do more, confronting a rising China with a "pivot" to Asia, and ostracizing a belligerent Russia. Whatever the merits of that strategy, it failed to produce quick results. Obama ended his presidency knowing that the job remained unfinished. "American leadership in this world really is indispensable," he wrote in a letter he left behind on the Resolute desk in the Oval Office for his successor. "It's up to us, through action and example, to sustain the international order that's expanded steadily since the end of the Cold War, and upon which our own wealth and safety depend."[13] It was heartfelt advice from the outgoing president. It was not advice that Donald Trump would take.

DONALD TRUMP RECOGNIZED many of the problems bedeviling America's role in the world. He had campaigned promising to solve them. But unlike all of his predecessors since Truman, he didn't see global leadership as the solution to what ailed America. To the contrary. He saw it as the problem. America's alliance commitments had, in his view, required the United States to "pay billions—hundreds of billions of dollars to supporting other countries that are in theory wealthier than we are."[14] America's trade policies had "de-industrialized America, uprooting our industry, and stripped bare towns like Detroit and Baltimore."[15] The result, as he put it in his inaugural address, was nothing less than an "American carnage."[16] Jobs had been lost, companies had closed their doors, and once-proud cities looked like ghost towns. Trump wasn't interested in securing the cooperation of other countries. He wanted to take back what they had taken from America.

Trump's disdain for American foreign policy had deep roots. He first aired his gripes in the 1980s, and he stuck to them over the subsequent decades, even as his positions on domestic issues seemingly changed with his moods and his audience. He put his criticisms at the core of his campaign. He vowed that "we will no longer surrender this country or its people to the false song of globalism."[17] None of the three pillars of American foreign policy—security alliances; open trade; and support for democracy, human rights, and rule of law—escaped his scorn. He said he would happily tell the other members of NATO, the most successful military alliance in history, "Congratulations, you will be defending yourself."[18] He suggested that Japan and South Korea acquire their own nuclear weapons. He denounced US trade policy, vowing to withdraw from the Trans-Pacific Partnership (TPP), renegotiate the North American Free Trade Agreement (NAFTA), and impose huge tariffs on China. He decried US efforts to lecture others about democracy and human rights because "we have to fix our own mess."[19]

What Trump was offering was a return to a foreign policy based on the logic of competition and domination. His predecessors spoke of American leadership routinely—and glowingly. He seldom mentioned it at all, except when delivering formal speeches written by aides that smoothed his rough edges. Instead, he continually spoke of winning—and he intended to win. Foreign policy experts surveyed the world and saw friends and enemies, allies and adversaries. When Trump surveyed the world, he saw only competitors, and they were seeking to take advantage of him and the United States. He would judge them not on sentimentalities about the past but on their willingness to make deals that he liked. His comment about world leaders just days before he took the oath of office made the point. "So, I give everybody an even start," he said. "Right now, as far as I'm concerned, everybody's got an even start."[20] No other American president would have equated the leaders of Britain and Australia with those of China and Russia.

The disdain Trump showed on the campaign trail for American leadership alarmed foreign policy experts in both major political parties. They breathed a collective sigh of relief, however, when he started his presidency by appointing foreign policy traditionalists like Mattis, Tillerson, and—after the short, unhappy tenure of Michael Flynn as national security adviser—Lieutenant General H. R. McMaster to critical national security positions and turning to free traders like Gary Cohn, the head of the National Economic Council, for top economics jobs. The praise for these appointments wasn't rooted in a belief that these picks had quick and easy solutions for a world in disarray. They didn't. Rather, the appointments were cheered because they, and the subordinates they hired, believed in the importance of American leadership—and what it could accomplish. This "axis of adults" in one telling, or "globalists" in another, would, or so the thinking went, curtail Trump's excesses and steer him on a more conventional path.

That hope rested on two questionable premises: that presidents change their views easily and that advisers matter more than the man they are advising. Trump quickly disproved both premises. He had said what he meant and meant what he said on the campaign trail. And no amount of expert advice was going to change things. He ended US participation in TPP, withdrew from the Paris climate agreement, initially refused to endorse America's alliance commitments, withdrew from the Iran nuclear deal, sought to renegotiate NAFTA, recognized Jerusalem as the capital of Israel, and curried favor with Russia even as his advisers argued, sometimes publicly, that he was undermining America's national interests and global leadership. Just as dangerous as what Trump did was how he went about doing it. He insulted allies and flattered adversaries. He routinely surprised his foreign policy team with his tweets and public statements, leaving them to clean up the diplomatic messes he had created. The president "has moved a lot of us out of our comfort zone," as McMaster delicately put it.[21] Trump, as he had said on the campaign trail, was more direct: "I alone can fix it."[22]

A few of America's friends applauded Trump's words and deeds. Israel and Saudi Arabia saw that he was giving them what they wanted and asking for nothing in return—a deal that was too good to pass up. But most of America's friends and allies were mystified and alarmed, even if they frequently preferred to keep their concerns private for fear of making themselves the target of Trump's outbursts. They wondered why he directed so much of his anger at America's friends while lavishing so much praise on its rivals. Their alarm didn't reflect unrealistic expectations about how relations with Washington should proceed. America's friends and allies were not strangers to epic confrontations with American presidents; American leadership had never generated unquestioned obedience. Even good friends can disagree strongly. Over the years, America's friends and allies had done just that on numerous issues, most memorably on the Vietnam War and the invasion of Iraq.

This time, though, felt different. Trump's first year and a half in office sent an unmistakable message. He had no interest in leading America's friends and allies. He was looking to beat them. His was not a win-win world but a world of winners and losers. "You hear lots of people say that a great deal is when both sides win," he once wrote. "That is a bunch of crap. In a great deal you win—not the other side. You crush the opponent and come away with something better for yourself."[23]

Trump was comfortable abdicating American leadership because he saw no value in it—just costs. In his view, America neither had exceptional responsibilities nor was an exceptional country. Rather, it was like every other nation, and as a result, it should pursue its own narrow interests, not mutual ones. "I will always put America first," he told world leaders gathered at the United Nations in September 2017, "just like you, as the leaders of your countries will always, and should always, put your countries first."[24] Most of America's friends in turn rejected his claims that the cooperative policies that had served them—and the United States—well for seven decades were now a danger. When he abandoned the Paris climate agreement, withdrew from the Iran nuclear deal, railed against multilateral trading arrangements, and overturned a range of other long-standing US policies, they forged ahead on their own. Trump might see opting out of the rules-based order as the ticket to America's renaissance. They, however, weren't about to follow him there.

Trump's retreat from global leadership was not lost on America's enemies—or its friends. A senior Japanese foreign policy official assessing Trump's policy in late 2017 said with sadness, "The throne is empty."[25] Long accustomed to looking to Washington for direction, Berlin, London, Paris, Seoul, Tokyo, and beyond now found that Trump had no interest in leading the Free World.

DONALD TRUMP WAGERED that the United States could secure the benefits of the world it created without bearing the burdens of leading it. That bet is unlikely to pay off. The world that America created after World

War II was not inevitable. It was the result of conscious policy choices made in the pursuit of a vision of how cooperation and leadership, rather than domination and competition, could benefit the United States. Consumed with the costs of that rules-based order, many of which he exaggerated, Trump couldn't appreciate its continuing and far greater benefits. Working with friends and allies multiplied American power far more often than constrained it. As a result, Washington, more so than any other country, got to be the rule maker in international politics and, with that role, won the power to shape outcomes to its liking. By choosing to act alone rather than mobilizing others in common cause, Trump was waging war on the world America had made.[26] He was also committing the very mistake he had accused his predecessors of making: taking on burdens others could have shared and squandering American power in the process.

The biggest beneficiary of Trump's decision to turn his back on American global leadership was China. It was the one country capable of filling the leadership vacuum he had created—and it was all too eager to do so. Trump "has given China a huge gift," a Chinese general crowed. "The U.S. is not losing leadership," a Chinese academic observed. "You're giving it up. You're not even selling it."[27] When Trump denounced trade deals and imposed tariffs, Beijing positioned itself as a defender of the open trading system it had exploited for years. When Trump abandoned the Paris climate agreement, Beijing strove to become the world leader in climate-friendly technologies. When Trump slashed US foreign aid, Beijing invested heavily in its "One Belt, One Road" initiative across Asia and beyond, looking to put China at the center of the global economy. When Trump undermined multilateral institutions, Beijing moved to set up competing ones. "The world needs China," the flagship newspaper of the Chinese Communist Party boasted in January 2018. "That creates broad strategic room for our efforts to uphold peace and development and gain an advantage."[28] China's vision for the world will not be friendly to the United States. The longtime rule maker could become a rule taker.

Even if China's bid for the mantle of global leadership fails, Trump's policies undermined America's security, prosperity, and values. By questioning America's alliance commitments, he emboldened foes and created uncertainty in the minds of friends about whether the United States would stand with them in a crisis. As he rejected multilateral trade deals, other countries forged ahead with writing their own. As the saying goes, if you're not at the table, then you're on the menu. Without Washington's involvement, the agreements they wrote put American businesses and workers at a disadvantage in the global marketplace. And by attacking democratic institutions at home and praising dictators and human rights abusers abroad, he encouraged antidemocratic trends the world over.

These are the dangers that Trump's advisers tried to warn him about in the Tank on that summer day in 2017. He wasn't impressed—or persuaded. As he said time and again during his first eighteen months in office, he didn't believe what the naysayers had to tell him. He was the self-described "very stable genius" who had won the presidency on his first try against long odds.[29] The experts hadn't foreseen his victory or, in his view, much else either. He didn't need detailed analyses or lengthy briefings. Those were for the weak, the timid, the indecisive. He had his gut. "I'm a very instinctual person," he explained, "but my instinct turns out to be right."[30] He knew less but saw more. Yet for all his talk about how he enjoyed hearing different viewpoints, as his presidency progressed, he increasingly surrounded himself with advisers who confirmed his view of himself rather than challenged it. Their role, as White House trade adviser Peter Navarro explained it in March 2018, was "to provide the underlying analytics that confirm his intuition. And his intuition is always right." This White House, Navarro went on, was like the New England Patriots football team: "The owner, the coach, and the quarterback are all the president. The rest of us are all interchangeable parts."[31]

When Trump surveyed the world in June 2018, he didn't see himself driving America's friends and allies away or ceding ground to China. He saw himself winning. He had in his imagination accomplished more than any other president in history. He had defeated the Islamic State in Iraq and Syria, even if his generals had done so largely by following the strategy developed under Obama. America's allies were spending more on defense, even though that too reflected decisions made before he came to office. He had been feted by the Chinese and Saudis, who had reviled the weak Obama. He had pushed a "maximum pressure" strategy that had compelled "Little Rocket Man" Kim Jong-un to meet with him in Singapore and promise to give up his nuclear arsenal. He had ended American participation in the jobs-killing Paris Agreement to combat climate change, which he had called a Chinese-created hoax. He had imposed tariffs on countries that had cheated the United States and stolen jobs from American workers. Trump saw himself doing what he had promised: making America great again. But his actions were in fact setting America on the road to a less secure and prosperous future—and, ironically for a president who insisted he was defending American sovereignty, one in which Americans would have less and not more control over their destiny.

2

Present at the Creation

The world was in crisis as President Franklin Roosevelt took the podium on January 6, 1941, to address a joint session of Congress. Europe had been at war for more than sixteen months. France had fallen, and Nazi Germany dominated the continent. Britain alone had held out. It had endured months of large-scale daylight bombing. Now it faced the Blitz, a terrifying nighttime bombing campaign. Britons desperately hoped for help from the United States, help that had not been forthcoming. Roosevelt wanted to change that. As Congress was gaveled to order, he had a simple goal: to persuade his fellow citizens that "the safety of our country and of our democracy are overwhelmingly involved in events far beyond our borders."[1]

Roosevelt faced a hard sell. For a century and a half, Americans had believed that their security rested on being faithful to the founding generation's admonition to stand apart from Europe's battles. They had broken with that faith only once. Twenty-four years earlier, they had marched off to fight imperial Germany in a war President Woodrow Wilson promised would make the world "safe for democracy."[2] It hadn't. The narrow, self-serving geopolitics of the old world had persisted. Looking back on the gap between what was promised and what was delivered, and struggling with the hardship of the Great Depression, many Americans had concluded that the Great War had been the Great Mistake. They turned inward, resisting the idea that they should fight and die once again on the battlefields of Europe. They clung to the belief that what happened over there would stay over there.

Roosevelt disagreed. He had worried for years that the storm clouds gathering in Europe would reach across the Atlantic. The time had long since passed, in his view, when the United States could ignore the dangers beyond its shores. It was "immature," he warned members of

Congress, many of whom bitterly opposed what he had to say, to think that "an unprepared America, single-handed, and with one hand tied behind its back, can hold off the world." The United States needed to create a "world founded upon four essential human freedoms": freedom of speech and expression, freedom to worship, freedom from want, and freedom from fear. It was a challenge America could meet. "Since the beginning of our American history, we have been engaged in change—in a perpetual peaceful revolution—a revolution which goes on steadily, quietly adjusting itself to changing conditions."[3]

The war that Roosevelt expected but didn't want came eleven months later when Japanese planes attacked Pearl Harbor. Over the next three and a half years, the United States and its allies fought and defeated the forces of fascism. Roosevelt, however, did not live to create the new world he sketched in his Four Freedoms speech. With his death in April 1945, that burden passed to Harry Truman, who had been vice president for little more than three months. The stakes were high and the chances of success unknown. Rather than shrink from the challenge, Truman embraced it. He was determined not to repeat the mistakes the United States had made after World War I. This time America would lead and not shirk. The work Truman began would be continued by successive administrations, both Democratic and Republican. The results proved far greater than he and others who were "present at the creation," as Dean Acheson, one of his closest advisers, later called this period, could have ever imagined.[4] Former foes became prosperous and steadfast friends as Europe and Asia rebuilt after years of devastating war. Confrontation with the Soviet Union ultimately ended without a shot being fired as the wall dividing East and West disintegrated. And, yet, winning the Cold War fueled a dangerous hubris over the next two decades. Unchecked by any other power, Washington sought to use its primacy to extend the world it had created in the West to the rest of the globe. That effort proved costly and led to several tragic failures. By the time of the 2016 presidential campaign, Americans across the political spectrum had come to question the cost of America's global leadership and what it had achieved.

WHEN WAR ERUPTED in Europe in September 1939, most Americans sympathized with the countries facing the Nazi onslaught but thought they could and should provide for their own security. In doing so,

Americans were reacting to turmoil overseas as prior generations had before them. Thomas Paine's pamphlet *Common Sense* had rallied colonists to the cause of independence by telling them that they had it in their "power to begin the world over again."[5] But the expectation always was that Americans would do so by the example they set rather than by the power of arms. George Washington had set down the great axiom of American foreign policy in his Farewell Address. "It is our true policy," he wrote, "to steer clear of permanent alliances with any portion of the foreign world." His reasoning was straightforward: "Europe has a set of primary interests which to us have none or very remote relation. Hence she must be engaged in frequent controversies, the causes of which are essentially foreign to our own."[6]

Americans would—with one great exception—adhere to Washington's guidance for the next century and a half, even as their country went from being a fragile experiment in self-government clinging to the Atlantic Coast to becoming a world-class industrial power that spanned a continent. The great exception was World War I. Even then, the United States entered the conflict grudgingly and late. When Europe went to war in August 1914, President Woodrow Wilson declared the United States neutral. Americans clung to their neutrality for more than two years, despite repeated German attacks on US merchant vessels and on passenger liners carrying American citizens. The refusal to fight only evaporated in April 1917 as Germany began unrestricted submarine attacks on American ships and news broke that Berlin had tried to persuade Mexico to attack the United States. The once-reluctant Wilson embraced the war with a zeal that matched that of any religious convert. He set out to remake American foreign policy and world politics with it. America would fight not just to stop German aggression but "to vindicate the principles of peace and justice in the life of the world as against selfish and autocratic power."[7]

The vehicle Wilson intended to use to make the world "fit and safe to live in" was a league of nations. It would provide "mutual guarantees of political independence and territorial integrity to great and small states alike."[8] Wilson traveled to the Paris Peace Conference in December 1918 to persuade his deeply skeptical European counterparts to adopt his radical vision of a new world based on collective security and rule of law. He eventually prevailed. The Treaty of Versailles, signed in June 1919, established a League of Nations that would "respect and preserve as against external aggression the territorial integrity and political independence of all."[9]

Wilson's success in Paris turned to failure at home. The idea that the United States would join with other countries to police disputes around the world, however unrelated to American interests and however far from America's shores, was a bridge too far for many Americans. Some opponents were isolationists who balked at the very idea of entangling alliances. But many wanted the United States to act as a great power, just not in the way Wilson proposed. They believed the United States should exercise a free hand in foreign affairs, not tie its fate to the whims and interests of others. Had Wilson been willing to accommodate his more reasonable opponents and had he enjoyed better health—he suffered a massive stroke while campaigning for the league—he might have triumphed. Neither was the case. The Senate rejected the Treaty of Versailles. The League of Nations formed without the United States. The moment when America might have led the world passed.

Americans slowly began to turn their backs again on the Old World. With the Great Depression and the rise of fascism in Europe, isolationist sentiment intensified. Americans increasingly questioned why they had fought in the Great War. Lofty sentiments about making the world safe for democracy gave way to dark suspicions about merchants of death. Wilson had been pro-British all along, so the argument went, and business leaders had pushed him toward war to line their own pockets. The lesson was clear: Americans should resist being dragged into another war that served the interests of others.

Franklin Roosevelt recognized the public mood when he kept the United States on the sidelines as the second great European war of the twentieth century began. But when he took modest steps to aid Britain in September 1940, isolationists coalesced behind the America First Committee. Started by students at Yale Law School, including a future president (Gerald Ford) and a future Supreme Court justice (Potter Stewart), the committee's argument was simple: American security lay in taking Washington's Farewell Address to heart. Separated from Europe by three thousand miles of ocean, blessed with abundant natural resources, and home to the world's largest economy, Fortress America would be invulnerable to attack.

It was a powerful and persuasive argument to many Americans. It was also wrong. Refusing to lead and choosing instead to stand alone didn't bring peace. It brought war. It was a lesson that the Roosevelt and his successors would remember.

FRANKLIN ROOSEVELT INTENDED to succeed where Woodrow Wilson had failed. He intuitively grasped what American leadership could accomplish and prevent. He was deeply familiar with the argument for the League of Nations. He had served for six years as Wilson's assistant secretary of the navy, at the time the number two position in what was then its own department. As the Democratic vice presidential nominee in the 1920 election, which Wilson had hoped would be a "great and solemn referendum" on his vision, Roosevelt had given hundreds of speeches defending the league. But where Wilson had stressed the moral rectitude of his vision, Roosevelt stressed its practical benefits. Neither set of arguments, it turned out, persuaded American voters; they voted overwhelming for the Republican ticket in one of the great electoral landslides in American political history. Roosevelt, however, was undaunted by the public's rejection of Wilson's vision. In 1923 he drafted his own "Plan to Preserve World Peace," fixing what he saw as the impracticalities in Wilson's plan.

Roosevelt returned to the question of what kind of world the United States should seek to create shortly after the country entered World War II. Although the failure to deter German, Italian, and Japanese aggression had discredited the League of Nations, Roosevelt clung to the idea that an effectively structured successor to the league could deter aggressor nations. "Unless the peace that follows recognizes that the whole world is one neighborhood and does justice to the whole human race," he told reporters early in 1943, "the germs of another world war will remain as a constant threat to mankind."[10] Just as important, Roosevelt recognized the need to tame the economic rivalries that had fueled the march to war. He convened forty-four allied nations in Bretton Woods, New Hampshire, in July 1944 to craft a blueprint for a new international financial order. "Economic diseases are highly communicable," he said in a message read to the delegates. "It follows, therefore, that the economic health of every country is the proper matter of concern to all its neighbors, near and distant."[11] In moving to place world politics on a new footing, Roosevelt was motivated as much by what he hoped to prevent as what he hoped to achieve. "Anybody who thinks isolationism is dead in this country is crazy," he worried. "As soon as this war is over, it may well be stronger than ever."[12]

Roosevelt did not live to see his vision of a new League of Nations realized. By the time the Senate consented overwhelmingly on July 28, 1945, to the treaty creating the United Nations, he had been dead for more than three months. And although Bretton Woods and the creation of the UN were monumental achievements that signaled that America would not retreat from the world scene as it had after World War I, Roosevelt had left many important questions about postwar American foreign policy unanswered. What should the peace look like? How would America define its interests? What threatened those interests, and how should it confront these threats? Harry Truman would be the one to answer those questions.

Truman was hardly prepared for the responsibilities he inherited. He had never drafted a plan for world peace, and he freely admitted he was "not a deep thinker."[13] He had had little exposure to foreign policy issues beyond having fought in World War I, and he had been a surprise choice to be Roosevelt's running mate in 1944. What Truman had in abundance, though, was the willingness to make decisions that filled in the details of the visions of American leadership that Wilson and Roosevelt had sketched. His decisions didn't flow from a master plan; he mostly reacted to events rather than drove them. But those decisions changed American foreign policy in two fundamental ways. For the first time in American history, the United States defined its interests globally rather than nationally or regionally. In March 1947, Truman stood before a joint session of Congress and declared what became known as the Truman Doctrine: "It must be the policy of the United States to support free peoples who are resisting attempted subjugation by armed minorities or outside pressures."[14] Three months later his administration unveiled the Marshall Plan to help rebuild Europe. Two years after that, he signed the treaty creating the North Atlantic Treaty Organization (NATO). American forces occupied Japan for four years before turning sovereignty back to Tokyo, and two years later both countries signed a mutual defense accord. By that time, US troops were leading a large UN-authorized coalition in defense of South Korea. Unlike in 1919, the United States was not turning its back on the world. It was instead building entangling alliances abroad.

As important as Truman's decision to define America's interests globally was the way he positioned the United States to lead. He could have imposed his choices on others by fiat. The United States had no peers. America enjoyed an atomic weapons monopoly. All the other major powers, whether victor or vanquished, were devastated. Instead, Truman calculated, in keeping with the visions of Wilson and Roosevelt, that the world would be far easier to lead if he embedded American power in multilateral arrangements that gave others a voice as well. Truman's presidency oversaw the creation of much of the institutional infrastructure of present-day global governance: the United Nations, the International Money Fund (IMF), the World Bank, and the General Agreement on Tariffs and Trade (the forerunner of the World Trade Organization), among others. Just as important, Truman encouraged other nations to build regional institutions that would regulate their relations in accordance with the rule of law. Embedded in all these efforts were the twin ideas that all countries, including the United States, should agree to be constrained by international law and that they would benefit from doing so.

Contrary to Roosevelt's great fear, isolationists did not mount a significant challenge to America's embrace of global leadership. The smoke pouring from the shattered remains of the USS *Arizona* at Pearl Harbor had discredited the idea that Fortress America could keep Americans safe, and the Soviet menace created fears that one totalitarian threat had replaced another. Congress repeatedly endorsed Truman's policies with lopsided bipartisan majorities. Wilson and Roosevelt had won. Most Americans agreed that the United States should lead the Free World.

For the next four decades, the political battles in the United States turned on tactics rather than on first principles. Was it feasible to liberate countries that had fallen under Soviet domination? Could Washington negotiate with the Kremlin? Did communist insurgencies in Vietnam and elsewhere threaten core US interests? Would America be more secure if it negotiated arms limitations with the Soviet Union? On these and a multitude of other questions, Democrats and Republicans fought with each other and among themselves. The debates were sometimes bitter. Nonetheless, a consensus held around basic principles. The United States had global interests it must be prepared to defend. American leadership advanced its security, prosperity, and values. International organizations, and especially military alliances, were a critical element of

American power. Friends and allies were essential because it was dangerous to be without them. Cultivating those relationships required taking
a long view rather than maximizing immediate gains.

American leadership resonated overseas. Rather than resisting it,
those countries that could followed it. The United States provided security and predictability, which in turn produced peace and prosperity. Disagreement and debate did not magically disappear. America and its allies
quarreled over issues large and small. Allies grumbled that Washington
failed to understand local concerns. Washington complained that allies
failed to pay their fair share. Yet even Vietnam, a war most American
allies opposed even as successive US administrations insisted it had to be
fought to demonstrate American credibility, couldn't break the bond that
had developed between leader and followers. The American-led order
worked too well for the countries that participated to think otherwise. It
produced unprecedented economic growth and one of the great geopolitical victories in world history—and with it the opportunity to broaden
the reach of the Free World.

"MR. GORBACHEV, TEAR down this wall!" Few who heard President
Ronald Reagan's demand in the shadow of the Brandenburg Gate on
June 12, 1987, expected to see the wall that had surrounded West Berlin for a quarter century come down in their lifetimes. But in November 1989, it did. Just two years after that, the Soviet Union itself fell.
With almost no advance notice, the unipolar moment had arrived—the
United States stood alone as the unchallenged superpower, perhaps even
a "hyperpower."[15] Washington suddenly saw the chance to prove Thomas
Paine right—America could remake the world anew. It would extend
the benefits of security, open economies, and rule of law that the West
had enjoyed to the rest of the globe.

The prize was enormous. "What is at stake is more than one small
country," President George H. W. Bush noted in his 1991 State of the
Union address, referring to the Iraqi invasion of Kuwait. "It is a big idea:
a new world order, where diverse nations are drawn together in common
cause to achieve the universal aspirations of mankind—peace and security, freedom, and the rule of law. Such is a world worthy of our struggle
and worthy of our children's future."[16] Bush's National Security Strategy
released that August went even further: "We have within our grasp an
extraordinary possibility that few generations have enjoyed—to build a

new international system in accordance with our own values and ideals, as old patterns and certainties crumble around us."[17]

Bush's optimism about what American leadership could achieve reflected the remarkable successes of the previous two years: German reunification, the Gulf War, and the collapse of the Soviet Union and communism. Ignoring the objections of Britain and France, both of which feared German dominance of Europe, and skillfully handling Soviet leader Mikhail Gorbachev, Bush helped midwife a new Germany less than a year after the Berlin Wall fell. The Gulf War epitomized Wilson's and Roosevelt's visions of collective security mobilized by American leadership. With the blessing of the UN Security Council, more than thirty countries joined what became an overwhelming military triumph. Bush showed similar deftness in handling the demise of the Soviet Union so that it went out with a whimper rather than a bang. Some critics objected that he should have pushed America's newfound primacy harder, whether by demanding more of Soviet leaders or by marching on Baghdad. But these complaints simply reinforced what seemed to be the more important lesson of Bush's foreign policy stewardship: the world, and not just the West, was ready to rally behind American leadership.

GEORGE H. W. BUSH did not, however, get the chance to build a new world order. Many Americans believed he had spent too much time worrying about problems overseas, and they voted him out of office in 1992. The opportunity to fashion a new world order instead fell to his two successors, Bill Clinton and George W. Bush. Born just seven weeks apart a year after the end of World War II, they came from different circumstances, championed different political philosophies, and showed scant interest in foreign policy before taking the oath of office. But their presidencies embraced similarly expansive—with the benefit of hindsight, excessively expansive—views of what American leadership could accomplish. Not only could America revamp global security, economics, and values, but its own security and prosperity depended on it.

That Clinton would end his presidency saying Americans had "no choice but to lead" was not obvious at its start.[18] He had campaigned for the White House by pledging to "focus like a laser beam" on America's domestic problems, and he stumbled badly early on with crises in Somalia, Haiti, Rwanda, and the Balkans.[19] His approach changed, however, after the massacre of eight thousand Muslim men and boys at Srebrenica, Bosnia, in July 1995 and a horrific bombing of Sarajevo the following month. Spurred to action after two years of hesitation in dealing with the Bosnia crisis, Clinton ordered air strikes on Bosnian Serb targets. That decision to finally intervene and demonstrate leadership created the political opening for the Dayton Accords, which ended Europe's bloodiest conflict since World War II.[20]

The success at Dayton showed Clinton what decisive American leadership could accomplish. He took to referring to the United States as the "indispensable nation"—it was the only country with the capacity, vision, and moral authority to mobilize the world to act in the face of pressing challenges. He turned to military force again in 1999, leading NATO in a war against Serbia over Kosovo. Unlike the Gulf War, it did not have the blessing of the United Nations and was fought over the objections of Russia and China. The war may have been "illegal" under international law, but to its defenders it was "legitimate." Even UN Secretary General Kofi Annan acknowledged that it created a new standard for humanitarian interventions, as "massive and systematic violations of human rights conducted against an entire people cannot be allowed to stand."[21] Secretary of State Madeleine Albright captured the sentiment that animated Clinton's willingness to bend the rules: "We see further than other countries into the future."[22] The United States had the might to do right.

Clinton's confidence about what America could achieve in promoting open economies and democratic values also grew over the course of his presidency. Rather than shrinking from globalization as a threat to American prosperity, he increasingly celebrated it. In 1993, he persuaded Congress to approve the North American Free Trade Agreement (NAFTA). The following year, he convinced Congress to support the creation of the World Trade Organization (WTO), which would have new powers to enforce international trade rules. Buoyed by increasingly robust economic growth at home—annual economic growth averaged 4 percent during his second term—Clinton touted the so-called Washington Consensus: the idea that countries should give markets freer rein and loosen the restrictions on the ability of goods and capital to cross borders. Seeing the success that the United States was enjoying, countries around the world began to scramble to adopt—or were compelled by the IMF and World Bank to adopt—these market-friendly policies, despite the disruption they caused and regardless of how well they suited their particular circumstances. Most consequentially, in 2000, Clinton convinced Congress to grant China the same treatment it gave other countries under WTO rules, paving the way for China to join the international trading system. "This is a good day for America," Clinton concluded after the House voted yes. "In ten years from now we will look on this day and be glad we did this. We will see that we have given ourselves a chance to build the kind of future we want."[23]

Clinton's faith in the power of markets was tied to an equally powerful faith that economic openness would beget political openness. In his first year in office, Clinton's national security adviser had laid out an ambitious Wilsonian agenda in which the United States would look to transform the world in its image. The course for America "must be a strategy of enlargement," Anthony Lake argued, "enlargement of the world's free community of democracies."[24] Lake's agenda gained little traction at first. But in the wake of the success at Dayton, Clinton committed himself to it. The immediate focus was enlarging NATO by drawing the Soviet Union's former satellite states into the alliance. "Now for the very first time since nation-states first appeared in Europe," he said, "we have an opportunity to build a peaceful, undivided and democratic continent."[25] But Clinton was increasingly persuaded by another assumption of Lake's enlargement strategy: "To the extent democracy and market economics hold sway in other nations, our own nation will be more secure, prosperous, and influential, while the broader world will be more humane and peaceful."[26] Countries that embraced the Washington Consensus would become not only more prosperous but also more democratic and more inclined to share America's interests and views. The ultimate prize was, of course, China. Encouraging it to adopt Western economic reforms would turn a potential adversary into a friend, relieving the United States of the burden of having to choose between its economic and security interests.

Clinton ended his presidency proclaiming, "Now we are at the height of our power and prosperity."[27] George W. Bush didn't disagree. But he thought Clinton had misused the power America had. On the campaign trail, he assailed Clinton's foreign policy, accusing him of "action without vision, activity without priority, and missions without end."[28] Clinton had, in his judgment, been too timid in using America's power, too willing to defer to American allies, too reluctant to stand up to America's foes, and too eager to engage in nation building abroad. Clinton had failed to recognize that America was Gulliver and, as a result, had allowed the Lilliputians to tie it down. Bush would not repeat that mistake. He believed in an America unbound.[29]

On a fundamental point, however, Bush agreed with Clinton. The United States should use its primacy "to turn these years of influence into decades of peace."[30] And like Clinton's, his presidency was irrevocably changed by a foreign policy horror, in his case September 11. The attacks on the World Trade Center and the Pentagon precipitated wars in Afghanistan and Iraq, the first as a matter of necessity, the second as a matter of choice. The two wars elicited different global reactions. The United Nations had unequivocally condemned the terrorist attacks, and NATO for the first time in its history invoked Article 5, its solemn obligation to come to the defense of a member under attack. There was broad international support for going into Afghanistan to capture Osama bin Laden and the other leaders of al Qaeda who had perpetrated the horrendous strikes. The Iraq War, though, enjoyed none of that global goodwill. Bush went to war despite the objections of even some of America's closest allies. Although critics argued that the decision would inflict lasting damage on American leadership, Bush and his advisers countered that how the United States went to war mattered less than what it accomplished. Once America emerged victorious—and it would—allies would praise Washington's decisiveness. Results, not process, would carry the day.

Bush also shared Clinton's vision of the economic and political benefits of open markets. Although he had criticized Clinton for treating China as a potential "strategic partner" rather than a "strategic competitor," he too believed that China's participation in the WTO would benefit both economies and help democratize Chinese politics. "The advance of Chinese prosperity depends on China's full integration into the rules and norms of international institutions," he said at a press conference with Chinese leader Jiang Zemin during his first trip to China as president. "And in the long run, economic freedom and political freedom will go hand in hand."[31] The immediate challenge was to encourage China to become a "responsible stakeholder" in the international system.[32] Bush was equally confident in America's ability to spread its values. In his second inaugural address, he channeled the grand ambitions of Wilson and Roosevelt by placing what he called his "Freedom Agenda" front and center in US foreign policy: "The survival of liberty in our land increasingly depends on the success of liberty in other lands."[33] Afghanistan and Iraq would demonstrate America's ability to refashion the world in its image.

Clinton and the younger Bush both promised that their vigorous exercise of American leadership in the unipolar moment would make America and its friends safer and more prosperous. By the end of Bush's second term in office, however, their confidence in the transformative power of American primacy looked more like hubris. Iraq had turned into a bloody occupation. The Afghanistan War showed no signs of ending. The Freedom Agenda had sputtered out. Rather than rally around the United States, many allies distanced themselves from US policy. Russia had accepted neither American primacy nor NATO expansion. It instead defended its sphere of influence by invading Georgia and intimidating other neighbors. China showed few signs of embracing Western political values or becoming a responsible stakeholder that would ratify decisions made in Washington. Clinton's boast of the benefits of China's entry into the world trading system looked like a bitter joke as manufacturers across the United States shuttered their doors or moved production overseas to compete with the flood of low-cost Chinese imports. Meanwhile, as Bush's time in office wound down, the United States plunged into the worst economic recession since the Great Depression, in good part because the pro-market, minimal regulation policies that US officials championed had backfired.

The unipolar moment had proven to be just that—a moment. It had begun with countries awed by what American primacy could accomplish. It ended with countries doubting the wisdom of American policies and wondering whether the United States would soon be eclipsed by China. The confidence that dominated Washington in the late 1990s and early 2000s had been misplaced. History hadn't ended after all. The next president would have to confront the consequences of that reality.

IRAQ BECAME A quagmire for the United States. For Barack Obama, however, it was a political gift. He had opposed the war from the start. "I know that even a successful war against Iraq will require a US occupation of undetermined length, at undetermined cost, with undetermined consequences," he warned with eerie prescience in October 2002. "An invasion of Iraq without a clear rationale and without strong international support will only fan the flames of the Middle East, and encourage the worst, rather than best, impulses of the Arab world, and strengthen the recruitment arm of al-Qaida."[34] Opposition to the war helped drive his rise to the Democratic nomination in 2008. He alone among the major candidates didn't have to apologize for supporting a war that six in ten Americans, and an even larger percentage of Democrats, had come to view as a mistake.[35]

Yet in criticizing the Iraq War, Obama didn't reject the idea of America as the indispensable nation. Abandoning "leadership is a mistake we must not make," he argued. "We must lead the world, by deed and example."[36] However, he had a tempered view of what American power could accomplish and believed that it needed to be placed on a sustainable footing after years of overreach. "We need to learn the painful lessons of the Iraq War," he said at the start of his presidential campaign, "if we're going to secure this country and renew America's leadership."[37] When asked which president he admired on foreign policy, he did not point to his fellow Democrat Bill Clinton and his ambitious view of what America could accomplish overseas. He instead pointed to George H. W. Bush, the Republican who had been criticized for his foreign policy caution.[38]

Obama hoped to renew American leadership through a "long game" that favored a more considered and measured use of US power abroad.[39] The strategy rested on three core convictions. The first was that the United States could achieve its goals overseas only in concert with others. Although America's absolute power continued to grow, its relative power was shrinking as globalization dispersed economic and political power and created thorny new problems. "In this new world, such dangerous currents have swept along faster than our efforts to contain them," Obama said in 2008. "That is why we cannot afford to be divided. No one nation, no matter how large or powerful, can defeat such challenges alone. None of us can deny these threats, or escape responsibility in meeting them."[40] The second conviction was that the United States could not change societies by military force. The Iraq War "should never have been waged" and could not be won because "only Iraq's leaders can settle the grievances at the heart of Iraq's civil war."[41] The third conviction was that the US commitment to the Middle East had distorted US foreign policy. "We cannot afford four more years of a strategy that is out of balance and out of step with this defining moment," he warned.[42] Far more attention needed to be paid to challenges like nuclear proliferation, climate change, and the rise of China.

Those three convictions explained the foreign policy objectives Obama outlined on the campaign trail. He would end America's wars overseas and be careful about using military force in the future. He would use US power judiciously and persuade others to carry more of the burden. He would revamp America's overseas commitments to enable it to tackle big new challenges like climate change. In all, his strategy could be summarized as do less militarily; do it with others; do big things.

Obama's approach, however, failed to renew American leadership and in many ways left it weaker. His failure wasn't for a lack of trying. He worked to rebuild relations in Europe and sought to pivot America's economic and military attention from the Middle East to Asia. He withdrew American troops from Iraq and, after a brief surge of force, sought to do the same thing in Afghanistan. He pushed to strengthen the G-20, conceived during the Great Recession of 2008 as the primary forum for managing the global economy, and tried to put US relations with Russia and China on a new, more cooperative footing. He sought to forge global coalitions to tackle nuclear proliferation and climate change. And he opened negotiations on broad new trade deals with Europe and Asia-Pacific countries in an effort to tie the major global economies more closely to the United States and pressure China to follow America's lead.

The world, however, didn't cooperate with Obama's strategy, and he failed to adjust accordingly. As much as he wanted to reduce the US commitment in the Middle East, the Middle East made it hard to exit. Iraq's leaders failed to settle their country's grievances, creating the opening for the Islamic State's rise. The Arab Spring threw the region into tumult, unleashing unrealistic expectations (including on Obama's part) that a democratic revolution was sweeping the region. In Libya, Obama put aside his reservations about America's ability to change other societies by force and actively supported regime change in response to British and French pleas for action. The result was a military intervention that toppled Muammar Gaddafi but left no functioning government in his place. Obama refused to intervene militarily in Syria after saying that "the time has come for President Assad to step aside" and drawing a red line on the use of chemical weapons.[43] Obama's judgment that a US military intervention would have made things worse in Syria may well have been right, but he failed to find a way to mitigate and confine the resulting humanitarian and refugee crises.

"Leading from behind," as one unnamed Obama official called the administration's approach, frequently failed to spur other countries to act.[44] Obama asked Europe to do more just as the Great Recession led Europeans to look inward and doubt the viability of the European Union. The Libyan intervention further showed that Europe's military capabilities had atrophied. While NATO allies bore the brunt of the bombing campaign, they needed American intelligence, surveillance, refueling, and targeting to get the job done. Several also had to rely on American resupply when they ran out of bombs and missiles.[45] When the fighting ended, Europeans, who had pressed for intervention, left the Libyans to their own devices. Obama had "focused on taking action multilaterally where our direct interests are not at stake" because "multilateralism regulates hubris," as he explained, but his "anti–free rider campaign" didn't work as well as he hoped.[46] European leaders in turn complained that Obama's soaring rhetoric all too often wasn't accompanied by equally impressive action.

Whereas friendly powers demurred on Obama's leadership efforts, rivals contested them. Emboldened by its rising power and sensing Obama's aversion to confrontation, China became more assertive, militarizing the South China Sea in violation of international law and intimidating neighbors that criticized its policies. The attempted reset with Russia failed. Obama dismissed Russia as a declining "regional power" that "doesn't produce anything that anybody wants to buy except oil and gas and arms," forgetting that weaker powers can spoil an agenda even if they can't set one.[47] The Kremlin did just that, invading Ukraine and annexing Crimea, intervening in Syria, and meddling in Western elections. Meanwhile, countries like Brazil, India, and South Africa focused more on enjoying the benefits of their status as rising powers than on bearing burdens to sustain the international order fueling their rise.

Obama similarly failed to build a political consensus at home for his long game. Much of the foreign policy establishment, including at times senior members of his own administration, saw his reluctance to use American military might not as prudence justified by recent history but as timidity and defeatism. On issue after issue, he found himself seeking to do less but being pushed by others in Washington to do more. At the same time, Obama had no solutions for the many Americans who saw themselves as the victims of globalization. The Great Recession, rapid technological change, and the flood of low-cost imports from China and elsewhere had upended their lives and left them doubting that tomorrow would be better than today. Seeing the growth of inequality and believing that no one in Washington understood their plight, they revolted against globalization and American leadership of the rules-based order. Their rejection of traditional foreign policy views and assumptions would become a defining theme of the 2016 presidential campaign.

Obama ended his presidency with American global leadership doubted by its friends, challenged by its rivals, and debated at home. He had corrected—his critics would say overcorrected—the hubris of his two predecessors. But the future of the rules-based order that Franklin Roosevelt had envisioned and Harry Truman had launched remained troubled. Finding a way to place American global leadership on a sustainable footing would fall to the next president—if he wanted to take up the challenge.

3

America First

New York Times readers had no reason to think the paper they picked up on the morning of September 2, 1987, had special significance. The stories on page 1 were unremarkable. Pope John Paul II had met with Jewish leaders angry he had received Austrian President Kurt Waldheim, who during World War II had served in a German Army unit that sent Greek Jews to Nazi death camps. The Food and Drug Administration had approved a new drug for treating high cholesterol. The chief of staff of the Philippine Army had warned that a mutiny had left the country vulnerable to a communist insurgency.

Sifting through the news of the day, even close readers of the *Times* might not have noticed the open letter "To the American People" that appeared on page A28. A Manhattan real estate developer who had owned the New Jersey Generals in the short-lived US Football League and was engaged in a public spat with New York City's mayor over tax abatements had paid $94,801 to run the full-page ad in the *Times*, the *Washington Post*, and the *Boston Globe*.[1]

The title minced no words: "There's Nothing Wrong with America's Foreign Defense Policy That a Little Backbone Can't Cure." The text was equally blunt: "The world is laughing at America's politicians." They had allowed America's friends and allies to play the country for a sucker. Japan, Saudi Arabia, and others were letting the United States sacrifice its blood and treasure "to protect *their* interests." While Washington was securing the Persian Gulf, "an area of only marginal significance to the United States for its oil supplies," it continued, these countries were getting rich. The solution to what ailed America was simple: "Make Japan, Saudi Arabia, and others pay for the protection we extend as allies." Placing a "tax" on these wealthy nations would generate the funds "to end our vast deficits," "reduce our taxes," and "help our farmers, our sick,

29

our homeless." The letter ended with a plea: "Let's not let our great country be laughed at anymore."

Times readers who noticed the ad had no reason to dwell on it. It
wasn't the first and wouldn't be the last open letter paid for by someone
with strong opinions and deep pockets. It certainly didn't change the
debate in Washington. US warships continued to patrol the Persian Gulf
to protect Saudi Arabia and to preserve the flow of oil to Japan and elsewhere. The ad's significance would become apparent only three decades
later. What appeared in the *Times* that September morning was the first
draft of the foreign policy platform that would help catapult Donald J.
Trump to an improbable victory in the 2016 presidential election.

MUCH HAPPENED TO Donald Trump between the penning of his open
letter and his descent down the Trump Tower escalator on June 16, 2015,
to announce his presidential run. The ad had no effect on US policy, but
it did achieve its immediate purpose: attracting attention to the launch
of his forthcoming book, *The Art of the Deal*. Released that November, it
spent fifty-one weeks on the *New York Times* best-seller list. Trump subsequently made and lost fortunes as the real estate market went through
booms and busts. He became a tabloid favorite along the way with his
marriages, affairs, divorces, and extravagant lifestyle. His fame reached
new heights in 2004 with the debut of the reality TV show *The Apprentice*.

Yet for all Trump had done since writing his letter, it quickly became
clear that his foreign policy views—and his resentments—hadn't changed.
Less than sixty seconds into his announcement speech, he complained
that the United States was losing to the Islamic State, to China, to Japan,
and to Mexico. Americans were "being ripped off by everybody in the
world" because of "stupid" leaders who were "selling this country down
the drain." American negotiators "don't have a clue," and the leaders of
the countries ripping America off "were smarter than our leaders." He
lamented that the Japanese "take our jobs, they take our money, and then
they loan us back the money, and we pay them in interest." He insisted
that "Saudi Arabia without us is gone."[2] Traditional politicians, however,
would "not bring us . . . to the promised land." Only Trump could "make
America great again." Doing that would require doing different things
in foreign policy and doing them differently.

Trump wasn't the first presidential candidate to run against Washington's foreign policy mistakes or to denounce America's overseas

commitments. So had the three men who occupied the White House before him. Clinton beat the elder Bush with a campaign that had the unofficial motto, "It's the Economy, Stupid." The younger Bush ran against nation-building abroad and promised to replace "diffuse commitments with focused ones."[3] Obama campaigned in 2008 on bringing US troops home from Iraq and in 2012 vowed to do more "nation-building right here at home."[4] But there the similarities ended.

The more significant difference was that Trump offered a fundamentally different prescription for how the United States should approach the world. Clinton, Bush, and Obama, like every major presidential candidate since World War II, believed the United States could best promote its security and advance its prosperity by leading others in creating a world that favored collective security, open economies, and democratic values. Talk about American leadership and global responsibilities peppered their speeches. They championed free trade and argued that the United States should seek to advance its values as well as defend its interests. They disagreed on specific policies, not over the fundamental strategy the United States should pursue in the world. They all shared the belief, as Bush once put it, that the United States had a "great and guiding goal: to turn this time of American influence into generations of democratic peace."[5]

Trump dismissed that approach as folly. He denounced how both Democrats and Republicans had bungled foreign policy since the end of the Cold War. "We failed to develop a new vision for a new time," he argued. The result was that "our foreign policy is a complete and total disaster. No vision. No purpose. No direction. No strategy."[6] As he had warned decades earlier in his open letter, the United States had "been disrespected, mocked, and ripped off for many many years by people that were smarter, shrewder, tougher. We were the big bully, but we were not smartly led. And we were the big bully who was—the big stupid bully and we were systematically ripped off by everybody."[7] Nowhere did he describe the United States as the indispensable nation that would lead others in creating a safer and more prosperous world.

From the very start of the campaign, Trump attacked all three pillars of American post–World War II foreign policy: alliances; free trade; and the promotion of democracy, human rights, and the rule of law. He routinely questioned the benefit of having allies. He described America's overseas military commitments as favors the United States did for others rather than as steps that served US interests. When asked if the United States benefited from having military bases overseas, his response was blunt: "I don't think so."[8] He called NATO "obsolete," suggested that he wouldn't protect member states that hadn't "fulfilled their obligations to us," and dismissed criticism of his demand that Europe spend more on defense by saying, "If it breaks up NATO, it breaks up NATO."[9] He was equally contemptuous of the US military commitment to Japan, asking "what are we getting out of" protecting Japan from an attack by North Korea, and he said he would consider withdrawing US troops from Japan and South Korea.[10] He insisted that "we get nothing out of the United Nations other than good real estate prices."[11] In all, Trump reduced America's security interests overseas to a commercial transaction: "If we're going to continue to be the policemen of the world, we ought to be paid for it."[12]

Trump was even more biting in criticizing US trade policies. He pressed the point he had been making since the 1980s: the international trade system that Washington had championed had killed American jobs. China had used its entry into the World Trade Organization (WTO) in 2001 "to rape our country" in "the greatest theft in the history of the world."[13] The North American Free Trade Agreement (NAFTA) with Canada and Mexico was "the worst trade deal ever signed in the history of this country and one of the worst trade deals ever signed anywhere in the world."[14] The Trans-Pacific Partnership (TPP), the trade deal that the Obama administration was negotiating with eleven other Pacific Rim countries, was "another disaster done and pushed by special interests who want to rape our country, just a continuing rape of our country."[15] The United States had lost at trade, Trump argued, because successive administrations had foolishly pursued multilateral trade talks that made it impossible for Washington to maximize its negotiating leverage. The better strategy was to "make individual deals with individual countries."[16]

The idea that the United States should defend and advance democratic values also held no sway over Trump. Rather than championing openness, diversity, and inclusion as great strengths, he staked out a hard-line anti-immigrant position that targeted Mexicans, Muslims, and refugees in particular. He made building a wall along America's southern border, which Mexico would miraculously pay for, a central plank of his campaign. He claimed that "Islam hates us," suggested he would support creating a national registry for all Muslims living in the United States, and endorsed a "total and complete ban" on Muslims entering the United States.[17] He called Syrian refugees "one of the great Trojan horses" of history and likened them to a woman in a 1960s song who took in an injured snake only to have it bite her.[18]

Democracy promotion came in for similar derision. It was, in Trump's eyes, a fool's errand. Other countries had no interest in what the United States was offering. Unrest in the Middle East began, he insisted, because Washington embraced "the dangerous idea that we could make western democracies out of countries that had no experience or interests in becoming a western democracy."[19] As a result, America ended up "trying to force democracy down their throat, we're spending trillions of dollars, and they don't even want it."[20] Even if foreign publics had wanted democracy, Trump argued, America wasn't a good role model. "When the world looks at how bad the United States is, and then we go and talk about civil liberties," he said, "I don't think we're a very good messenger."[21]

Trump doubled down on his dismissal of efforts to promote democracy with an unusual admiration for authoritarian strongmen around the world. He hailed China's leaders for being "much smarter than our leaders."[22] He argued that the world would be "100 percent" better off if Saddam Hussein and Muammar Gaddafi were still alive.[23] He marveled at how North Korea's youthful leader, Kim Jong-un, had consolidated power, saying, "You gotta give him credit."[24] He lavished praise on the Egyptian dictator Abdel Fattah el-Sisi, calling him "a fantastic guy" who "took control of Egypt. And he really took control of it."[25] Not mentioned was the fact that these leaders brutalized their people, ignored the rule of law, and tolerated if not benefited from corruption.

Trump's most effusive praise, though, was for Russian President Vladimir Putin. Trump's admiration for Putin long predated his decision to run for president. In 2007, he hailed the Russian leader "for doing a great job."[26] Six years later, he told a reporter that Putin had done "a really great job outsmarting our country."[27] A year after that, he called Russia's invasion of Ukraine "so smart" and said Putin had "done an amazing job of taking the mantle."[28] Trump's willingness to dismiss Putin's long list of misdeeds continued during the campaign. When a TV anchor noted that Putin had ordered journalists killed, Trump responded, "Our country does plenty of killing, also."[29] Calls from fellow Republicans for a tougher line on Russia didn't move Trump. "Why do I have to get tough on Putin?" he asked. "I don't know anything other than that he doesn't respect our country."[30] Even an FBI briefing on how Russia had hacked the Democratic National Committee's emails in a bid to influence the election had no effect. That crime, Trump insisted surreally, could have been carried out by "somebody sitting on their bed that weighs 400 pounds."[31]

In all, Trump made it clear on the campaign trail that he had no intellectual or sentimental attachment to the alliances that the United States had built after World War II; to the multilateral trade system that had generated global prosperity and lifted millions out of poverty; or to America's role in championing democracy, human rights, and the rule of law. Trump's vision was of a dog-eat-dog world in which every country pursued its narrow interests in a fight to be a "winner" rather than a "loser." Trump wasn't proposing to navigate this zero-sum world by positioning the United States as the leader of a global coalition of like-minded states advancing common interests and shared values. To the contrary. In his view, America's friends were as dangerous as its adversaries—if not more so. The alliances and trade deals that Clinton, Bush, and Obama had seen as critical to American security and prosperity weren't the solution. They were the problem.

Trump's critics routinely described this worldview as isolationist. But that wasn't quite right. He did appeal to isolationist sentiments with his criticisms of misguided military interventions and his attacks on efforts to promote democracy and defend human rights. He wasn't, however, looking to withdraw the United States from the world, either militarily or economically. His views differed significantly from those of his GOP rival, Senator Rand Paul, who did advocate curbing America's appetite for military intervention and shrinking its overseas military footprint. Trump said on multiple occasions that he wouldn't make blanket statements about when he would or wouldn't use military force overseas. He also said he was open to ordering the American military to stop humanitarian crises, noting that "it depends on the country, the region, how friendly they've been toward us."[32] He didn't call for allies to spend more on defense so the United States could spend less; he vowed to spend more on defense regardless of what they did. Indeed, the premise underlying his calls for allies to spend more was that America *wouldn't* come home if it got a deal that made it worth staying abroad. Whether

Trump intended it or not, he was effectively suggesting that American power should be up for sale and thereby turning the US military into modern-day Hessians.

Instead of withdrawing from the world, Trump was proposing to shed what he saw as the delusion of American global leadership. He wanted a foreign policy that would be more self-promoting, more nationalist, and utterly transactional. He wasn't looking to build relationships. He was looking to make deals, great deals. In doing so, he would worry about the United States "before we worry about everybody else in the world."[33] In short, he was promising to put "America First."

FOREIGN POLICY EXPERTS derided Trump's embrace of "America First" as his foreign policy slogan. They noted that the original America First movement had sought to keep the United States out of World War II and had been discredited for attracting Nazi sympathizers. Trump showed no sign that he knew the term's origin or its association with anti-Semitic voices—or that it bothered him if he did. For him the slogan stated the obvious. The United States should do what all other countries do: put itself first.

The origins of "America First" were also lost on most Americans. They didn't know their history either. What mattered was that Trump's message had an innate appeal to many voters. Throughout the Cold War and into the post–Cold War era, a segment of the American public had always doubted the wisdom of an activist foreign policy. The exact percentage varied with the poll question and the immediate political context, but over the decades around a third of Americans across the political spectrum wanted the United States to play at most a minor role in world affairs.[34] Rarely, however, had major-party candidates argued for throwing off the mantle of global leadership. When they had, as Patrick Buchanan did in the 1992 and 1996 Republican presidential primaries, they lost badly. Trump, then, was giving voice to political views that had long been marginalized.

Yet Trump's appeal wasn't just to those who wanted the United States to do less in the world. He was also saying aloud what many voters who favored an active role sensed: America's foreign policies weren't working. The promised "cakewalk" in Iraq had turned into a prolonged occupation in which nearly forty-five hundred US service members died. Iraqis weren't grateful for America's sacrifice. Afghanistan had turned into

America's longest war, with no end in sight. The Arab Spring had not yielded the democratic advances that experts had predicted. And defense officials from both parties had been saying for years that too many allies were "willing and eager for American taxpayers to assume the growing security burden left by reductions in European defense budgets."[35] Indeed, the same week that Trump declared NATO obsolete, *The Atlantic* magazine published an interview in which Obama complained, "Free riders aggravate me."[36]

Trump's criticisms of US trade policy resonated for similar reasons. To be sure, trade received far more blame than it deserved for America's economic ills. Trade didn't trigger the Great Recession of 2008–2009, and the relentless advance of technology did far more to eliminate high-paying blue-collar jobs. (US manufacturers produced 40 percent more in 2016 than they did just twenty years earlier with five million fewer workers, thanks to productivity improvements.)[37] That said, successive administrations oversold the job-generating benefits of US trade deals while downplaying the fact that greater foreign competition would hurt some industries even as the overall economy grew. Most important, policy makers were slow to recognize how badly China's entry into the WTO had damaged US manufacturing. Workers living in Akron, Flint, and Scranton, however, had felt the impact of "the China shock" immediately and directly.[38] Washington's recognition that something needed to be done came too late to help them.

And by attacking immigrants and refugees, Trump tapped into strong strains of xenophobia and racism in American political life. As much as Americans celebrated being a nation of immigrants, many of them also feared it. Over the course of American history, surges in immigration into the United States had repeatedly triggered a backlash against newcomers. The recent wave of immigration was no different. Trump stoked and exploited simmering resentments across the country.

In running against the core tenets of postwar American foreign policy, Trump benefited from being a political outsider. He bore no responsibility for previous failures, a point he made time and again. He was helped by the fact that he could portray himself as having opposed the Iraq War. Whether he actually did was debatable; he certainly didn't oppose "it very strongly" from the start, as he often said.[39] But most of his rivals couldn't make even a debatable claim to having opposed the invasion. A strong majority of Americans may have supported the war at the start;

more than a decade later, an equally large majority saw it as a mistake. Trump was telling those voters he had foreseen what the experts had missed. And if experts had gotten Iraq wrong, they were likely wrong on other important matters as well.

But Trump wasn't just campaigning on what he hadn't done. He was also campaigning on what he could do. He made that point in his campaign announcement: "This is going to be an election that's based on competence."[40] Trump vowed that he would bring real-world common sense to a government long run by incompetents. He regularly belittled foreign policy experts as "dummies."[41] It was their utter disregard for how America's pocket was being picked that had left the country in its imperiled state. Ignoring their advice would improve US foreign policy: "If our presidents and our politicians went on vacation for 365 days a year and went to the beach," Trump said, "we'd be in much better shape right now in the Middle East."[42] In contrast, Trump insisted that the skills that had made him a great businessman would translate easily into the world of foreign policy. He could get things done in the White House because he had gotten things done in the cutthroat world of real estate.

One final aspect of America First increased its appeal. As with his open letter three decades earlier, Trump wasn't an American Churchill promising only "blood, toil, tears, and sweat."[43] Precisely the opposite. He insisted Americans could win without making sacrifices. As one newspaper headline put it, "In Donald Trump's Worldview, America Comes First, Everyone Else Pays."[44] The allies would spend more on defense. Middle East oil would pay to defeat terrorists. New trade deals would send jobs flooding back to the United States. Although experts denied there was free lunch to be had, Trump understood better than his critics what many Americans wanted to hear. As one perceptive analyst wrote of his all-gain-no-pain claims, "he sensed that the public wanted relief from the burdens of global leadership without losing the thrill of nationalist self-assertion."[45] What policies, then, would put America First?

ON THE CAMPAIGN trail, Trump was crystal clear about who was to blame for America's troubled foreign policy: politicians who didn't stand up for America's interests, experts with foolish ideas and bad judgment, and ungrateful allies that bit the hand that fed them. But as specific as Trump was in his diagnosis, he was vague in his prescription for what would produce "so much winning" that Americans might "get bored with winning."[46] To an extent unparalleled in modern American politics, he avoided laying out detailed policies or describing how his remedies would work. Indeed, for as much as he talked about America's "horrible" trade deals, he never said what a good trade deal would look like or what the United States might need to give up to get it.

What Trump offered in the place of traditional campaign policy proposals was attitude. Strength, in his view, was the coin of the realm. He would be the strong leader America lacked. He would compel concessions from others. Time and again, he said he would create "the strongest military that we've ever had" and be prepared to wield it without regard to the diplomatic niceties other presidents had observed. He argued that the United States should simply use its "tremendous economic power over China" to force Beijing to trade fairly.[47] The fact that military power was irrelevant to many of the challenges the United States faced overseas and that China could retaliate against American companies mattered little to his thinking.

When Trump did venture into policy specifics, he offered simplistic and often contradictory ideas. He said he would destroy the Islamic State by bombing "the hell out of the oil fields" that it controlled, though few military experts believed such a strategy would work.[48] He further ventured that he would defeat the terrorist group "with very few troops on the ground."[49] But he also said that "we really have no choice" but to send up to thirty thousand troops to fight the Islamic State.[50] He repeatedly complained that Obama had botched US policy in Libya and Syria. But he had called for the United States to overthrow Muammar Gaddafi and encouraged Obama to "stay the hell out of Syria."[51] He vowed to punish China for artificially depressing the value of its currency to gain a trading advantage. By the time he became a candidate, however, China was actively intervening in currency markets to prop up the value of the renminbi.[52]

When journalists pushed Trump for specifics or noted his contradictions, he had a ready-made response: he had plans, but it would be foolish to reveal them. "I have a plan," he said when asked about how he would defeat the Islamic State, but "I don't want to broadcast to the enemy exactly what my plan is."[53] Indeed, he went further to argue that refusing to discuss specifics would give him the upper hand in his dealings abroad. "We are totally predictable," he complained. "We tell everything. We're sending troops. We tell them. We're sending something else. We have a news conference. We have to be unpredictable."[54] He never explained why the unpredictability that would intimidate America's adversaries wouldn't also unnerve its allies, who were looking not for surprises but for steadiness from Washington.

Trump was hardly the first candidate to skirt tough questions about details, trade-offs, and costs in his foreign policy proposals. Nor was he the first to suggest he had a secret plan to win a war. Richard Nixon had done so in 1968 on Vietnam. Campaigns, after all, are about visions and promises, not about decisions and choices. And being vague on the campaign trail has virtues. Many presidents found once they reached the Oval Office that they had boxed themselves in by what they had promised during the campaign. But shying away from specifics helps only if candidates know what they want to do and that it can in fact be done. In the absence of either, vagueness is a recipe for chaos and confusion.

As IMPORTANT AS what Trump proposed to do in foreign policy was how much he knew about it. For decades he had expressed strong opinions about what the United States did abroad. But on the campaign trail he showed time and again that he had a lot to learn about economics and foreign policy. He was often wrong on details. He said that America's gross domestic product, a measure of the country's total economic output, was "below zero."[55] When asked how he would modernize the US nuclear triad—the land-, sea-, and air-based components of the US nuclear arsenal—his rambling answer suggested he didn't know what it was.[56] He argued that US nuclear weapons were "obsolete" because "we have not been updating" them, even though a modernization program had been under way for several years at a total projected cost of $1 trillion.[57] In an interview with a friendly conservative radio talk show host, he confused Iran's Revolutionary Guards Quds Force with the Iraqi Kurds and admitted that he didn't know the names of the leaders of al Qaeda, Hezbollah, and the Islamic State.[58]

More important, though, he was also often flat wrong on major matters. NATO wasn't obsolete. Contrary to what he claimed, fighting terrorism had been one of its primary objectives since September 11. He seemed not to know that US allies typically subsidized the presence of American military forces on their soil. As a result, bringing the troops back home would cost the United States, not save it money. He failed to acknowledge that the livelihoods of hundreds of thousands of American workers depended on trade and that imposing tariffs on other countries would potentially cost workers their jobs. He refused to recognize how Washington's promotion of democracy, human rights, and the rule of law had inspired democratic activists, helped topple authoritarian regimes, and curtailed human rights abuses around the world. The list went on.

Trump was hardly the first presidential candidate to voice foreign policy opinions that outpaced his actual knowledge. In his first race for the presidency, George W. Bush famously failed a foreign policy pop quiz sprung on him by a TV reporter. (He couldn't name the leaders of India, Pakistan, or Chechnya.) What distinguished Trump was how he reacted to charges that he didn't know enough. Bush freely admitted he wasn't a foreign policy expert. "This is a big world," he said, "and I've got a lot to learn."[59] Trump insisted, against all available evidence, not only that he knew a lot but that he knew more than anyone else.

It didn't matter what the subject was; the candidate who had made a career as a property developer and a reality TV star claimed to know more than people who had devoted their lives to the topic—whether it was foreign policy generally ("I know more about foreign policy than anybody running"); the Islamic State ("I know more about ISIS than the generals do"); trade policy ("Nobody knows more about trade than me"); the Iran deal ("I've studied it in great detail. I would say, actually, greater by far than anybody else"); or alternative fuels ("I know more about renewables than any human being on Earth").[60] In the few instances in which he admitted he didn't know something, he said that once he became president he "would know more about it . . . and believe me, it won't take me long."[61] Trump's supreme confidence in what he knew, or would quickly learn, led to supreme confidence in his ability: "I'm the only one who knows how to fix" America's failed foreign policy, he declared in April 2016.[62]

Trump ignored another standard move out of the presidential campaign playbook: assembling a team of foreign policy advisers to brief the candidate on world events, produce policy papers explaining what the candidate proposed to do, and act as surrogates on television and radio. Instead, Trump flew solo. As soon as his campaign started, reporters asked who was advising him. He repeatedly said he would be "announcing something very soon."[63] When he finally named five advisers in March 2016, many foreign policy experts wondered who they were.

Three of the advisers had no significant government experience; one was a 2009 college graduate who cited participation in Model UN as one of his qualifications.[64] None of the five was close to Trump, and none was heavily involved in drafting speeches or writing policy papers. The truth was that Trump didn't have a team of foreign policy advisers. And he didn't have one because he didn't think he needed one. He was being candid when he said, "My primary consultant is myself and I have a good instinct for this stuff."[65]

Most Republican foreign policy experts wouldn't have rushed to advise Trump even if he had been willing to accept advice. The positions he had staked out alarmed his GOP rivals, leading them to call him variously a "jackass," a "kook," and a "race-baiting, xenophobic, religious bigot" (Lindsey Graham); "a jerk" (Jeb Bush); a "con artist" and a "lunatic" (Marco Rubio); and "amoral" and a "pathological liar" (Ted Cruz).[66] Disdain for Trump ran even deeper among the GOP foreign policy establishment. In March 2016, 122 Republican foreign policy experts signed an open letter arguing that he "would use the authority of his office to act in ways that make America less safe, and which would diminish our standing in the world."[67] Shortly after Trump won the Republican nomination, fifty Republican national security leaders signed another open letter saying he "would be a dangerous President and put at risk our country's national security and well-being."[68]

Trump not surprisingly ignored the complaints of the "Never Trumpers." After all, these were the people who in his view had created the problems he had vowed to fix. But in alienating the GOP foreign policy establishment, Trump created a problem for himself. If he won, he could not govern alone. He would need to staff a government and fill hundreds of foreign policy posts. The Never Trumpers knew how to make government work. But even before he had taken his oath of office, many of the people his administration would need had already taken themselves out of the running. And even if they wanted back in, Trump was not a man to forgive or forget. By accident, design, and declaration, the new foreign policy team would be a band of one: the new president himself.

4

A Very Organized Process

At two thirty in the morning, November 9, 2016, Wisconsin was called. To the surprise of the country, the world, and almost certainly himself, Donald J. Trump was elected president. Until Election Day, Trump had focused on running for president and maybe dreamed a little about winning. But he hadn't thought about governing at all. Having won the election, he now had seventy-three days to get ready for the moment he would become the leader of the United States and the Free World.

Throughout the long campaign, Trump had refused to think about the day after the election, concerned it would send the wrong signal and hurt his chances of victory. "Remember Romney?" Trump asked of his campaign staff, referring to the 2012 Republican candidate. "He was walking around in khakis with his transition team, and what the hell did it get him? I'll tell you what! He lost!"[1] Fortunately, even as Trump refused to think about governing while still on the campaign trail, a seasoned team of former officials had been working for months to get ready for the day he would win. Thick binders full of possible candidates for the many positions that need to be filled, detailed timelines, and extensive plans for the first days and weeks of a new administration had been assembled by the team, which was led by New Jersey Governor Chris Christie. The day after the election, Christie's team was ready to turn planning into practice.

Trump and his closest advisers had other ideas, however. They sidelined Christie and largely ignored his team's work from the summer. A new team decided to start over, essentially making it up as they went along. Trump boasted on Facebook about the "very organized process taking place as I decide on Cabinet and many other positions."[2] But the reality was otherwise. Beyond selecting his cabinet, Trump showed little interest in any of the transition details. Much like the campaign that preceded it, the transition was chaotic. Trump didn't care. In winning the presidency, he had done what no one thought he could. Now he would govern the same way.

THE UNITED STATES is unusual among democracies. In most democratic governments, only a handful of senior positions change after an election. In the United States, however, the entire top level of government turns over when one president gives way to another. The personnel changes involve not just prominent posts, like cabinet secretaries and ambassadors, but also thousands of jobs held by little-known officials across every government department and agency. The turnover is especially dramatic in the White House, where an almost entirely new staff starts work the same day a new president first sets foot in the Oval Office.

The scale of the turnover when the presidency changes hands is enormous, as is the potential for turmoil and even catastrophe as new officials learn their job while events march on. Having lived through the horror of the 9/11 terrorist attacks, George W. Bush recognized how vulnerable a new administration might be and sought to ensure as seamless a transition as possible in 2009. His staff worked for months to prepare the next president, from the moment he entered office, for whatever might happen. They wrote detailed transition briefs and hosted a crisis simulation to help their successors better understand the challenges they would face after Inauguration Day.

Barack Obama deeply appreciated Bush's effort. He worked with Congress to make what Bush had done voluntarily a matter of law. In August 2016, after the Republican and Democratic parties had selected their presidential nominees, that process went into effect for the first time. The Trump and Clinton campaigns each set up transition efforts on separate floors in a government-run building on Pennsylvania Avenue, a stone's throw away from the White House. Trump tapped Christie to head his transition effort, and the New Jersey governor set out to prepare for a possible Trump presidency.

By late September, about one hundred people were part of the Trump transition team. In ten weeks, they generated enough documents to fill thirty binders. Some of the documents contained the names and résumés of potential candidates for six hundred of the most senior appointments. Others created detailed "landing teams" that, during the transition,

would work with current senior officials at each of the executive departments and agencies to prepare for the new administration. Still other
documents were drafts of executive orders and policy pronouncements
that Trump might issue. There was a timeline for the transition itself. The
aim was to complete all cabinet appointments by early December and
other top-level appointments by the end of the year. Christie's team also
developed specific action plans for day one, day one hundred, and day
two hundred of a Trump presidency. All of it had been shared with the
campaign in weekly updates that top campaign officials regularly discussed. Even if few thought Trump would win the election, his transition
team at least was ready.

ON NOVEMBER 9, everything seemed in place for a smooth transition. Two
days later, Trump upended the process and made Vice President–elect
Mike Pence the chair of the transition. A new executive committee
was appointed. It consisted of Trump's children and son-in-law, an
assortment of Trump friends and acquaintances, and a number of senior
campaign advisers. With a few exceptions, none had any government
experience, and except for Christie (who was relegated to one of six
vice chairs), none had been involved in the transition team's prior work.
Indeed, many of the people Christie had hired to staff the transition
effort were summarily dismissed, replaced by campaign aides and others
close to top Trump advisers. And the thirty binders of carefully prepared
documents were thrown in the trash.

Trump never explained why he shook up his transition team. Some
said he worried about having too many Christie cronies around. Others
pointed to the conviction of two Christie aides as part of the "Bridgegate"
scandal days earlier. Jared Kushner, Trump's son-in-law and a ubiquitous
presence during the campaign, no doubt had a role. A decade earlier,
Christie had prosecuted Kushner's father for corruption, sending him to
jail. Whatever Trump's reasoning was, it was clear that the decision had
little to do with the transition itself. The president-elect showed little
interest in the process. And neither he nor many on his team understood
the scope of the transition. "How many of these people stay?" Kushner
asked when he strolled through the West Wing two days after the election.[3] The answer was none. All of them would be gone on January 20.

Although process and planning—and outlining policy options—had
been top of mind for Christie and his team before the election, the only

things that mattered now with Christie gone were people and power. Finding the right people, and jockeying for position, became the singular focus for the next seventy days.

When Trump sat down with Obama in the Oval Office two days after the election, he asked him for a list of names for possible top national security positions.[4] Obama said he would get him a list, and he ordered his staff to prepare one within thirty-six hours. But he made clear that one person shouldn't be on it: Michael Flynn. The retired general, Obama warned Trump, was ill suited for a senior position. In 2014, the White House had ordered Flynn's firing as director of the Defense Intelligence Agency (DIA) citing managerial incompetence. Since then, Obama argued, Flynn's publicly declared hard-line views on Islam and his financial connections to Russia disqualified him from a top job. Interestingly, Christie shared Obama's view, and he had left Flynn's name off his list of potential candidates for national security adviser.[5]

None of the names on the list Obama sent Trump was ever seriously considered for a position in the new administration. A week after the Oval Office meeting, Trump ignored Obama's warning and announced he had picked Flynn as his national security adviser. Trump's choice was not surprising. Flynn had been an early supporter of his campaign and warmed up crowds before Trump's campaign speeches. The incoming president knew the general better than any other potential national security official. At one point, he had even considered making Flynn his running mate. Trump also valued loyalty, and above all, Flynn had been loyal, barnstorming the country for Trump during the election and even giving an electrifying speech at the Republican National Convention, in which he joined the crowd in chanting, "Lock her up! Lock her up!"

Aside from loyalty, Flynn saw the world in much the same way Trump did. Both believed Iran and radical Islamic terrorism posed existential threats to America, and both believed Russia could be a valuable partner in addressing those threats. "We can't do what we want to do unless we work with Russia, period," Flynn told the *New York Times* before the election. Moscow's illegal invasion of Ukraine and bombing of civilians in Syria was "besides the point." Improving relations with Moscow was vital to winning what Flynn called a "world war" against Islamists. "What we both have is a common enemy," he insisted. "The common enemy that we have is radical Islam."[6] Like Trump, Flynn believed that the problem wasn't that America and Russia had different objectives in Syria or the Middle East but that Obama had been too weak in addressing the terrorist threat. Putin responded to strength, and Trump would demonstrate strength through an unapologetic use of American military power to destroy Islamic radicalism. That would place America and Russia on the same side.

Appearing strong was important to Trump, and he sought top advisers who conveyed strength. That was another reason he chose Flynn, a retired three-star general, to be his national security adviser. It also led him to meet with a series of other retired generals and admirals to discuss key positions in his administration. One was former US Army vice chief of staff General Jack Keane, who had advised the campaign and transition teams. In their first meeting, Trump offered Keane the job of defense secretary. Keane declined, citing personal reasons (his wife of fifty-one years had recently passed away), and suggested Trump consider retired generals James Mattis or David Petraeus, both former commanders of US forces in the Middle East.[7]

During the campaign, Mattis had talked to every candidate, except Trump. When the two met at Trump's golf course in Bedminster, New Jersey, on November 19, Mattis told Trump he had major disagreements with his positions on critical issues, including on torture, NATO and Russia, immigration, and trade. The meeting concluded after forty minutes, and Mattis didn't think he would be offered a job. But Trump was impressed. "General James 'Mad Dog' Mattis, who is being considered for Secretary of Defense, was very impressive yesterday," he tweeted the next morning. "A true General's General!"[8] Days later Trump recounted how Mattis had convinced him that waterboarding and other means of torture were ineffective. "I was very impressed by that answer," Trump told the *New York Times.* Torture is "not going to make the kind of a difference that a lot of people are thinking."[9]

Mattis's candidacy to head the Pentagon was atypical. All but one of the previous secretaries of defense had been civilians. The exception was the legendary George C. Marshall, who had been chief of staff of the army during World War II and served as Truman's secretary of state before moving over to the Pentagon. But the choice of Mattis made sense for Trump. Like Flynn, Mattis had had his disagreements with the Obama administration, notably over how hard a line to take with Iran, as a result of which he had been replaced as head of US Central Command before his full tour had been completed. "Iran is not a nation-state," he told a Washington think tank in 2016. "It's a revolutionary cause devoted to mayhem [and] the single most enduring threat to stability and peace in the Middle East."[10] Mattis also worried about the consequences of America's retreat from the region. After leaving active duty, he told Congress that Obama's "policy of disengagement in the Middle East" had fueled the rise of the Islamic State. The United States needed to "come out from our reactive crouch and take a firm, strategic stance in defense of our values."[11]

Trump no doubt was also attracted to some of the mythology surrounding Mattis. A hard-charging marine, he had led his troops in the failed pursuit of Osama bin Laden into the Tora Bora mountains in late 2001. He had also commanded the 1st Marine Division in the 2003 invasion of Iraq. "I come in peace. I didn't bring artillery," Mattis would tell local Iraqi leaders. "But I'm pleading with you, with tears in my eyes: if you fuck with me, I will kill you all."[12] Trump loved the nickname "Mad Dog" and announced his decision to nominate Mattis as defense secretary at a campaign-style rally. Trump called him "the closest thing we have to General George Patton," the storied general who fought Field Marshal Erwin Rommel's army in the African desert and helped lead the liberation of Europe in World War II.[13]

The real-life Mattis was rather different from the mythology, however. To his friends, Mattis was better known as the "warrior monk" than by the "Mad Dog" moniker he disdained. A lifelong bachelor, he was an avid reader who traveled with his thousands of books from one military assignment to the next. "Thanks to my reading, I have never been caught flat-footed by any situation," he told a colleague in 2003. "It doesn't give me all the answers, but it lights what is often a dark path ahead."[14] This, for example, was how he explained his thinking about counterinsurgency: "You're as well off if you've read 'Angela's Ashes' and Desmond Tutu's writings, and if you've studied Northern Ireland and the efforts for rapprochement there, and in South Africa following their civil war, as you are if you've read Sherman and, obviously, von Clausewitz."[15]

A patriot, Mattis agreed to serve as Trump's secretary of defense. He made clear, however, that he would always remain his own man. They could disagree in private, Mattis told the president-elect, but if he were ever criticized in public, he would leave the same day. Same if he was ordered to do something illegal or immoral. "If I ever thought it was something immoral," he told Congress during his confirmation hearings, "I'd be back fishing on the Columbia River tomorrow."[16]

ALTHOUGH TRUMP QUICKLY settled on Flynn and Mattis, the search for his secretary of state proved more challenging. Rudy Giuliani had strongly supported Trump during the campaign, and he thought he was a shoo-in for the job. But Trump didn't like people who tried to steal the limelight from him, and when stories about Giuliani's foreign business entanglements and large speaking fees emerged, the president-elect looked elsewhere. One possible candidate was South Carolina Governor Nikki Haley, a rising star in the GOP. Although she had supported Marco Rubio during the campaign and had been a late convert to Trump, their first meeting at Trump Tower went so well that the president-elect offered her the job. Haley was flattered. But she realized that her foreign policy résumé was too thin and declined the offer. "I'm very aware of when things are right and when they are not," she told CNN a few months later. "I just thought he could find someone better."[17] Instead, Trump made her his ambassador to the United Nations.

Next, Trump flirted with a host of other possible candidates, including former CIA Director David Petraeus, former UN Ambassador John Bolton, former Utah Governor Jon Huntsman, and Senate Foreign Relations Committee Chair Senator Bob Corker. All of them traipsed through the lobby of Trump Tower to meet with the president-elect, and afterward he would tweet how well he thought of them. Perhaps the most surprising of the candidates Trump considered was Mitt Romney, the 2012 Republican nominee, who had been a fierce critic of Trump during the campaign. Although Trump seemed to take to Romney, saying he "looks the part," many of his strongest supporters rose up in loud protest, dooming any chance of Romney ending up at Foggy Bottom.[18] On the advice of Robert Gates, the former secretary of defense and CIA director, Trump next considered someone who had not been on anyone's radar screen—Rex Tillerson, the soon-to-retire CEO of Exxon. "If you want to understand Rex Tillerson," Gates explained, "and it may be a corny thing to say, but you've got to understand that he's an Eagle Scout."[19] When Tillerson first met with Trump, the president-elect was "blown away" by the oilman and immediately offered him the job.[20] "The president puts a ton of weight on first impressions,"

Steve Bannon, Trump's campaign chair, later recounted. "As soon as Rex walked in the room, I knew the job was his."[21]

Tillerson was a surprising choice as secretary of state. Although Trump noted that he was "much more than a business executive; he's a world-class player," Tillerson was the first nominee for the job who had neither government nor military experience.[22] Instead, he had worked at Exxon since graduating with an engineering degree from the University of Texas in 1975. A company man through and through, Tillerson had come to know world leaders, especially in the Middle East and Russia. But his focus had been on deals that made money—not the underlying complexities involved in diplomacy. He admitted as much in a town hall meeting in late 2017. "When I came to the State Department," Tillerson explained, "I didn't know anything about your culture, I didn't know anything about what motivates you, I didn't know anything about your work, I didn't know anything about how you get your work done."[23] Nor, three months out from retirement, was he all that interested in being secretary of state. "I didn't want this job. I didn't seek this job," he told a reporter in his first interview after arriving at Foggy Bottom. "My wife told me I'm supposed to do this."[24]

The biggest issue facing his nomination, however, wasn't his desire for the job or his aptitude for it but his views on Russia. Exxon had been deeply invested in Russian energy development, and Tillerson had worked closely with Russian President Vladimir Putin. In 2013, Putin had awarded Tillerson the Order of Friendship, and the following year, when the United States and European Union imposed sanctions on Moscow for its invasion of Ukraine, the Exxon chief had argued for leniency toward Russia. And although he skipped the St. Petersburg economic forum in 2014 and 2015, he had returned in 2016 and appeared all chummy on a panel with Putin crony Igor Sechin, the head of Rosneft, the state-run oil company. The same year, Tillerson told students at his alma mater that he had "a very close relationship" with the Russian president.[25]

Given how Trump had bent over backward to be nice to Putin during the campaign, many worried about a secretary of state who appeared to share such sentiments. This is "a matter of concern to me," Senator John McCain said in reacting to Tillerson's possible nomination. "Vladimir Putin is a thug, bully and a murderer, and anybody else who describes him as anything else is lying."[26] Senator Marco Rubio weighed in via

Twitter: "Being a 'friend of Vladimir' is not an attribute I am hoping for from a #SecretaryOfState."[27] Although Tillerson would ultimately assuage those concerns sufficiently to win confirmation, forty-three senators voted against him, the largest number of negative votes ever for any secretary of state nominee.

WHAT WAS NOTABLE about Trump's national security team was that he had known so few of them before Election Day. He met most of them for the first time during the transition, and those meetings invariably ended in job offers. Trump wasn't looking for a cohesive team of advisers who shared a common perspective on the world or even for a creative team of rivals. He was looking for people from central casting—often tall, broad-shouldered men—preferably with combat experience. Mattis fit the bill. So did John Kelly, like Mattis, a retired four-star Marine general, who had last served as commander of Southern Command. Trump briefly considered Kelly for State but, attracted by the general's southern border experience, nominated him instead to run Homeland Security, the department in charge of countering terrorism at home and defending America's borders from threats abroad. For CIA director, Trump selected a Tea Party congressman from Kansas, Mike Pompeo, who had graduated from West Point. Though Tillerson lacked a military background, he conveyed strength as a Texas oilman and world-class deal maker who had little in common with the striped-pants caricature of the State Department diplomat.

In contrast to his predecessors, who had always looked for experience at the highest levels of government to staff the senior most national security positions, Trump did not place much value on knowing how to operate in Washington. Indeed, most of his picks lacked deep Washington experience. Pence and Pompeo had served on Capitol Hill, not in the executive branch. Tillerson spent his life moving up the ranks at Exxon. Most of the retired military spent their time in the field rather than in bureaucratic battles inside the Beltway, as had past generals like Colin Powell and Brent Scowcroft, who had help top national security positions. Flynn's career was in military intelligence, and his first managerial experience as DIA director had ended badly. Mattis had avoided policy positions at the Pentagon during his forty-four years in the Marine Corps. And although Kelly spent a year working the Hill and served as the senior military assistant for Robert Gates and Leon Panetta, he too was not a Washington creature.

Other presidents might have compensated for this lack of Washington experience by surrounding themselves in the White House with advisers who had walked the corridors of powers for years. Yet, here too, the New York real estate mogul opted to rely on people who had never served in the executive branch. As his chief of staff, Trump appointed Reince Priebus, a political operative from Wisconsin who had worked his way up to head the Republican National Committee. Trump appointed Steve Bannon as his chief strategist, a position he made explicitly coequal to the chief of staff. Bannon had a sharp intellect, but he was a flamethrower who had run Breitbart, the alt-right news site. The final power center in the White House was occupied by Jared Kushner, Ivanka Trump's husband, who was appointed the president's special adviser. During the campaign, Kushner had been responsible for interacting with foreign diplomats and officials, a practice he extended during the transition. Once in the White House, the thirty-seven-year-old real estate developer would take on responsibility for Middle East peace as well as being the point man in bilateral relations with China, Mexico, and Saudi Arabia—all matters that normally would fall under the purview of the secretary of state.

The members of Trump's national security team shared some important commonalities. Most of them had spent years dealing with the Middle East; they had far less exposure to Asia or Europe. Most of them believed in using hard power, especially the military, to get things done. Flynn, Kelly, and Mattis had all served under Obama and clashed with a president they saw as weak. All saw a need to respond more strongly to terrorism at home and to destroy the Islamic State and other terrorist threats abroad. They viewed Iran as a particularly destabilizing presence in the Middle East, though some, like Mattis and Tillerson, thought it best to stick with the nuclear agreement with Iran that Trump had railed against during the campaign.

But they disagreed on many more issues. The main division was over America's role in the world. The newcomers to Trump world—Mattis, Tillerson, Pompeo, and even Pence—held traditional foreign policy views, believing in American leadership of a rules-based order founded on security alliances; free trade agreements; and support for democracy, human rights, and the rule of law. They saw a resurgent Russia in adversarial terms and worried about rising strategic competition from China. These were mainstream views in Washington. Trump and many of his closest White House advisers, however, roundly rejected them, castigating the traditional national security worldview as "globalist," in contrast to their "nationalist" perspective. Among the most prominent nationalists were Bannon and Trump's trade advisers, including Peter Navarro, who was appointed to head the new National Trade Council at the White House; Robert Lighthizer, who served as the US trade representative; and Secretary of Commerce Wilbur Ross. These nationalists all shared Trump's view that existing multilateral trade arrangements had benefited other countries at the expense of American jobs and growth; that China in particular posed the gravest economic threat; and that rewriting trade deals with allies in North America, Europe, and Asia should take priority over security cooperation. This America First view had been central to Trump's campaign and to his victory—and it would be central to his governing as well.

Trump saw no problem in these conflicting views among his senior advisers. Globalist and nationalist views would live alongside each other in a Trump administration, leaving the ultimate decision on policy to the president. As he said later, "Hey, I'm a nationalist and a globalist. I'm both. And I'm the only one who makes the decision, believe me."[28]

THE TRUMP TEAM approached the transition much as they would a hostile takeover. There was little, if any, contact between those who were coming in and the Obama officials who were leaving. Mattis had a brief courtesy call with Defense Secretary Ashton Carter. Tillerson didn't even go that far; he never talked to Secretary of State John Kerry—before or after his confirmation. Flynn did meet four times with Susan Rice, but mainly because the outgoing national security adviser insisted she brief him on sensitive matters he needed to know before taking office. He didn't come with a note taker or take many notes himself. Things were little better below the top levels. The Trump team had three different people heading the transition for the National Security Council (NSC) and its staff during the seventy-three days between the election and inauguration. It took two weeks for anyone to begin the NSC transition process, and when the first Trump group arrived at the White House, only two of the six had security clearances. Over at the State Department, the process was even less involved. The department had set up a large transition office just off the C Street entrance to the Harry S. Truman Building. There was space for fifty people. Fewer than a dozen ever showed up. Contact with officials in the department was sparse and largely discouraged. When Haley contacted senior State officials to ask about some of the details of her office and residence, the transition head called the officials and told them never to speak to an incoming person again.[29]

Rather than preparing for governing—or filling out the large slate of politically appointed positions with nominations—the Trump team was eager to actually begin governing. So eager, in fact, that on several occasions, the president-elect and his team wanted to make policy even before they were in office. Trump's predecessors had sought to make clear to foreign governments—friends and foes alike—that, as Bill Clinton put it following his election in 1992, "America has only one President at a time, [and] that America's foreign policy remains solely in his hands."[30] That was not how Trump and his team saw it. From congratulatory phone calls with foreign leaders to direct interference on sensitive policy issues with foreign diplomats, Trump's team sought to put its stamp on foreign policy well before his inauguration.

Foreign leaders were eager to talk to the incoming president. Few of them knew him, and many were worried about the positions he had taken during the campaign. They needed reassurance. The president-elect himself was just as eager to receive their congratulatory calls. He talked to thirty-two of them in the first few weeks of the transition. But he did so in ways that broke with precedent and confused rather than reassured many foreign leaders. In past transitions, the incoming team would prioritize whom the president-elect would talk to, making sure critical allies and partners were the first to connect with him. Calls would be routed through the State Department Operations Center, which is staffed around the clock by career foreign service officers, to ensure that the foreign leaders on the other line were who they said they were and to provide translators and note takers as necessary. And before any call, the transition team would normally work with State Department experts to prepare short briefing papers that would give the president-elect a heads-up on issues that might be raised and suggest ways to respond or deflect. All of these procedures had been laid out in a memo contained in one of the binders Christie's team had prepared before the election.[31]

Trump and his team ignored all of these standard practices. They made no attempt to connect with or use the State Department in handling the large number of calls that were coming in to congratulate Trump on his victory. Leaders who called the State Department were told that the staff did not know how to connect them with the president-elect, leaving them to try to find a way to reach him on their own. Some proved inventive. Australian Prime Minister Malcolm Turnbull reached Trump on his cell phone after he got the number from golfer Greg Norman.[32] Others called Trump Tower in the hope that they might get through. For his part, Trump took incoming calls in no particular order and without vetting the callers. He didn't request briefings on the issues that other leaders might raise, and no note takers recorded what was said.

The result was a series of early missteps, most minor but some with more lasting consequences. The first call to get through was from Egyptian strongman Abdel Fattah el-Sisi. The only NATO ally Trump spoke with on his first day as president-elect was Turkey's President Recep Tayyip Erdogan.[33] British Prime Minister Theresa May, who had been first on the Christie-prepared list of calls, was unable to get through until the next day. Trump reassured her that Britain was "a very special place for me and my country." However, rather than issuing a formal invitation to visit the White House, he told her, "If you travel to the US, you should let me know."[34] Other foreign leaders happily released their own version of their conversations with Trump, often painting themselves in the most favorable possible light. The government of Kazakhstan, for example, noted that Trump "stressed that under the leadership of Nursultan Nazarbayev," who had been in power for a quarter century, Kazakhstan "had achieved fantastic success that can be called a 'miracle.'"[35] The Pakistani prime minister's office issued a press release indicating Trump had accepted an invitation to visit Pakistan, saying he "would love to come to a fantastic country, fantastic place of fantastic people."[36] And Philippine President Rodrigo Duterte, whose cold-blooded war on drug traffickers had killed thousands, reported that Trump was "quite sensitive" to "our worry about drugs" and that he thought the crackdown was being conducted in "the right way."[37]

Without a note taker on the US end, there was no way to counter these characterizations. Most commentators dismissed them as the stumbles of a newly elected president who was not yet fully staffed. But there were more consequential cases, as when Trump in early December spoke to President Tsai Ing-wen of Taiwan, becoming the first president or president-elect to do so since 1979, when the United States broke diplomatic relations with the Chinese island nation. "The president of Taiwan

CALLED ME today to wish me congratulations on winning the Presidency," Trump tweeted in response to the uproar.[38] Yet the transition had planned the call for some time, with the goal of gaining leverage over Beijing by suggesting the Trump administration might not adhere to the long-established "One-China" policy, under which Washington recognized only Beijing, not Taipei, as representing China. "I took a call," Trump said a few days later. "I fully understand the One-China policy. But I don't know why we have to be bound by a One-China policy unless we make a deal with China having to do with other things, including trade. . . . I don't want China dictating to me."[39] Even if deliberate, the policy change was not well thought out, and the transition was hardly the optimal moment to announce such a consequential change. Moreover, within weeks of taking office, Trump reversed himself after Beijing let it be known that there would be no further high-level contact unless the president recommitted the United States to the One-China policy.[40]

The phone calls and public statements all left an unsettling impression abroad. Yes, Trump was new at governing, and he would hopefully learn the ropes over time. But the dominant sense overseas was that they now faced a president who had little knowledge of the world, little discipline in dealing with foreign leaders, and little staffing to help set him straight. All of a sudden, the leadership of the Free World was in the hands of someone who did not appear to comprehend the responsibility attendant to such a role. It was a concern shared in the Obama White House, leading Obama to declare that his "advice to [Trump] has been that before he starts having a lot of interactions with foreign governments other than the usual courtesy calls, that he should want to have his full team in place, that he should want his team to be fully briefed on what's gone on in the past and where the potential pitfalls may be, where the opportunities are."[41] Sound advice. The incoming team didn't follow it.

RATHER THAN WAIT for the inauguration, Trump allowed, if not encouraged, his advisers to make their voices heard on foreign policy matters during the transition in at least two notable instances. The first concerned Israel. In the second half of December, the UN Security Council considered a resolution criticizing Israeli settlement activities as an obstacle to achieving a two-state solution to the conflict with the Palestinians. Israel strongly opposed the resolution, but the Obama administration signaled it might abstain from the vote as a sign of its displeasure with continuing settlement expansion—as previous administrations had done on other occasions. Trump's transition team put on a full-court press to stop the vote. Kushner directed Flynn to call members of the Security Council, including Russia, to see if they would halt consideration of the resolution or, failing that, vote against it. This was a top priority for Trump, Kushner told Flynn.[42] Trump himself called Egypt's President Sisi, whose government had sponsored the resolution, asking him to drop it and suggesting that a vote would harm Egypt's relations with the new administration.[43] At the State Department, the transition team asked for cell phone numbers and email addresses for the ambassadors and foreign ministers of the fourteen other Security Council members. Nikki Haley tried to reach Ambassador Samantha Power, whom she was slated to succeed, to ask her to postpone the vote. And on December 22, Trump went public. "The resolution being considered at the United Nations Security Council regarding Israel should be vetoed," he tweeted, noting it "is extremely unfair to all Israelis."[44]

The collective attempts to interfere in the UN deliberations had some effect.[45] Following Trump's call, Cairo dropped its sponsorship of the resolution, though the other cosponsors (Malaysia, New Zealand, Senegal, and Venezuela) continued to push for a vote. Russia at the last minute asked that the vote be postponed until after Christmas, arguing in part that a new US administration was on the way in. The vote nonetheless proceeded. The final outcome was fourteen votes in favor and one abstention—by the United States. At most, the Trump team could claim its effort had nudged Britain a bit. Even though it had played a critical role in drafting the resolution, after the vote, London sought to move closer to the incoming administration by taking a far more critical tone of the Obama administration, including issuing a sharply worded critique of a major end-of-the-year speech by John Kerry on the resolution and peace process.[46]

The Trump team's pressure had more success in the second case, concerning Russia. In the fall of 2016, the US intelligence community had concluded that, at Putin's direction, Russia had interfered in the presidential election campaign by hacking email accounts and publishing their contents online.[47] Following the election, Obama ordered the intelligence community to review Russian activities, both in order to determine what had happened and to help prevent future interference. On December 29, Obama ordered the closure of two Russian diplomatic compounds outside Washington and New York, which the FBI had long seen as intelligence gathering facilities, and expelled thirty-five suspected Russian spies from the United States as punishment for Moscow's actions.[48]

Trump viewed the entire discussion of Russian interference as an attempt by Democrats to discredit his unexpected victory. Before and after the elections, he consistently downplayed the possibility of a Russian role in the election. "I think it's ridiculous. I think it's just another excuse. I don't believe it," he said, adding, "They have no idea if it's Russia or China or somebody . . . sitting in a bed some place. I mean, they have no idea."[49] The accusations also ran counter to Trump's desire to improve relations with Russia and build a strong relationship with Putin, which, he had argued during the campaign, would serve America's interests well.

Given Trump's views, top members of his transition team connected with top Russian officials, including its ambassador to the United States, Sergey Kislyak, to reassure Moscow that a different policy was forthcoming. In early December, Kushner and Flynn met with Kislyak and asked about the possibility of setting up a secure communications link between the Trump transition team and the Kremlin using Russian diplomatic facilities. The Russians turned down the request.[50] More consequential was the Trump team's response to the sanctions Obama imposed. Fearing Russia would retaliate and cause a "tit-for-tat escalation" that would make it more difficult to improve relations with Moscow, Kushner told Flynn to connect with Kislyak and urge Moscow not to respond to the new sanctions, as they could be revisited after the inauguration.[51] The next day, Putin announced that Russia would not retaliate, indicating that he would wait and see how relations with the United States would proceed under President Trump.[52] "Great move on delay (by V. Putin)," Trump tweeted that day. "I always knew he was very smart!"[53]

TRUMP'S DECISION TO interfere in the conduct of US foreign policy after the elections was symptomatic of a larger issue—the reality that the president-elect and much of his team were unprepared for the task they were about to confront, that of governing at home and leading abroad. The chaotic transition served as a warning, to the country and the world, that the first days and weeks of the new administration would be tumultuous. Few could have guessed the extent to which this would be the case.

5

A Fine-Tuned Machine

Donald Trump used his inaugural address to underscore how much of a new beginning he intended to deliver now that he was the president of the United States. The bulk of his speech presented a dark vision of American challenges at home: "rusted-out factories," struggling families, "the crime and the gangs and the drugs." He declared, "This American carnage stops here and stops right now." He also had a loud and clear message for those abroad: "For many decades, we've enriched foreign industry at the expense of American industry; Subsidized the armies of other countries while allowing for the very sad depletion of our military; We've defended other nation's borders while refusing to defend our own." America spent "trillions of dollars overseas," which "made other countries rich while the wealth, strength, and confidence of our country has disappeared over the horizon." The future would be different. "From this moment on, it's going to be only America First."[1]

Although discussion of the inauguration was soon overtaken by Trump's insistence, contrary to all evidence, that the crowd size that day had been the largest ever, the speech left many wondering about the new direction America would be taking. "That was some weird shit," former President George W. Bush was overheard saying after Trump concluded his remarks.[2] German Vice Chancellor Sigmar Gabriel warned of a "rough ride," saying that "what we heard today were highly nationalistic tones" that would require Europe and Germany to stand together "to defend our interests." China's official daily editorialized that Trump's address put the world on notice that "frictions between the US and its allies, and trade tensions between the US and China, seem inevitable within the four years ahead."[3] Mexico's president felt compelled to say, "Sovereignty, national interest and protection of Mexicans, will guide relations with the new government of the United States." And French President François Hollande warned that Trump's inauguration "opens up a period of uncertainty [that] must be faced with lucidity and clarity."[4]

Trump was undaunted. "The time for empty talk is over. Now arrives the hour of action."[5] And action there was. In the hours, days, and weeks following his inaugural call to arms, the president and his administration issued a flurry of statements, orders, and initiatives intended to overturn the status quo and attack long-accepted policies and principles. "We are moving big and we are moving fast," Steve Bannon declared. "We didn't come here to do small things."[6] The swiftness and scope of the change left Washington gasping for air, mobilized large-scale demonstrations across the country, and caused incredulity abroad. The impact on US influence overseas was significant, as America's friends and foes alike sought to adjust to a global power that seemed bent on unmaking the very world it had made.

Although part of the tumult was a deliberate attempt at disruption, Trump's first few weeks in office underscored broader management problems of an inexperienced team that scorned governing experience. The president started out managing his White House much as he had his private business—with himself at the center, surrounded by multiple voices competing for his attention and power. Neither the way decisions were made, nor the way they were announced and ultimately implemented, followed a predictable path. And none of the top people surrounding the president—his chief of staff, his chief strategist, his chief counselor, his daughter and son-in-law, or his vice president—had much of an idea of how to institute regular order. Michael Flynn, the original choice to be national security adviser—the person charged with running the foreign policy process in the West Wing—lasted less than three weeks on the job. And although all new administrations come in wary of Washington's permanent bureaucracy, the Trump team seemed determined to blow it up.

It fell to a few senior officials to try to steer the ship of state to steadier waters. James Mattis at the Pentagon, Rex Tillerson at State, John Kelly at Homeland Security, and Lieutenant General H. R. McMaster, who replaced the ousted Flynn as head of the NSC staff in February, emerged as the administration's national security wise men to help the president make better choices, keep some of the wilder ideas at bay, and reassure the country and the world that the United States could still be counted upon to lead, as it had for the past seventy years. That, at least, was their goal. The president would listen and at times follow their guidance. At other times, he would go with his own instincts, convinced he knew best. Many in Washington, throughout the nation, and across the world, wary about the president's instincts, instead hoped that "the Committee to Save America," as two veteran Washington reporters christened the wise men, would find ways to prevail over the mercurial president.[7] Ultimately, though, whether they did or not would be the president's call.

It took only a few days for the country and the world to learn that the tone of the inaugural speech had set the tone for the new administration—and that President Donald Trump would be no different from Candidate Donald Trump. In terms of both style and substance, Trump was committed to upending the status quo. In the process, he called into question America's core commitment to openness—of its borders, of its markets, and even of its society and democracy.

The first indicator of change came on the issue of immigration, which had long been central to America's self-definition as an open country, built by immigrants and, as Ronald Reagan had pledged in his farewell address, "open to anyone with the will and the heart to get here."[8] Trump had campaigned on a strong anti-immigration platform, promising to build a "big, fat, beautiful wall" at the southern border; ensure "extreme vetting" of foreigners; establish a "deportation force" to round up and deport those in the country illegally; and institute a "total and complete shutdown on Muslims entering the United States."[9]

The opening shot was an executive order temporarily banning travel to the United States by citizens from seven Muslim-majority countries and by all refugees—including indefinitely barring refugees from Syria, where more than half the population (eleven million people) had been displaced as a result of a six-year-long civil war. The order stated that future refugee admissions should give preference to Christians over Muslims. "We don't want them here," Trump said during a signing ceremony at the Pentagon, referring to "radical Islamic terrorists," although anyone thinking he was referring to all Muslims could easily be excused. "We want to ensure that we are not admitting into our country the very threats our soldiers are fighting overseas."[10]

The travel ban created widespread chaos at US airports and other points of entry as immigration officers sought to implement the hastily drawn-up order, volunteer lawyers tried to address the plight of those arriving from abroad, and demonstrators flooded airport arrival halls all over the country. Even as the chaos was playing out on television screens around the nation and the world, Trump saw the turmoil as proof of his power, both over a Washington system he had long criticized and over the direction of the nation's policy. "It's working out very nicely," he told reporters in the Oval Office the next day.[11] Bannon suggested that it all had been deliberate. "You had to be a disruptor and keep people on their back heels," he later explained.[12] Even so, questions about the order's constitutionality led the acting attorney general, Sally Yates, to instruct the Justice Department not to defend the order, which was quickly challenged in federal courts around the country.

Frustrated by a system that stood in his way, Trump fired Yates and railed on Twitter about the unfairness of judicial interventions. "What is our country coming to when a judge can halt a Homeland Security travel ban and anyone, even with bad intentions, can come into U.S.?"[13] The problem, of course, was the indiscriminate nature of the ban, not the right to bar those who pose a threat from entering the country. Since 9/11, the United States had subjected refugees and visa applicants to strict vetting procedures, forcing those who were admitted to wait as long as two years before being allowed to enter the country. There was no evident need for a new system, let alone a blanket ban. American allies weighed in to make that point. "The necessary and resolute fight against terrorism in no way justifies a general suspicion against all people who share a certain faith," declared German Chancellor Angela Merkel, who in 2015 allowed nearly one million refugees to enter her country.[14] "This can only worry us," warned French Foreign Minister Jean-Marc Ayrault. "Welcoming refugees who flee war and oppression is part of our duty."[15] Canadian Prime Minister Justin Trudeau took to Trump's favorite medium to express his views, tweeting, "To those fleeing persecution, terror & war, Canadians will welcome you, regardless of your faith. Diversity is our strength."[16] Together, these comments reflected a deep concern that America, long a beacon of freedom and human rights, was turning inward and sending a clear message that foreigners were no longer welcome.

Immigration law was but one of the areas Trump tackled in his first days in office. Trade was another. On his first full workday as president, he signed a memorandum withdrawing the United States from the twelve-nation Trans-Pacific Partnership (TPP) agreement. "My Administration," the memo declared, will "deal directly with individual countries on a one-on-one (or bilateral) basis in negotiating future trade deals."[17] Ten years in the making, the TPP agreement lowered tariffs and barriers to trade and investment and set new environmental and labor standards for twelve nations that rimmed the Pacific, which together accounted for 40 percent of global gross domestic product (GDP) and one-third of global trade. By tying the major market economies of Asia and the Americas together into a single agreement, its framers had aimed to set the global standards and rules for trade and unify America and its major partners in the region in the face of a rising China. None of that seemed to matter to Trump, who instead focused squarely on the need to negotiate better, bilateral deals "to promote American industry, protect American workers, and raise American wages."[18]

Although Trump had campaigned against TPP, arguing that it "would make it easier for our trading competitors to ship cheap sub-sidized goods into U.S. markets," he withdrew from the pact without any internal review of its consequences or the diplomatic outreach to other partners that would normally occur with such a decision.[19] Many of America's most important allies and trading partners were affected, including Australia, Canada, and Japan, but that mattered little to the new president. Indeed Trump's intended message went far beyond TPP. For all practical purposes, his decision signaled that the era of multilateral trade deals, which the United States had championed since Harry Truman was president, was effectively over.

Trump's other favorite campaign target was the North American Free Trade Agreement (NAFTA) among the United States, Mexico, and Canada, which he called "the single worst trade deal ever approved."[20] He had repeatedly threatened to withdraw from the agreement because of the large deficit the United States ran with Mexico in particular. Once in office, he pushed to get out of the agreement but was persuaded by both his Mexican and Canadian counterparts and his cabinet members to give negotiations a chance. Even so, Trump frequently warned, "If we can't come to a satisfactory conclusion, we'll terminate NAFTA."[21]

Trump had also long complained about trade with Europe. The European Union (EU) rather than individual European countries had primary responsibility for trade matters, but Trump wasn't interested in dealing with the EU, which he insisted had been "formed to beat the United

States in trade."[22] Instead, he wanted to focus on individual countries and negotiate bilateral deals. With Britain having voted to leave the EU, Trump supported negotiating an agreement with London. "I'm a big fan of the UK, we're gonna work very hard to get it done quickly and done properly," he said.[23] But his real focus was Germany, an export juggernaut, which he thought dominated the EU. "You look at the European Union and it's Germany. Basically a vehicle for Germany."[24] So when Merkel visited Trump at the White House in March, the president rebuked Germany for running a large trade surplus with the United States and insisted the two countries broker a new deal. Merkel explained that as an EU member she did not have the authority to enter trade talks, that only the EU could negotiate a bilateral deal with the United States. "That's great," Trump responded. "Wilbur, we'll negotiate a bilateral trade deal with Europe," he said, turning to Wilbur Ross, his commerce secretary.[25] Of course, the Obama administration had been trying to negotiate just such a deal, the Transatlantic Trade and Investment Partnership, for four years, only to founder on growing European opposition. Ross would soon find out that reviving the talks would be no easy matter.

THE FIRST DAYS of the Trump administration alarmed America's allies around the world. They were unaccustomed to interacting with a US president who was bent on a transactional approach to international politics and who dismissed the value of long-standing relationships. Within days of his inauguration, Trump got into a public spat with his Mexican counterpart, Enrique Peña Nieto, over the border wall he had promised to build, with Mexico picking up the bill. Jared Kushner had worked with the Mexican foreign minister to secure an early visit to Washington by the Mexican president to help rebuild a relationship damaged by the campaign. But for Trump, the wall took precedence, and he signed a directive ordering its construction on January 25. That forced Peña Nieto to go on national television to express his strong opposition to the wall and make clear Mexico would never pay for it. "If Mexico is unwilling to pay for the badly needed wall," Trump tweeted in response, "then it would be better to cancel the upcoming meeting."[26] The visit was canceled, and the Mexican president would not visit Washington in Trump's first year and a half in office (though they did meet briefly on the sidelines of the G-20 Summit in Germany, where Trump again reiterated that Mexico would "absolutely" pay for the wall).[27]

Some of the early, congratulatory phone calls with allied leaders also proved strained, in part because of strong foreign opposition to Trump's travel ban. But none was as contentious as Trump's call with Prime Minister Malcolm Turnbull of Australia, one of America's closest allies, whose troops had fought alongside American forces in every war since World War I. The president got into a heated exchange over a commitment the Obama administration had made to take in 1,250 refugees who had been refused entry into Australia. "I think it is a horrible deal, a disgusting deal that I would have never made," Trump fumed. After an extended argument, Trump said, "I have had it. I have been making these calls all day and this is the most unpleasant call all day. Putin was a pleasant call. This is ridiculous."[28] He then ended the call. When word leaked out that he had hung up on Turnbull, Trump was unapologetic. "When you hear about the tough phone calls I'm having, don't worry about it," he said. "They're tough. We have to be tough. It's time we're going to be tough, folks. We're taken advantage of by every nation in the world, virtually. It's not going to happen anymore."[29]

Not all interactions with allied leaders started off badly. British Prime Minister Theresa May was the first foreign leader to come to Washington, a visit that went off without a hitch. May invited Trump to come to Britain for a state visit with the queen, which the president greatly appreciated. Although the bilateral conversations did not follow a set agenda and none of the US participants appeared to take notes, May left Washington sensing that the special relationship between the countries, now more important because of the British decision to leave the EU, was still solid.[30] Japanese Prime Minister Shinzo Abe also established a strong, personal rapport with the president, in part based on their mutual interest in golf. Abe had hurried to the United States nine days after Trump's election to ensure the two allies remained close, and he presented the president-elect with a gold-plated driver. In February, shortly after Trump's inauguration, they played twenty-seven holes near Mar-a-Lago during Abe's first official visit. The visits paid off, with Trump reiterating America's strong commitment to the US-Japan security alliance. "The unshakable U.S.-Japan Alliance is the cornerstone of peace, prosperity, and freedom in the Asia-Pacific region," a joint statement noted. "The U.S. commitment to defend Japan through the full range of U.S. military capabilities, both nuclear and conventional, is unwavering."[31]

Yet, even as Trump was reaffirming the alliance with Japan, he continued to question the pillars of America's engagement with Europe, both NATO and the EU. The Atlantic Alliance had been America's most important security pact since the end of World War II, and any questions about the US commitment to defend European allies would inevitably raise questions about its security commitment everywhere. Trump had doubted the value of NATO during the campaign, and he did so again days before assuming office. "I said a long time ago that NATO had problems. Number one it was obsolete, because it was designed many, many years ago. Number two the countries aren't paying what they're supposed to pay." This last point, in particular, stuck in Trump's craw. "I think [it] is very unfair to the United States."[32]

Within days of coming to the White House, Steve Bannon asked the NSC staff to compute how much European allies had been underspending on defense.[33] They calculated that if the European NATO members had spent 2 percent of their GDP on defense since 2006, their overall spending would have been $1 trillion more than what they actually spent over the ensuing decade. Trump saw this gap as something that was owed the United States, believing that Washington had spent more because the allies had spent less.[34] In calls and meetings with allied leaders, Trump made clear he wanted this money back. "Chancellor, you're terrific," Trump told Merkel at the end of their first meeting at the White House in March, "but you owe me one trillion dollars."[35] The day after the visit, the president went public with his demand. "I had a GREAT meeting with German Chancellor Angela Merkel," Trump tweeted. "Nevertheless, Germany owes vast sums of money to NATO & the United States must be paid more for the powerful, and very expensive, defense it provides to Germany!"[36] Of course, that is not actually how NATO works. America is not a mercenary army, and individual allies determine for themselves how much to spend on defense. As for the 2 percent requirement, NATO leaders had agreed to it only in 2014, following Russia's invasion of Ukraine, and as a goal to be achieved by 2024. Trump's insistence that Europeans owed large sums of money left many allies, not least in eastern Europe, with a deep sense of foreboding about whether the American president would stand with them in case of a threat from Russia or elsewhere. "In those early days, we feared for NATO and whether America would be there for us," worried one senior Baltic official.[37]

Trump's views of the EU were equally disturbing to many Europeans. Unlike Obama, who had urged Britain to stay in the Union, Trump had supported Brexit, even claiming he had predicted the outcome of the vote.[38] Shortly after his election, he met with Nigel Farage, a leader of the Brexit campaign, and suggested that London appoint Farage as the UK ambassador to the United States.[39] Trump wasn't alone in pushing a sharply different view of the EU. When Michael Flynn, the incoming and short-lived national security adviser, met with a senior French official during the transition, he left the diplomat stunned by asking, "When are you leaving the EU?"[40] A German diplomat meeting with Kushner in early 2017 was equally taken aback by the young adviser's perspective on the Union. When the diplomat explained that the EU was much more than a trading bloc, not least its role in overcoming European divisions that had produced a century of war, Kushner responded, "That may have been ok for the first twenty-five years, but now the EU is our opponent."[41] On another occasion, Kushner told a European diplomat, "I'm a businessman, and I don't care about the past. Old allies can be enemies, or enemies can be friends."[42]

Trump's challenge to the Europeans came at a particularly difficult time for a Europe that at the outset of 2017 faced a growing list of problems. Russian aggression in Ukraine, China's economic assertiveness, war and unrest in the Middle East, a growing terrorist threat, and large numbers of migrants from Africa heading northward all posed significant challenges. Add Brexit and a growing populist surge on the European continent—which in some countries produced governments that were skeptical, if not actually opposed, to the EU—and Europe clearly had its hands full.

For decades, Washington had been a partner in addressing many of these challenges. Now, leaders in Brussels, Berlin, Paris, and beyond were starting to question that partnership. In a letter to EU leaders, the president of the European Council, Donald Tusk, wrote that the Trump administration represented a threat to Europe similar to Russia, China, and turmoil in Africa and the Middle East. "The change in Washington puts the European Union in a difficult situation," Tusk wrote his colleagues, "with the new administration seeming to put into question the last 70 years of American foreign policy."[43] As a consequence, Europe would have to deal with America differently than it had in the past. "I think we are entering into a different phase of our relationship,"

Federica Mogherini, the EU's de facto foreign minister, said after visiting Washington in early February. "A more transactional approach means Europeans will be more transactional, and we will base our approach on our interests."[44]

THE SCALE, SCOPE, and speed of change left people in Washington and other capitals around the world breathless. Much of that was deliberate—a forceful attempt to upend the status quo and overthrow conventional wisdom. Although the establishment, in Washington and abroad, might well protest, that was in part the point. "This is a president who ran against the foreign policy establishment pretty explicitly," NSC spokesman Michael Anton explained. "So I don't think that it should surprise anyone that the foreign policy establishment isn't supportive. It's a sign he's following through on what he said he would do."[45] But even if that was the intent, the execution left much to be desired. For most of the new initiatives, there had been little if any preparatory work—no communication strategy; no active attempt to build support for the new direction; and in many cases, no vetting, consultation, or review by other parts of the government. Mattis and Kelly, for example, were only told about the contents of the travel ban shortly before Trump signed the document. Tillerson was never consulted, despite the major foreign policy ramifications. Top intelligence leaders were left in the dark.[46] And the White House did not prepare any press guidance or talking points or prep any of its surrogates to defend the new policy on television.

News accounts in these first few weeks highlighted the chaos the White House was creating. Trump, of course, pushed back. "It is the exact opposite," he said in his first press conference. "This administration is running like a fine-tuned machine."[47] Perhaps that was the view from the Oval Office. But seen from elsewhere, the chaotic beginning of the administration reflected a lack of appreciation for process—which, like it or not, is how Washington works. No one in position of authority in the Trump White House had ever worked in the executive branch, and few had ever worked in Washington. The president and his team, moreover, confused policy pronouncements with actual policy, mistaking a statement for its implementation. The travel ban, for example, was announced on January 27, but it needed two major revisions and endless court reviews before a much weaker version was finally put into force in December.

The early weeks of the administration were beset by predictable problems with how it made decisions. One concerned the role of the NSC and its adviser in the White House. Since John F. Kennedy was president, the NSC had stood at the center of national security policy making, and its head had been the senior White House adviser to the president on national security matters.[48] This changed in the early days of the Trump White House. When Michael Flynn occupied the large corner office on the first floor of the West Wing, he was forced to compete with others for a say over policy. Part of this was by design. Trump appointed a homeland security adviser, Tom Bossert, who effectively operated on a par with Flynn, as had been the case during the Bush administration. Under Obama, however, the homeland security adviser had been subordinated to the national security adviser, as it had proven difficult to separate responsibility for the two areas in practice.

But the problem went beyond organizational design. Of much greater consequence was the fact that two top advisers, Kushner and Bannon, were also critical national security players in the Trump White House. Even though Kushner had no foreign policy experience, Trump had looked to his son-in-law to manage some of the most sensitive relationships, including with China and Mexico. He also put Kushner in charge of trying to negotiate a peace between Israel and the Palestinians, a goal that had eluded even the most seasoned negotiators for decades. Kushner's outsized foreign policy role did not pose a problem only for the secretary of state, who traditionally is the president's principal representative to foreign governments. It also effectively diluted Flynn's authority because many foreign interlocutors now sought out the president's son-in-law rather than his national security adviser as the best route to the Oval Office.

Whereas Kushner's authority was informal, Bannon secured a formal role in the NSC decision-making process. He was made a member of the NSC and given a standing invitation to attend all meetings of the NSC Principals Committee (PC), which brought the heads of the departments and agencies responsible for national security together on a regular basis.[49] Never before had a political strategist achieved such formal authority in foreign affairs—not George W. Bush's strategist, Karl Rove, who never attended a NSC or PC meeting, and not Obama's chief strategist, David Axelrod, who did so only occasionally as a backbencher. To enhance their influence over policy, Kushner and Bannon also set up a separate entity in the White House—the Strategic Initiatives Group—that was intended to be a source of fresh policy thinking separate from the NSC, which was largely staffed by professionals—the permanent bureaucrats—on loan from other agencies.[50]

Although there is competition for power in every administration, the problems in the Trump White House were accentuated by the way the president operated. Supremely confident in his abilities and knowledge, Trump placed himself at the hub of a many-spoked wheel. He liked people competing for attention and influence, and he saw himself as the sole decision maker on all matters, large and small. A good number of staff could walk into the Oval Office at will, normally a privilege that was strictly controlled and limited to avoid overwhelming the president with information and providing him with potentially conflicting advice. Rather than putting a single person in charge of running the White House, Trump had made Bannon an equal to Chief of Staff Reince Priebus and anointed Kushner and his daughter Ivanka Trump as a third pole of power. Given such multiple access points, and lacking a clearly agreed upon and regulated process for the flow of paper (the lifeblood of effective governance), the president was presented with advice from many different sources, and that advice had never been vetted or reviewed, let alone synthesized into a coherent set of options. Add to such a process a president who lacked discipline, suffered from a short attention span, and sought to communicate his immediate thoughts to a wide public audience via Twitter, and the chaos and dysfunction that befell the White House in the early days and weeks of the administration were difficult to avoid.

A final process problem stemmed from the new team's deep distrust of the establishment and Washington bureaucracy, the people and agencies that operate the government on a day-to-day basis. Trump had run against Washington and all it stood for. He brought to the Oval Office a profound sense that the permanent bureaucracy was a large part of the problem, a point his inaugural speech stressed:

> For too long, a small group in our nation's Capital has reaped the rewards of government while the people have borne the cost. Washington flourished— but the people did not share in its wealth. Politicians prospered—but the jobs left, and the factories closed. The establishment protected itself, but not the citizens of our country. Their victories have not been your

victories; their triumphs have not been your triumphs; and while they celebrated in our nation's Capital, there was little to celebrate for struggling
families all across our land.

"That all changes—starting right here, and right now," Trump
concluded.[51]

To be effective required more than a change of president; it required
what Bannon called "the deconstruction of the administrative state."[52]
The new team viewed the permanent bureaucracy, not as an apolitical
civil service, but as a "deep state," aligned with past administrations
and determined to oppose the changes Trump was seeking to make.
Career civil servants were derided and dismissed as "Obama holdovers,"
although in nearly all instances they had served multiple presidents of
both parties. When a thousand diplomats and State Department civil
servants signed a memorandum voicing their dissent to the travel ban,
using a long-established mechanism designed to bring alternative viewpoints to the attention of senior leaders, the administration's reaction
was predictable. "These career bureaucrats have a problem with it?"
asked Sean Spicer, the White House press secretary. "They should either
get with the program or they can go."[53] Either way, they would just be
ignored. The White House put little stock in the expertise that resided
in government, whether regarding complex scientific issues like climate
change and infectious diseases (eighteen months into his administration,
Trump had yet to nominate his White House science adviser) or the
analysis of intelligence on the purpose and aims of foreign governments.

THE CHAOS THAT marked the administration's first few weeks in office
worried some of the more senior members of the administration—
notably Kelly, Mattis, and Tillerson. Together they sought to right the
ship of state, bringing a sense of regular order at home and reassuring
allies and partners abroad that the administration knew what it was
doing and would continue to adhere to long-standing precepts of American foreign policy. McMaster's appointment as national security adviser
also helped to reassure many who were concerned about the direction of
American foreign policy. By April insiders and outsiders alike pointed to
the emergence of this "Axis of Adults" as reason for hope that the conduct
of America's relations abroad would return to a more normal pattern.[54]
Senator Bob Corker, chair of the Foreign Relations Committee, even

went so far as to say that these officials were "people who help separate our country from chaos."[55] There were plenty of indications in support of that contention.

Kelly, for instance, was livid that the White House had issued the travel ban without soliciting his input or giving his team at Homeland Security guidance on how to enforce the order. Worse, he felt blindsided when it turned out that the president was signing the order at the very moment he was on a conference call with the White House, being briefed on its main provisions.[56] Kelly had no problem with efforts to strengthen the border, up the degree of vetting, and limit entry to the United States. But he wanted to be involved in the decisions. The disastrous rollout of the travel ban was an early indication that the White House needed supervision from outside—including from him and his department when it came to matters of immigration. Although he told Congress that responsibility for the chaos was "all on me," his message to the White House was more direct: "That's not going to happen again."[57] From then on, major policy pronouncements on immigration—including revisions of the travel ban—were vetted and reviewed by Homeland Security, Justice, and other agencies involved in their execution.

For their part, Mattis and Tillerson were also determined to undo some worrying perceptions about the new direction in foreign policy that had emerged during the campaign and continued into the transition. Both used their confirmation hearings to strike a strong tone regarding Russia, as Trump had refused to do throughout the campaign. "I'm all for engagement, but we also have to recognize reality," Mattis told senators when asked about Trump's desire for good relations with Russia. He added, "There's a decreasing number of areas where we can engage cooperatively and increasing numbers of areas where we're going to have to confront Russia."[58] Tillerson referred to Russia as "a danger" to the United States and NATO, insisting that Moscow "must be held accountable." He didn't think America and Russia would ever be friends. "Right now they're clearly in the unfriendly adversary category," he added.[59]

Mattis was also determined to reassure America's allies that, notwithstanding what Trump had said during the campaign, they could continue to count on the United States. He used his first overseas trips to visit South Korea, Japan, and NATO and publicly reiterated America's commitment to their security and defense. In Tokyo, Mattis stressed that the US-Japan "defense treaty is understood to be as real to us today as it was a year ago, five years ago and as it will be a year and ten years from now."[60] In Brussels, he noted that "NATO is the fundamental bedrock for keeping the peace and defending the freedoms we enjoy today."[61] Vice President Pence took the same message to the annual Munich Security Conference in mid-February, telling a large audience of European security officials, "Today, on behalf of President Trump, I bring you this assurance. The United States of America strongly supports NATO and will be unwavering in our commitment to this transatlantic alliance."[62] In subsequent trips abroad, Mattis and Pence continued to stress America's fundamental security commitments. European and Asian allies embraced the statements as welcome signs that the fundamentals of their relationships with Washington would remain unchanged. Even so, they longed to hear the same reassurances from Trump himself and worried that statements by his advisers might not reflect his actual views.

Just three weeks into the administration, Trump fired Flynn as national security adviser because of charges that he had misled the vice president and other officials about the content of his discussions with Russian Ambassador Sergey Kislyak during the transition. It later turned out that Trump had serious questions about Flynn's judgment almost immediately, which made his ouster that much easier.[63] It's rare for presidents to get an early do-over, but Flynn's dismissal provided Trump with the opportunity to appoint a more seasoned professional to the job. He quickly settled on yet another military officer, Lieutenant General H. R. McMaster.

McMaster came strongly recommended by much of the national security establishment. The pick was widely hailed on Capitol Hill and elsewhere. John McCain called McMaster "an outstanding choice," a sharp contrast to Flynn. "I could not imagine a better, more capable national security team than the one we have right now."[64] McMaster had excelled on the battlefield, both while serving as a tank commander during the Gulf War and in launching a successful counterinsurgency campaign in northern Iraq after Saddam Hussein had been ousted from power. His doctoral dissertation on the failure of the Joint Chiefs of Staff to push back against political considerations dominating White House strategy during the Vietnam War had been published to much acclaim, and it offered hope to some of Trump's critics that he would put his penchant for speaking truth to power into practice. At the same time, there were also some concerns about his appointment. The most success-ful national security advisers were those with close personal connections to the presidents they served. Trump had never heard of McMaster until a week before his appointment, and he had only met the general once before hiring him. McMaster's decision to remain on active duty also had implications for his relationship with the president, his commander in chief, and with Mattis, to whom he formally reported as an active-duty officer and who would have a say on his promotion to a four-star general. Although McMaster no doubt would offer the president and others his unvarnished advice, it is in the nature of the military to do as ordered, whether one likes it or not.

Early indications, however, were that McMaster would be his own man and put his own stamp on the NSC and its staff. At his first all-staff meeting, the new national security adviser said that the label "rad-ical Islamic terrorism" was unhelpful because the acts these terrorists engaged in were "un-Islamic."[65] This stood in sharp contrast not only to the views of his predecessor but to those of the president, who during the campaign had castigated Hillary Clinton for refusing to use the term. McMaster also began to weed out Flynn's eccentric appointments to the NSC staff (who were informally known as the Flynnstones) and brought in more seasoned, and mainstream, national security experts.

McMaster revised a presidential memorandum outlining the workings of the NSC and the membership of critical committees that were more in line with the procedures of previous administrations. The new memo made clear that McMaster was responsible for both national and home-land security matters, as had been the case under Obama, thereby plac-ing the homeland security adviser in a subordinate position. The chair of the Joint Chiefs of Staff and director of national intelligence were once again standing members of the NSC and the PC, and, crucially, Bannon no longer had a seat on either committee.[66] Therefore, formally at least, McMaster had restored the position of the NSC head as the principal White House adviser to the president for national security affairs. A few weeks into his tenure, McMaster showed why this mattered.

AIRCRAFT ROARED OVERHEAD as bombs fell on the rebel-held town of Khan Sheikhoun in Syria. It was early in the morning, April 4. Soon video footage circulated around the world showing women and chil-dren frothing at the mouth and gasping for air, suffering from what UN officials later determined was a sarin nerve gas attack by Syrian forces. That morning, military, intelligence, and national security advisers briefed President Trump on what had happened. The graphic pictures shocked the president. "When you kill innocent children, innocent babies, little babies, with a chemical gas that was so lethal," Trump said later, that "crosses many lines, beyond a red line, many many lines."[67] The "red line" referred to a similar situation four years earlier, when after another Syrian chemical weapons attack, Obama had failed to enforce his red line. Trump was determined not to make the same mistake, and in the next sixty hours, the NSC would meet four times to go over options on how to respond to the nerve gas strikes. As President Trump arrived at Mar-a-Lago for a meeting with Chinese President Xi Jinping on April 7, he ordered a strike against the airfield from which the Syrian planes had departed to drop their bombs on innocent civilians. Over dessert, Trump told Xi that fifty-nine cruise missiles were just then destroying the Syrian airfield.[68]

In contrast to almost every other policy matter discussed in the early days of the Trump White House, the decision to strike Syria followed a textbook process. Information on what had happened was gathered and evaluated, and intelligence analysts determined what chemical agent was used and who had executed the attack. Different options for responding were developed, evaluated, and discussed. The president repeatedly met with all of his advisers, and on the basis of the best information available, he made the final call—a proportionate retaliation against the forces most directly responsible for what Trump rightly called this "heinous" attack.[69] His decision, careful and deliberate, was widely supported at home and abroad. And to many it marked a turning point for his presidency—after two months of turmoil, the administration was finally on track. "Trump is making gains because he has assembled a competent national security team—and listens to its advice," commented David Ignatius, the doyen of foreign policy commentators in Washington. "There was a consensus among his top advisers for a quick, limited strike on a Syrian air base, and Trump took the recommendation. He didn't amplify, augment or otherwise disrupt it with his own tweets. He allowed the process to work."[70]

6

Peace through Strength

On April 8, 2018, President Trump and his national security team gathered for an emergency meeting in the White House Situation Room. A day earlier, Syrian forces had used chemical agents in their brutal effort to put down an uprising, killing dozens of civilians and injuring hundreds more. The cruise missile strike he had ordered a year earlier in response to a similar chemical attack had deterred Syrian President Bashar al-Assad only for a while. Trump was determined to punish Assad. He warned on Twitter of a "big price to pay." The missiles "will be coming, nice and new and 'smart!'"[1] On April 13, the United States, this time joined by Britain and France, attacked three chemical weapons facilities in Syria in a strike that aimed, as the president put it, "to establish a strong deterrent against the production, spread, and use of chemical weapons."[2]

As before, Trump only considered one response to Syria's brutal actions: military force. He was happy to condemn the "Animal Assad" on Twitter and to raise the issue in the UN Security Council. But there was only one way to demonstrate strength and decisiveness. The president put little stock in diplomacy. In Trump's view, that had been Obama's big mistake. He had been too reluctant to wield America's military might and too reliant on diplomacy. To Trump and his advisers, Obama's decisions to withdraw US troops from Iraq, set a timetable for drawing down US forces in Afghanistan, refuse to intervene decisively in Syria, and let allies lead in Libya had demonstrably weakened the United States. Trump vowed to reverse that decline by demonstrating strength.

Trump saw the military as the most absolute expression of strength. As president, he promised to deliver "one of the greatest military buildups in history," producing a military that was "bigger and better and stronger than ever before. . . . We believe in peace through strength."[3] His first budget proposed increasing defense spending by nearly 10 percent, and he proposed paying for a small part of the increase by slashing funding for the State Department by almost a third.[4] "It is not a soft-power budget," Mick Mulvaney, the budget director, said when explaining the president's priorities. "This is a hard-power budget, and that was done intentionally. The president very clearly wants to send a message to our allies and to our potential adversaries that this is a strong-power administration."[5]

Overwhelming military power had been at the core of America's global leadership since World War II. But leadership depended on more than military might. It also rested on strong diplomatic engagement and a commitment to promote democracy, human rights, and the rule of law. Trump downplayed both. He saw little value in diplomacy, and he said little about the importance of democracy or human rights abroad. Yet, in ignoring these vital diplomatic and political underpinnings of America's global engagement, Trump risked undermining the effectiveness and legitimacy of using military force. Force, on its own, could only accomplish so much. Lasting solutions, whether in Syria, Afghanistan, or elsewhere, would require diplomatic engagement and long-term support for building stable societies.

FROM THE OUTSET, Trump put the military's stamp on his administration. Generals filled many of the national security positions, not only at the top but at lower levels of the administration as well. They at least were united by common experience and common vision for the country. James Mattis, John Kelly, and H. R. McMaster were the first generals of the post-9/11 era, cutting their command teeth in multiple tours in Afghanistan and Iraq. They viewed the use of force as essential to achieving America's objectives against critical threats in the region—above all terrorism and Iran. And they had criticized Obama's retreat from the region—exemplified by his refusal to enforce the red line he drew on Syria's use of chemical weapons—both when they served in his administration and afterward. Now, they were united in their commitment to reverse course.

Iran topped the list of their concerns. Quite apart from the shortcomings of the Iran nuclear deal, Mattis and his colleagues believed Obama had failed to see Iran as a strategic threat to the region. By focusing on Tehran's nuclear weapons potential, Obama had done too little to reverse its growing influence in the region (including in Iraq, Syria, and Yemen) and downplayed the threat it posed to Israel. America's friends in the region had become increasingly dismayed by Obama's policy, and one of the first orders of business for the new team was to reassure them that the Trump administration had their back. Within days of coming to office, Flynn declared that the United States was "officially putting Iran on notice," after it had tested a ballistic missile and attacked a Saudi vessel.[6] The Israeli prime minister and Saudi crown prince were among the first foreign leaders to visit the White House after Trump came to office, and the president opted to start his first overseas trip with visits to both countries.

Trump's generals also thought Obama had been deeply mistaken in withdrawing American forces from Iraq in 2010, believing that even a small contingent of a few thousand troops could have prevented the revival of Islamic extremists. "We saw with the precipitous withdrawal of U.S. forces from Iraq, and the subsequent fall of Mosul, what can happen when you withdraw before making your military gains permanent," McMaster explained shortly after becoming national security adviser.[7] Similarly, the generals believed that Obama had been too cautious in addressing the conflict in Syria, arguing that the failure to support the resistance to the Syrian regime had opened the door to the Islamic State and its subsequent conquest of a large swath of territory across Syria and Iraq. And they viewed Obama's belated decision to go after the Islamic State as too little, too late.

Like many of their military colleagues at the time, McMaster and Mattis had also criticized Obama's decision to put a time limit on the US troop surge into Afghanistan in 2009. Although the surge, which at its height consisted of more than 150,000 US and allied troops, had reversed the gains made by the Taliban, the rapid drawdown of US forces from 2011 onward prevented the consolidation of the security gains over the longer term. By the time Trump came to office, fewer than 10,000 US troops remained, and the Taliban was once again making headway. One of McMaster's most pressing priorities as national security adviser would be to address the rapidly deteriorating situation in Afghanistan.

To Mattis, Obama's actions all added up to a seeming reluctance of the United States to lead in the world. "You can call it disentanglement," he told the *New Yorker*. "From the enemy's point of view, the U.S. is inclined to lose."[8] Although Trump may not have agreed with all of the nuances of the generals' critique of Obama (he had taken very different positions on Iraq and Afghanistan, for example), he clearly shared their belief that the United States could never afford to lose. His administration would be different. "We weren't fighting to win," Trump explained, talking about the fight against the Islamic State. "We were fighting to be politically correct."[9] All of that would change.

DURING THE CAMPAIGN, Trump had promised to convene "my top generals and give them a simple instruction. They will have 30 days to submit to the Oval Office a plan for soundly and quickly defeating ISIS."[10] A week after entering the White House, Trump signed an order tasking the Pentagon to prepare such a plan by the end of February. Mattis delivered it on time. His blueprint essentially stuck to the strategy the Pentagon had pursued since 2014, when Obama promised "to degrade, and ultimately destroy" the Islamic State.[11] It would use airpower, deploy advisers, and provide arms and training in support of local forces to defeat the terrorist group in Syria and Iraq and more selectively in other parts of the Middle East and North Africa. The United States would continue to encourage a large coalition of countries to contribute to the overall effort, although it would still have to carry much of the burden.

Even though the strategy represented more continuity than change, the new plan sought four major changes in its execution. First, Mattis proposed streamlining the decision-making process for conducting the campaign against the Islamic State; under Obama, that process had been laborious to ensure strong White House control. At the Pentagon chief's urging, Trump delegated essential authority over military operations to Mattis, who, in turn, delegated authority down to the commanders in the field. Although the goal of destroying the group remained unchanged, "no longer will we have slowed decision cycles because Washington D.C. has to authorize tactical movements on the ground," Mattis told the Pentagon press. "I have absolute confidence as does the president, our commander in chief, in the commanders on the ground as he's proven by delegating this authority to me with the authority to further delegate it" to local commanders.[12]

Mattis also sought to increase the scale and scope of the campaign against the Islamic State. The number of air strikes in Syria alone increased two and a half times in 2017, compared to 2016. The bombardments were particularly intense in the summer of 2017, when US airpower supported local forces in the liberation of the Islamic State's self-proclaimed capital of Raqqa.[13] But it wasn't only in Syria that US efforts intensified. The president also agreed to ease restrictions on air strikes and ground operations in Yemen and Somalia by declaring both countries "areas of active hostilities." And in October 2017 he accepted a recommendation to further ease restrictions on lethal drone strikes against not only terrorists who were deemed to pose an imminent threat to Americans but terrorist foot soldiers as well.[14] As a result, the number of strikes tripled in Yemen and doubled in Somalia in 2017, compared to the previous year.[15] The administration further embarked on a deliberate extension of the scope of the campaign against the Islamic State. Originally focused in Syria and Iraq (which was still the main effort), the fight extended quite quickly to other areas, including to North and West Africa. There was a notable increase in bombing of terrorist targets in Libya. And Niger had become a major base of operations, with the United States deploying nearly a thousand troops and drones in support of counterterrorism operations throughout the region.

A final significant change was the adoption of what Mattis called an "annihilation" strategy. Instead of flushing Islamic State fighters out from urban areas and allowing them to redeploy elsewhere, the strategy sought to encircle urban centers before attacking them to ensure extremists couldn't escape to fight another day. Rather than "shoving ISIS out of safe locations in an attrition fight," Mattis explained, the new tactic involved "surrounding the enemy in their strongholds so we can annihilate ISIS. The intent is to prevent the return home of escaped foreign fighters."[16] Although the capture of urban areas now involved more intense fighting and much greater destruction, the result was to limit the capacity of the Islamic State to bolster its defenses elsewhere in Syria and Iraq and to reduce the number of fighters who might escape to Europe.

The intensified and expanding effort against the Islamic State produced results. In March, Iraqi forces recaptured the city of Mosul after a six-month fight. It was the sudden fall of Mosul in 2014 that had awakened the Obama administration to the threat posed by the Islamic State. By October, Syrian opposition forces had liberated Raqqa, with support from US airpower. While the cost paid by the local populations during the occupation was immense—with public executions and rapes of young girls and women gravely damaging every family that remained— the liberations came with their own costs. Long-term bombardments left the cities in ruin and in need of massive rebuilding, and the increase in US and coalition airpower also inevitably increased the cost in terms of civilian casualties. The war was brutal, but its end was hardly a stable peace.

By the end of 2017, 98 percent of the territory once held by the Islamic State had been liberated, including 61,500 square kilometers (about the size of West Virginia) in 2017 alone.[17] Trump claimed full credit. "I totally changed rules of engagement. I totally changed our military, I totally changed the attitudes of the military and they have done a fantastic job," Trump said after the fall of Raqqa. "ISIS is now giving up." Asked why now and not before, the president was quick to answer. "Because you didn't have Trump as your president."[18]

Although Trump's desire to claim credit was understandable, the overall result was long anticipated. The changes he and Mattis introduced were important, but they altered neither the course nor the outcome of the conflict. More important, some of the major shortcomings of the Obama effort remained unaddressed by the new administration. Like his predecessor, Trump singularly focused on defeating the Islamic State, leaving other developments in Syria and Iraq to be addressed at a later stage. As a result, while US and coalition forces were pummeling the Islamic State and assisting local forces, Russia, Iran, and the Assad regime were steadily retaking control of much of Syria.[19] The essential contradiction in US policy toward Syria that had marked Obama's policy—wanting to defeat the terrorist group without strengthening Assad's hold on power—remained unresolved in Trump's approach.

The bigger problem, though, was that in focusing on how military power could be brought to bear against the Islamic State, the Trump administration (much like Obama's before) failed to tie its military strategy to a specific political outcome. "The problem with this campaign from the beginning was that our military dominance was patched on top of political quicksand," the *Washington Post*'s David Ignatius wrote after the fall of Raqqa. "That's still true. Obama never had a clear political strategy for creating a reformed, post-Islamic State Syria and Iraq; neither does Trump. Our military is supremely effective in its sphere, but the enduring problems of governance, it cannot solve."[20] At the beginning of the campaign, Mattis defined success as destroying the Islamic State "to a point where the locals can handle that and it's no longer a trans-regional, transnational threat."[21] Yet that was an end state defined in military or security terms, not political ones. The group emerged out of the civil conflict in Syria and Iraq—it was mainly the product of a failure of governance, not a failure in security—and if that broader political problem was not addressed, any victory would likely prove temporary.

Lacking a clear political strategy, Trump officials opted for security measures instead. In Iraq, Mattis made clear, the United States would retain a military presence. We "will continue standing by the Iraqi people and their military," the defense secretary promised when visiting the country in August, "to maintain the stability that has been earned at a very, very high price."[22] The same logic would apply to Syria. "The United States will maintain a military presence in Syria focused on ensuring ISIS cannot re-emerge," Tillerson said in early 2018. "Our military mission in Syria will remain conditions-based. We cannot make the same mistakes that were made in 2011 when a premature departure from Iraq allowed al-Qaida in Iraq to survive and eventually morph into ISIS."[23]

There were, however, two problems with this strategy. First, it was far from clear how the continued military presence would foster a political outcome that would produce stability, a necessary condition for preventing the reemergence of terrorist groups. Having criticized Obama for withdrawing American troops from Iraq and failing to do more in Syria, Mattis, McMaster, and other senior advisers didn't want to repeat that mistake. But that did not mean they had a clear sense of how keeping some American troops in place would actually help promote long-term stability. More important, the president himself made very clear that, no matter what his senior national security advisers believed, he wanted American troops to come home as soon as the Islamic State was destroyed. "I want to get out" of Syria, Trump told reporters in early April 2018. "I want to bring our troops back home."[24] A few hours later Trump was in the Situation Room listening to Mattis and his top generals argue for more time. He grudgingly agreed to hang on so long as what was described as a cleanup operation took months and not years—and so long as the Gulf States were put on notice that they had to start picking up the slack on stabilization and reconstruction in the liberated areas.[25]

TRUMP HAD BEEN just as skeptical in July 2017, when he had gone to the Situation Room to decide his administration's policy on Afghanistan. "We're losing," Trump told his national security team. "What does success look like?" he asked.[26] It was an accurate observation about the state of the conflict and a good question about the endgame of what by now was America's longest war. The United States had gone into Afghanistan a month after 9/11 to take out the Taliban regime that had given refuge to Osama bin Laden, the man responsible for the attacks that killed three thousand people on American soil. Even the Bush administration had given little thought to what success in Afghanistan would look like; the focus was on getting bin Laden, destroying the al Qaeda terrorist network he led, and ousting the Taliban from power.[27] What followed was sixteen years of continuous conflict, with periodic surges of forces and increased American attention, then force drawdowns and reduced interest in the country's fortunes. At the end of the Bush administration, America's top military officer told Congress he was "not convinced that we're winning it in Afghanistan."[28] The verdict at the end of the Obama administration was little different, with the US commander in the country warning of a "stalemate."[29]

Afghanistan was a priority for McMaster when he came to the White House in February 2017. Like many in the military, he believed that Obama's 2009 decision to set a date certain for drawing down the large surge in US and allied forces had been deeply mistaken. He wanted a do-over—sending more troops to help train Afghan forces and take the fight to the Taliban and a growing network of foreign terrorists. And this time without a deadline.[30] He pushed hard to convince Trump to accept his recommendation. But the president was wary, and he would become increasingly resentful of McMaster's constant lobbying on the issue. He had largely ignored the conflict during the campaign and had previously indicated that the American involvement had lasted long enough. "I agree with Pres. Obama on Afghanistan," Trump had tweeted in 2013. "We should have a speedy withdrawal. Why should we keep wasting our money—rebuild the U.S.!"[31] Trump wasn't ready to follow the advice of his generals just yet.

McMaster was undeterred. First, he beat back opposition from Steve Bannon and Jared Kushner, who, knowing Trump didn't want to stay in Afghanistan, had pushed various alternatives. One was a harebrained scheme developed by Erik Prince, the founder of Blackwater, a security firm that had made hundreds of millions of dollars in Iraq, to send private security forces, instead of US soldiers, to Afghanistan.[32] McMaster convinced Trump that outsourcing America's national security effort to private interests made no sense. Next, McMaster had to get Mattis and

Tillerson to support his proposal to send some four thousand additional US troops to Afghanistan and also seek additional commitments from NATO allies. The force increase would improve training of Afghan forces and assist in directing airpower and rocket fire in support of Afghan-led military operations. Importantly, the additional commitment would be open ended, deployed for as long as necessary. McMaster's strategy also envisaged increased pressure on Pakistan to go after terrorist safe havens on its territory and entice India to provide greater economic support to Kabul.

When Trump came down to the White House Situation Room for the National Security Council (NSC) meeting on Afghanistan on July 19, his principal advisers hoped to get his blessing for the proposal. It wasn't to be. A day earlier, the president had met with four veterans of the Afghanistan War. That discussion had bolstered his instinct that it was a no-win situation and that America was better off getting out. During the meeting in the Situation Room, Trump railed against his generals for failing to produce a clear strategy, complained about NATO allies not doing enough, asked why China and not the United States was getting Afghanistan's mineral wealth, and repeatedly suggested that the top US commander in the field be fired for failing to win the war. After delivering a two-hour scolding that left Mattis visibly upset, Trump left without making a decision on the way forward in Afghanistan.[33]

That decision came a month later, after Trump had appointed John Kelly as his chief of staff to replace the ousted Reince Priebus. Kelly's writ was to smooth the White House operation, and he took to it as a retired four-star Marine general would. He imposed strict controls on access to the Oval Office. Everyone would report to the chief of staff— no more multiple channels into the Oval Office. Decisions would be well prepared before being presented to the president. And one of those decisions dealt with Afghanistan. McMaster further refined the strategy, adding some benchmarks to gauge progress on its implementation. Kelly invited the national security team to Camp David, where they led Trump through the details and to a final decision to accept the proposed course of action.

"My original instinct was to pull out—and, historically, I like following my instincts," Trump told a military audience when announcing his decision in August 2017. "But all my life I've heard that decisions are much different when you sit behind the desk in the Oval Office." He had been convinced that a "hasty withdrawal would create a vacuum that terrorists, including ISIS and al Qaeda, would instantly fill, just as happened before September 11th"—and, he added, as happened after America had withdrawn from Iraq in 2011. "We cannot repeat in Afghanistan the mistake our leaders made in Iraq." So, America would stay in Afghanistan. More troops would be deployed as necessary, and restrictions on the use of force would be lifted. And, "in the end, we will win."[34]

But what constituted success? Trump asked his advisers. He gave his definition of victory: "attacking our enemies, obliterating ISIS, crushing al Qaeda, preventing the Taliban from taking over Afghanistan, and stopping mass terror attacks against America before they emerge."[35] But although that might have been a win in Trump's eyes, such achievements hardly constituted a success. It had long been clear that there was no military solution in Afghanistan. "We can't kill our way to victory," Admiral Michael Mullen, then chair of the Joint Chiefs of Staff, had famously declared in 2008.[36] That was the lesson of Vietnam. The United States had devastated North Vietnamese forces, won virtually every major battlefield engagement, and still lost the war. More bombing in Afghanistan wasn't going to bring about a different outcome. Instead, the goal for many Trump advisers was to force the Taliban to the negotiating table. "This entire effort is intended to put pressure on the Taliban," Tillerson said the following morning, "to have the Taliban understand: You will not win a battlefield victory. We may not win one, but neither will you."[37] Slightly more force, and an open-ended commitment, would get America there.

As in Syria and Iraq, the Trump approach in Afghanistan was all military. Tillerson and other officials may have thought about diplomacy, but Trump would have none of it. "We don't want to talk to the Taliban," the president said after a particularly brutal bombing in Kabul in early 2018. "We're going to finish what we have to finish, what nobody else has been able to finish, we're going to be able to do it."[38] Once again, force would solve all problems. And Trump wasn't alone in that view. McMaster, Mattis, and Kelly all had worked to convince the president to embark on a course over which he had his doubts and which he reluctantly accepted only because he didn't want to follow in his predecessor's footsteps and hastily withdraw US troops. Even Tillerson wasn't really preparing for diplomacy. The US embassy in Afghanistan was without an ambassador, the State Department office set up to deal with Afghanistan under

Obama had closed down, and there was not even an acting assistant secretary of state in the bureau responsible for the region. That pointed to a bigger problem. While Trump didn't have much use for diplomacy, neither, it turned out, did his secretary of state.

DIPLOMACY IS LIKE gardening, former Secretary of State George Shultz often said. "The way to keep weeds from overwhelming you is to deal with them constantly and in their early stages."[39] In diplomatic terms, such weeding requires a strong American diplomatic presence overseas to tend to relations with other countries and to advance American interests and values. It also requires the secretary of state and other senior officials to travel around the world, to attend global forums and regional conferences, to confer frequently with allies and partners to ensure they all stay on the same course, and to engage with adversaries to try to bridge differences. And it requires a major engagement in Washington to ensure that diplomacy has a voice in interagency policy deliberations and that US officials interact with foreign diplomats and officials who work in and travel regularly to the nation's capital. All such gardening, moreover, is essential to effective global leadership—to building coalitions, maintaining international institutions, and managing critical relationships.

During his fourteen-month tenure as America's top diplomat, however, Rex Tillerson showed little interest in tending gardens. That much became clear a few weeks after he entered office, with the release of a White House budget blueprint that cut funding for the State Department and foreign assistance by nearly a third and overall staffing by 8 percent. Tillerson hadn't objected to the proposed cuts, and once the blueprint was released, he defended it as an "unmistakable restatement" of the country's requirements and changing priorities.[40] He argued that the State Department's budget had grown too big, too fast under the previous administration and was "simply not sustainable." The cuts also reflected a presumption "that as time goes by, there will be fewer military conflicts that the U.S. will be directly engaged in" and that "we will also be attracting resources from other countries, allies, and other sources." Moreover, the department needed reform, which, once implemented, would allow it "to be much more effective, much more efficient, and be able to do a lot with fewer dollars."[41]

The first three of these arguments seemed clear rationalizations for doing less. It wasn't obvious that executing a $50 billion budget—less than one-tenth the size of the Pentagon's—was unsustainable given global requirements; that there would be fewer military conflicts under a Trump administration; or that allies who were already spending proportionally more than the United States on development assistance would commit additional resources. But the reform argument held sway with Tillerson. The ex-CEO was the quintessential organization man. He had led three large reorganizations during his career. It was something, he said he enjoyed doing.[42] So revamping the State Department became the singular focus of his tenure. "The most important thing I can do is to enable this organization to be more effective, more efficient, and for all of you to take greater satisfaction in what you do day in and day out," he told US embassy staff in London.[43] Yet eleven months into the effort, after $12 million had been spent on outside consultants, Tillerson announced technical and human resource changes that were hardly groundbreaking—putting the department's email system in the cloud, integrating global address lists, improving medical evacuation and temporary duty travel procedures, and ending a freeze on hiring family members he had imposed early on.[44]

The bigger problem, though, wasn't a singular focus on remaking the State Department or cutting funding. Indeed, Congress rejected the administration's budget cuts as a "doctrine of retreat" that "serves only to weaken America's standing in the world," and kept funding level with previous years.[45] The problem was that Tillerson—just like the Trump team at the White House—showed little interest in the expertise and experience of career officials residing in his building. He centralized decision making on the seventh floor by insisting he be the final authority on even the most mundane matters.[46] He also established a top-down policy-making process that discouraged ideas or input from lower levels, undermining a long-standing practice of relying on experts with decades of experience and encouraging the development of ideas from below. "I never briefed the secretary and many of my counterparts never briefed him either," said Patricia Haslach, who served as the acting assistant secretary of economic and business affairs until December 2017.[47] It was a complaint heard frequently around the building.

The first year of Tillerson's tenure also saw a huge number of senior officials departing the State Department. Rather than waiting until replacements were confirmed, as had been the norm in prior administrations, the new team dismissed or reassigned many senior career officials, often with just a few days' notice. Others, seeing the writing on the wall, decided to retire on their own volition. One was Dana Shell Smith, who quit as the US ambassador to Qatar amid the mounting crisis with Saudi Arabia, citing the "complete and utter disdain for our expertise." Another was Nancy McEldowney, director of the Foreign Service Institute, who spoke of "a toxic, troubled environment and organization."[48] Adding to the woes, Tillerson and the White House were slow to fill the many positions left vacant by departing officials. Tillerson wanted to complete his departmental redesign effort before deciding which critical positions needed to be filled. And when he did decide on nominees for senior slots, the White House rejected many of his suggestions because they included people who had opposed Trump during the campaign. At the end of Tillerson's tenure in March 2018, two-thirds of the top thirty-six positions at the State Department were without a Senate-confirmed head. Fifteen positions were without even a nominee. And many dozens of ambassadorial slots remained unfilled well into the second year of the administration.[49]

EMPTY OFFICES AND low morale seemed to have little effect on Tillerson. "I walk the halls, people smile," he told Bloomberg ten months in. "If it's as bad as it seems to be described, I'm not seeing it, I'm not getting it."[50] Perhaps that was because Tillerson, like Trump, had a constricted view of what diplomacy should aim to accomplish. He was particularly reluctant to promote democracy, human rights, and the rule of law, long mainstays of America's involvement overseas. There were early signs that democracy promotion would no longer occupy pride of place in the Trump administration's foreign policy. A new draft State Department mission statement was similar to statements in previous administrations, except that it dropped the words "justice" and "democracy."[51] The change reflected Tillerson's belief, as he told a department town hall meeting, that the promotion of democracy, human rights, and other values "creates obstacles to our ability to advance our national security interests, our economic interests."[52] Instead, Tillerson's top policy chief later explained, the United States should use human rights to castigate America's adversaries but leave these issues aside when dealing with America's friends and allies. "Allies should be treated differently—and better—than adversaries," Brian Hook wrote. "Otherwise, we end up with more adversaries, and fewer allies."[53]

Such thinking, defended as a return to realism in foreign policy, had significant flaws, which critics quickly pointed out. Tillerson's notion that these values were uniquely American, rather than universal in their application, ignored the fact that "America didn't invent human rights," as Senator John McCain put it. "Those rights are common to all people: nations, cultures and religions cannot choose to simply opt out of them."[54] That, indeed, was the point of the Declaration of Independence and its insistence on the self-evident truth "that all men are created equal, that they are endowed by their Creator with certain unalienable Rights, that among these are Life, Liberty and the Pursuit of Happiness." To suggest, moreover, that human rights should be used as a cudgel against adversaries but ignored when it came to allies undermined the very idea of human rights and of democracy itself.

Even so, Trump had no interest in being evenhanded. He denounced countries like Iran, North Korea, and Venezuela, at least as long as their behavior constituted a threat the president sought to deal with. But he said nothing when friendly nations like Egypt or Saudi Arabia trampled on human rights. He was quick to tweet his disagreement with long-standing democratic allies like Canada, Germany, and South Korea, and equally quick to cheer authoritarian leaders as they consolidated their power. He was the first Western leader to congratulate President Recep Tayyip Erdogan for winning a constitutional referendum that concentrated power in the presidency in ways that bordered on authoritarian control.[55] He praised President Xi Jinping for becoming, in Trump's own words, "president for life," adding, "I think it's great. Maybe we'll have to give that a shot some day."[56] He ignored the warning "DO NOT CONGRATULATE" written on his briefing papers for his call with President Vladimir Putin following an election that was fraught with fraud and that excluded any credible opposition.[57] He lauded President Rodrigo Duterte for doing an "unbelievable job on the drug problem," even though the Philippine president had launched a horrific campaign of extrajudicial killings that had left thousands dead.[58] And Trump wasn't alone in this enthusiasm for authoritarians. After visiting Saudi Arabia in May, Wilbur Ross praised how the president and his team had been treated. "There was not a single hint of a protester anywhere there during the whole time we were there," he told CNBC. "Not one guy with a bad placard."[59] Of course, the kingdom was hardly known for tolerating dissent, which can be punishable by death.

Trump's embrace of strongmen and his administration's unwillingness to defend democracy and human rights had consequences: strengthening those hostile to core values and undermining those who had been fighting for such values for many years. Whenever the president rejected a news story that he did not like as "fake news," other leaders had new excuses to limit press freedom or inquiries into corruption and abuse. Democracy and freedom were increasingly on the defensive, a trend that predated Trump's victory in 2016 but had continued since. America, for all its faults, has long been a beacon for those who seek freedom and a better way of life. The Statute of Liberty at the entrance to New York Harbor commands the world beyond its shores to "give me your tired, your poor, your huddled masses yearning to breathe free, the wretched refuse of your teeming shore." It is a message that has given people the world over hope of a new and better future—a hope that gets lost when American leaders no longer think it important to defend and uphold these values.

EVEN THOUGH TILLERSON shared Trump's sense that America needed to put its economic and security interests first in its engagement abroad, differences in personality, perspective, and style ultimately doomed their relationship. "I'm an engineer by training," Tillerson explained. "I'm a very systems, process, methodical decision maker. He's an entrepreneur. Different mind-set. He makes decisions differently."[60] Much as he tried, Tillerson could never adjust his operating style to the president's. For Trump, though, the problem between the two men went far beyond differences in style. Over time, the president grew increasingly concerned that Tillerson was "totally conventional" in his approach to issues.[61] Trump wanted to break out of that kind of establishment thinking, which he thought had cost America so much. On a whole range of issues— trade agreements, the Iran nuclear deal, climate change, the status of Jerusalem, and others—Tillerson argued for continuity where Trump demanded change. In March 2018, after months of rumors, Trump fired Tillerson. By tweet, of course.

Though Tillerson's tenure as secretary of state was brief, the damage he inflicted on American diplomacy is difficult to overstate. Woody Allen once said that 80 percent of life is showing up. And so it is in diplomacy. But America under Trump and Tillerson was showing up less and less. Tillerson traveled to fewer places and for shorter periods than his predecessors. He had little backup because many of the top officials who normally spend time on the road, visiting other countries to work out differences and help bring them along in addressing common challenges, weren't in place. With no ambassador in Australia, Egypt, Jordan, Saudi Arabia, or Turkey during Trump's first eighteen months in office, America's voice in these critical countries was heard less often and less persuasively. Fewer American diplomats attended major international gatherings than in the past, leaving the playing field for other countries, notably the Chinese, to fill.

Across a range of conflicts, from Syria to South Sudan, Venezuela to Myanmar, and more, America's involvement was notable only for its absence. In previous decades, American diplomats would have met with all parties, worked to contain conflict, and sought to frame diplomatic outcomes. Yet, even while American warplanes were bombing in Syria, Russia joined with Turkey and Iran to search for a diplomatic solution, leaving the United States on the sidelines. Far from helping to find a solution to the humanitarian and political crisis in Venezuela, Trump mused about a possible military invasion and then skipped a summit meeting of leaders of the Americas that was intended to address the issue. And in the Middle East, where Trump had hoped to help resolve the conflict between Israel and the Palestinians, the decision in December 2017 to recognize Jerusalem as Israel's capital effectively sidelined any further US diplomatic efforts. It all added up, one foreign diplomat observed with some understatement, to the reality that the United States "is a bit less important than before."[62]

7

America Alone

In May 2017, Donald Trump embarked on a five-nation trip abroad, his first as president of the United States. The trip was filled with indelible images—including an all-male sword dance with Saudi royals, Trump's white-knuckled handshake with newly elected French President Emmanuel Macron, and his shoving of Montenegro's prime minister to get to the front row at a photo op. But two images captured the essence of the nine-day trip. In Riyadh, Trump stood with King Salman bin Abdulaziz Al Saud of Saudi Arabia and President Abdel Fattah el-Sisi of Egypt, their hands spread above a brightly glowing orb that cast sinister shadows on their faces. And during the Group of Seven (G-7) Summit in Italy, the leaders of Britain, Canada, France, Germany, Italy, Japan, and the European Union (EU) strolled along the cobblestone streets of Taormina, Sicily, with Trump following behind alone in a golf cart. The Middle East tableau showed Trump's tight embrace of two of the region's most autocratic, even if friendly, governments. The Sicily shot showed Trump isolated from America's most important allies.

The Middle East leg of the trip was a roaring success. Saudi Arabia and Israel, long-standing American friends who had been sharply critical of Barack Obama, were both eager to embrace the new president. The remainder of the trip proved less congenial. A brief meeting with Pope Francis turned frosty, with the pontiff repeating his earlier criticism of the president's immigration policy and emphasizing his deep belief in the need to address the threat of climate change. A new American president's first meetings with NATO, the European Union, and G-7 allies normally present occasions to celebrate the strength and depth of the partnerships. Trump, however, used those meetings to cast doubt on the US commitment to NATO, free trade, and curbing greenhouse gas emissions.

"This historic trip represented a strategic shift for the United States," H. R. McMaster and Gary Cohn, the president's national security and economic advisers, wrote in the *Wall Street Journal* upon returning to Washington. "America First signals the restoration of American leadership and our government's traditional role overseas—to use the diplomatic, economic and military resources of the U.S. to enhance American security, promote American prosperity, and extend American influence around the world."[1] But European leaders and commentators didn't see the trip or Trump's emerging presidency that way. The American president only appeared interested in satisfying America's immediate interest—no matter the damage to US alliances, ideals, or credibility. Friends and rivals were increasingly persuaded that the United States under Trump was abandoning its role as leader of the Free World.

DONALD TRUMP'S ELECTION was greeted with immediate doubts and concerns in most world capitals—but not in Riyadh or Jerusalem. Both the Saudi and the Israeli governments had long soured on Obama. It had started in 2011, during the Arab Spring, when Obama sided with the protesters gathering in Tahrir Square to demand the ouster of Hosni Mubarak, Egypt's long-serving president and a close friend of the United States. Israel worried that after thirty years of peace with Egypt, a more radical regime would pose a new threat along its southern border. Saudi Arabia wondered whether Washington's abandonment of a close friend in Cairo might signal its own impending abandonment. Israel and Saudi Arabia were further upset by Obama's failure to intervene in Syria, which created an opening for their archenemy Iran to extend its influence in the region. Both were furious about the Iran nuclear deal, which they believed would at most postpone Tehran's inevitable quest for nuclear weapons and regional dominance.

Little wonder, then, that Israel and Saudi Arabia applauded Obama's departure from the White House. After the elections, both governments reached out to Trump Tower to establish a new relationship. For Riyadh, Mohammed bin Salman, the king's son and soon-to-be-named successor as crown prince (often referred to by his initials, MBS), was the point man for the outreach, connecting early on with Trump's son-in-law, Jared Kushner. Prime Minister Benjamin Netanyahu also reached out directly to Trump and to Kushner, whose family had long-standing ties to the Israeli leader. MBS and Netanyahu were each early visitors to the White House. The first two stops on Trump's first trip overseas were Riyadh and Jerusalem.

The Saudis went all out when Trump arrived after a long overnight flight to Riyadh on May 20. King Salman met the American president personally at the airport, which he hadn't done when Obama visited a year before. The arrival was given red-carpet treatment, with military bands and a flyover of American-built fighter jets. Giant pictures of the president and king lined the highways from the airport and were projected onto the exterior of the Ritz-Carlton, where Trump stayed. King Salman presented Trump with Saudi Arabia's highest civilian honor, the Collar of Abdulaziz al Saud, an ornate necklace and medal. The president also met with the leaders of the Gulf Cooperation Council, who pledged strong cooperation on addressing the terrorist threat in the region, and with leaders from more than forty Muslim countries, who had come to Riyadh for the occasion. He delivered a well-received speech on the "battle between good and evil," which, he emphasized, was "not a battle between different faiths, different sects, or different civilizations."[2] And the Saudis also agreed to buy $110 billion worth of weapons, including naval ships, tanks, and advanced antimissile defense systems, which Trump greeted as "tremendous investments in the United States . . . and jobs, jobs, jobs."[3]

The Saudis couldn't have been more pleased with the visit. "Today was a truly historic day in the relationship between the Kingdom of Saudi Arabia and the United States," Foreign Minister Adel al-Jubeir exclaimed, adding that it was also "a turning point in the relationship between the United States and the Arab and Islamic world."[4] Both countries were completely aligned on Iran, with the United States pledging its support for the Saudi-led military intervention in Yemen, where Iranian-backed rebels had overthrown the sitting government. Riyadh and Washington insisted that they were also aligned in a common fight against extremism, terrorism, and terror financing, with the American guests saying little about past Saudi support for extremist teachings around the world.

Importantly, whereas previous American leaders had criticized Saudi human rights abuses, including its imprisonment of political opponents, its treatment of women, and its denial of the right of non-Muslims in the kingdom to worship, Trump assured his hosts that he had a different agenda. "We are not here to lecture—we are not here to tell other

people how to live, what to do, who to be, or how to worship," he told the
gathering of Muslim leaders. Rather, "we must be united in pursuing the
one goal that transcends every other consideration. That goal is to meet
history's great test—to conquer extremism and vanquish the forces of
terrorism."[5] For Trump, the fight against terrorism took precedence over
the fight for human rights.

During the two-day visit, the king and the president, as well as their
respective son and son-in-law, established a close relationship. The Saudis came away from the visit persuaded that the White House was now
back firmly, even unquestioningly, on their side. That much became clear
a few weeks later, when the Saudis, with the backing of Bahrain, Egypt,
and the United Arab Emirates, imposed a blockade on neighboring
Qatar. Overnight, the Saudis and their allies cut off diplomatic relations
with the small emirate, closed their land borders and airspace to Qatari
traffic, and ordered Qatari citizens to leave their countries while calling all of their own citizens back home. Even twelve thousand camels
grazing on Saudi land were forced back across the border.[6] The precip-
itating cause looked to be the Qatari emir's criticism of Saudi Arabia's
embrace of Trump and of the strong anti-Iranian tone of the Riyadh
meeting of Muslim leaders. But the deeper reason was long-standing
Saudi displeasure with Qatar's support for political Islamist groups that
Riyadh detested (including Hamas and the Muslim Brotherhood), its
relationship with Iran (with which Qatar shared its vast gas field), and
its support for Al Jazeera (the Doha-based broadcaster, which often criticized Saudi rulers).

The blockade was a brazen move by Riyadh, not least because Qatar
was also home to the largest US air base in the Middle East, which
housed more than ten thousand American service members and was
a critical asset in the fight against the Islamic State. Secretary of
Defense Jim Mattis and Secretary of State Rex Tillerson worried that
the embargo would undermine the unified effort against terrorism and
threaten US military operations in the region. Trump didn't share their
concern. "So good to see the Saudi Arabia visit with the King and
50 countries already paying off. They said they would take a hard line
on funding extremism," Trump tweeted. "All reference was pointing to
Qatar. Perhaps this will be the beginning of the end to the horror of
terrorism!"[7]

The president's advisers, however, were focused on finding a way to defuse the situation as quickly as possible. After consulting with Mattis, McMaster, and even the president, Tillerson made a public appeal to all parties, endorsing a Kuwaiti mediation effort, calling on the Saudis and their allies to ease the blockade of Qatar, and insisting that Doha move "more quickly" to end financing of terrorism.[8] But Trump remained firmly in the Saudis' corner. "Qatar, unfortunately, has historically been a funder of terrorism at a very high level," he said an hour after Tillerson spoke. He went on to note that during his visit to Saudi Arabia, "nations came together and spoke to me about confronting Qatar over its behavior." He had endorsed "hard but necessary action."[9] Tillerson tried a mediating effort a few weeks later, shuttling between the parties, but to no avail. The Saudis didn't budge, knowing that Trump backed them. It was a lesson they would apply in other circumstances, including months later, when MBS moved against some of the richest Saudis and potential opponents to solidify his power. "I have great confidence in King Salman and the Crown Prince of Saudi Arabia," Trump tweeted in support of the move, "they know exactly what they are doing."[10] As far as the White House was concerned, Saudi Arabia could do no wrong.

TRUMP'S SUCCESSFUL STOP in Saudi Arabia set the stage for the next leg of his trip—his visit to Israel. Although conflict between Israel and the Arab world had persisted for decades, the administration believed there was a new opportunity for cooperation. For the first time, the main Arab countries appeared to be more concerned with deterring Iran and fighting terrorism—long Israel's priorities—than with supporting the Palestinian cause. "We are witnessing a reassessment of regional relationships, most notably between Israel and a number of our Arab partners—all friends of America, but too often adversaries of each other," McMaster said shortly after the trip's conclusion. "Today their interests are converging. This is an opportunity."[11] This realignment, Trump's team believed, also offered new hope for resolving the Israeli-Palestinian conflict. They would pursue an "outside-in" approach to peace, long favored by Netanyahu, with Israel and the Arab countries working together to bring the Palestinians on board, rather than rely on the "inside-out" approach, in which Israel and the Palestinians worked out a deal as a condition for peace with the Arabs.

Trump was eager to make what he called the "ultimate deal," telling the *Wall Street Journal* days after his election that "as a deal maker, I'd like to do . . . the deal that can't be made."[12] He put Kushner in charge of the effort. While in Israel, Trump met with leaders of both sides to discuss the way forward, only to discover what most everyone knew: the deep differences separating the parties would be difficult to bridge. The issues of security, final borders, the rights of refugees, settlements, and the status of Jerusalem had stymied peace efforts for decades. As Trump left Israel, he still expressed some optimism. "I've heard it's one of the toughest deals of all," he said, "but I have a feeling we're going to get there eventually. I hope."[13] But as Colin Powell would frequently say, "Hope is not a strategy."

Kushner, though, was undeterred. He returned in August for another visit to the region and came back believing a deal could be made. At a breakfast with a top European diplomat in September, Kushner explained he was pressing both sides for their bottom line. Once he got that, a deal could be struck. "I am confident we will get there," he said.[14] Kushner told a group of congressional interns it was hard getting to the bottom line because both sides continually talked about how the other had wronged them in the past. "But how does that help us get peace?" he asked. "We don't want a history lesson. We've read enough books. Let's focus on, how do you come up with a conclusion to the situation?"[15] Kushner failed to understand the wisdom in William Faulkner's observation that "the past is never dead. It's not even past." Understanding the history of the Israeli-Palestinian conflict was essential to resolving it. But Kushner, like Trump, was so confident in his deal-making abilities that he thought that nothing, not even history, could get in his way.

Some knowledge of history might have made Kushner more skeptical about the monumental decision Trump made in December 2017 to recognize Jerusalem as Israel's capital. Trump, like many of his predecessors, had promised to do so during the campaign. But once in office, the rest had chosen not to follow through. The reason was simple: of all the issues dividing Israelis and Palestinians—indeed Muslims, Jews, and Christians—none was more full of symbolism or more fraught with danger than the status of the holy city of Jerusalem. In siding with Israel, Trump forfeited America's status as an honest broker in the peace process. "The U.S. has pulled itself out of the diplomatic process and can no longer be a mediator or sponsor," declared Mahmoud Abbas, the president of the Palestinian Authority, after what he called Trump's "sinful" decision on Jerusalem.[16]

The Palestinians were not alone in condemning the decision. So did all Arab leaders, including the Saudis. The UN Security Council voted 14–1 on an Egyptian resolution calling on the United States to rescind its decision; the lone US vote against the resolution vetoed its passage. After Trump threatened to cut off aid to any country that voted in the UN General Assembly to condemn the US decision, the resolution passed 128–9, with 35 abstentions. Trump was unmoved. Meeting with Netanyahu in Davos in January 2018, the president maintained that the recognition would make it easier to negotiate a deal. "We took Jerusalem off the table, so we don't have to talk about it anymore. They never got past Jerusalem. We took it off the table."[17] Yet, with his decision, Trump had not only taken Jerusalem off the table; he had effectively taken away the negotiating table altogether, and with it any prospect for negotiating the "ultimate deal."

THE PRESIDENT'S VISIT to Europe proved less cordial than his stops in the Middle East. Unlike the Saudi and Israeli governments, European leaders viewed Obama's tenure more positively and worried about Trump's stance on issues like NATO, climate change, trade, and Russia. Trump failed to offer much reassurance during his visit, and after five days of meetings with America's staunchest allies, he left behind a continent fearful about the direction he had set.

Trump was the first president since NATO's founding in 1949 to enter office having questioned the value of the alliance, which had stood as the cornerstone of America's global engagement for seventy years. Even before his trip, European leaders had visited Washington to impress on him the importance of supporting NATO and the US treaty commitment, enshrined in Article 5, to come to the defense of allies if they were attacked. Britain's Prime Minister Theresa May told the press after her first meeting with Trump that he had expressed his support for NATO, though he himself stayed silent on the matter. A few weeks later, Trump did express to German Chancellor Angela Merkel his "strong support for NATO," but he coupled that with an even stronger statement that Germany and European allies needed to spend much more on defense. When NATO Secretary General Jens Stoltenberg visited in April, the president conceded that NATO was "no longer obsolete," but he dropped the declaration of support for Article 5 that his aides had included in his prepared remarks.[18]

The meeting with NATO leaders in Brussels in late May presented the perfect opportunity to rectify this omission. The leaders had gathered at NATO's new headquarters. At the entrance to the building stood two monuments commemorating important milestones in the alliance's long history: a section of the Berlin Wall, which symbolized NATO's victory in the Cold War, and a giant piece of steel from the Twin Towers, a reminder of the only time NATO had invoked Article 5. Merkel, who had grown up in East Germany behind the wall, used the occasion to thank the NATO allies for standing by Germany and helping achieve its reunification, united, as she said, "in the trust that it is not isolation and the building of walls that make us successful but open societies that share the same values."[19]

Trump followed Merkel as the only other NATO leader to speak. The draft text of his speech contained a strong reaffirmation of Article 5, and his aides had assured both allies and the press that he would use the occasion to make that point.[20] But he didn't. To the amazement of those gathered at the new headquarters—and of his top national security advisers as well—Trump again scrapped the line. Instead, he praised King Salman ("a wise man who wants to see things get much better rapidly") and lectured America's closest allies on not spending enough on defense. "This is not fair to the people and taxpayers of the United States," he intoned. "Many of these nations owe massive amounts of money from past years and not paying in those past years." Only five of twenty-eight nations had met the long-term NATO spending goal, but "even 2 percent of GDP is insufficient to close the gaps in modernizing, readiness, and the size of forces. We have to make up for the many years lost."[21] Later, at a private dinner with his counterparts, the president returned to his lecture, suggesting that what the alliance really needed was nations spending 3 percent of GDP on defense. The United States wasn't going to fill the gap. "This will end," the president declared emphatically.[22]

In the days that followed, Trump's top advisers argued that the president had affirmed America's commitment to NATO's collective defense, even if he didn't say the exact words. His very presence at the meeting, they said, reaffirmed his "commitment to NATO and all 13 articles that make up that treaty."[23] To the allies, such rationalizations sounded hollow. If it was so obvious, why not say it? News reports that Trump had himself decided to delete the sentence from his draft speech only heightened concern about his true commitment to NATO.[24] So when he finally did affirm Article 5 some weeks later, the damage in terms of trust and confidence had been done.[25] Although European allies wanted to believe him, his overall critical posture toward NATO made it difficult for them to do so.

Trump had a point when it came to defense spending by America's allies. At the turn of the century, non-US NATO countries spent about 2 percent of their collective GDP on defense. That figure declined to below 1.5 percent even before the financial crisis of 2008 and continued to decline thereafter.[26] Successive US administrations had pushed the Europeans to reverse that trend, but it wasn't until 2014, following Russia's invasion of Ukraine, that alliance leaders agreed to halt spending cuts and instead "aim to move towards the 2% guideline within a decade."[27] Trump was right to hold the alliance to this standard. But NATO is more than how much every nation spends on defense. It is above all a political and military alliance of shared values and shared interests—indeed, the longest and most successful such alliance in history. Countries contribute to the collective enterprise in many different ways—deploying troops to defeat terrorists in Afghanistan and deter Russia in the Baltics, ships to protect sea lanes from terrorists and pirates and help refugee flows, airplanes to provide surveillance for the coalition effort against the Islamic State and air defense of Iceland, and peacekeepers in the Balkans. Those actions, as much as spending on defense, are what make NATO the bedrock of transatlantic security.

Although past presidents had lectured Europe on paying its fair share, European leaders were worried that Trump's focus on how much each ally spent on defense distorted his understanding of the alliance. "Two percent is America's stock answer to every problem raised at the North Atlantic Council," one European diplomat complained. "We are not focusing on the big strategic issues and what NATO can do about them."[28] America's European allies increasingly worried that Trump was turning the transatlantic alliance into the transactional alliance—where the US willingness to commit would be decided by how much some allies were spending rather than by how serious the shared threat was or by what collective action could accomplish to defend shared interests and promote shared values.

THE SCOLDING IN Brussels was followed by major disagreement over two other issues: trade and climate change. These issues were the main topics of the G-7 Summit in Taormina, which opened the day after the NATO visit. The meeting offered Trump his first opportunity to interact extensively with leaders of America's closest and most important allies. Originally formed as an informal gathering of leaders to discuss the global economy, the G-7 had evolved into the principal annual meeting of Western leaders to consider the most pressing issues of the day and coordinate policy going forward. The Taormina Summit also provided an opportunity for the other leaders to take the measure of the man now occupying the Oval Office. What they discovered, to the dismay of many, was that the Donald Trump they met in private wasn't any different from the Donald Trump they saw in public—and that his beliefs were as strongly held and unswayable as ever.

Trade was high on the agenda because Trump's early actions and statements had left America's top economic partners deeply troubled. He did nothing to reassure them on this trip. In Brussels, while meeting with EU leaders, the president declared that the "Germans are bad, very bad," complaining about the "millions of cars they are selling to the US. Terrible. We will stop this."[29] It was an old complaint, and it ignored the fact that a growing portion of German cars sold in the United States were made there. Many US-made German cars were also exported to China, thus improving the overall US trade balance. Rather than fight over the issue, the G-7 leaders sought to paper over their differences. Recognizing that "free, fair, and mutually beneficial trade and investment" were "engines for growth and job creation," they reiterated their "commitment to keep our markets open and to fight protectionism, while standing firm against all unfair trade practices."[30]

There was no way to paper over the differences on climate change, however. During the campaign, Trump had railed against the Paris Agreement that 196 countries had negotiated in 2015 to reduce greenhouse gas emissions, increase the ability to adapt to adverse consequences of a changing climate, and help finance these global efforts. The agreement contained no binding targets or enforcement mechanisms and left it up to each nation to decide how it would reduce its emissions—facts that Trump conveniently ignored, insisting the agreement was "bad for US business" and promising to "cancel" US participation.[31] Back in Washington, Trump's aides had debated the wisdom of sticking to Paris or walking away. His principal national security and economic advisers, including the secretaries of state and defense, as well as his daughter and son-in-law, had urged him to stay with the agreement because they deemed it a much-needed response to the global threat of climate change. Others within the administration, including the head of the Environmental Protection Agency and Steve Bannon, argued that the agreement would destroy American jobs and hurt American competitiveness. And they contested the validity of the underlying science that had formed the globally accepted basis of the Paris Agreement. Trump's sympathies lay with the skeptics. The Taormina meeting would put those sympathies to the test.

"His views are evolving," Gary Cohn told reporters as the president arrived in Sicily. "He came here to learn. He came here to get smarter."[32] The other leaders were willing teachers. Macron argued that climate change was real and had to be addressed before it was too late. Justin Trudeau suggested that previous experience with eliminating the dangerous gasses that produced a hole in the ozone layer showed that industries were adaptive and could take the necessary steps to reduce greenhouse gas emissions without major economic impact. Merkel argued that there was a global race to dominate the renewable energy sector, one that the United States was well positioned to win but that China and India would otherwise lead. Trump was unmoved. "For me, it's easier to stay in than step out," he said rather unconvincingly. The issue for him was jobs, American jobs, and the agreement he insisted, contrary to all available evidence, was bad for jobs.

In the end, the six allies could not change Trump's mind. The declaration released at the conclusion of the summit summarized the state of affairs. "The United States of America is in the process of reviewing its policies on climate change and on the Paris Agreement and thus is not in a position to join the consensus on these topics," it stated.[33] "There is a situation where six—if you take the E.U., seven—stand against one," Merkel said after the meeting concluded.[34] The G-7 had become a G-6 + 1. "Now China leads," a resigned Macron concluded.[35]

In any other administration, an American president so isolated on a major issue might have taken another look. Not so Trump. In fact, the combined pressure from the other leaders may have hardened his position. Disappointing the Europeans was "a secondary benefit" of walking away from Paris, one White House official explained.[36] Days later he strode into the Rose Garden and declared, "We're getting out." The reason was the same one he had told the G-7 leaders. "The Paris Agreement handicaps the United States economy in order to win praise from the very foreign capitals and global activists that have long sought to gain wealth at our country's expense. They don't put America first. I do, and I always will." Worse, Trump continued, "the same nations asking us to stay in the agreement are the countries that have collectively cost America trillions of dollars through tough trade practices and, in many cases, lax contributions to our critical military alliance." No more. "We don't want other leaders and other countries laughing at us anymore. And they won't be. They won't be. I was elected to represent the citizens of Pittsburgh, not Paris."[37]

Foreign leaders pushed back hard this time. Macron took to the airwaves minutes after having told Trump by phone that "nothing is renegotiable in the Paris accords."[38] He called on American scientists, entrepreneurs, and others disappointed in Trump's decision to come to France and work toward common solutions and "make our planet great again."[39] Merkel was equally firm. "Since the decision by the United States of America to quit the Paris climate accords, we are more determined than ever to make it a success," she told German lawmakers a few weeks later. "We will and must take on this existential challenge and we cannot and will not wait until every last person in the world can be convinced of climate change by scientific evidence. In other words: The climate treaty is irreversible and is not negotiable."[40]

AMERICA'S ISOLATION ON the climate change issue was underscored when Trump returned to Europe for the G-20 meeting in Hamburg in July. There, the other nineteen delegations confirmed their continued support for the Paris Agreement. "The negotiations on the climate issue reflected dissent," Merkel, the meeting's host, noted in her closing press conference. "Everyone against the United States of America."[41]

But the bigger issue in Hamburg wasn't climate change or even the clash over Trump's trade policies, real though those were. It was his relationship with Vladimir Putin. During the campaign, Trump had spoken positively about Putin and the potential for improving US-Russian relations. "I have always felt that Russia and the United States should be able to work well with each other towards defeating terrorism and restoring world peace," Trump had said, "not to mention trade and all of the other benefits derived from mutual respect." Putin had returned the favor. "He says that he wants to move to another level of relations, to a deeper level of relations with Russia," the Russian president said of Trump. "How can we not welcome that? Of course we welcome it."[42]

Trump's election had generated great excitement in Moscow, and it was even greeted with a standing ovation in the Russian Duma when the news broke.[43] "Nobody believed he would win except for us," a confident Putin noted at his 2016 end-of-year news conference.[44] Putin's enthusiasm was matched by Trump, who hoped to achieve a grand bargain with Moscow once in office. In return for Russia's cooperation on eliminating the Islamic State in Syria and resolving the conflict in Ukraine, Trump indicated he would favor lifting the sanctions Obama had imposed on Moscow for its invasion of Ukraine and interference in the US elections. "If you get along and if Russia is really helping us, why would anybody have sanctions if somebody's doing some really great things?" Trump asked.[45]

Trump's desire for a rapprochement faced major obstacles at home and abroad. One was the conclusion by the US intelligence community that Russia had interfered in the elections. "We assess Russian President Vladimir Putin ordered an influence campaign in 2016 aimed at the US presidential election," the unclassified report on Russian hacking concluded in early January 2017. "Russia's goals were to undermine public faith in the US democratic process, denigrate Secretary Clinton, and harm her electability and potential presidency. We further assess Putin and the Russian Government developed a clear preference for President-elect Trump. We have high confidence in these judgments."[46] Senators John McCain and Ben Cardin mounted a bipartisan push to enact additional sanctions to punish Russia for its interference. Indeed, the more the White House appeared interested in accommodating Moscow, the more inclined Congress was to legislate against it.

Another obstacle was the fact that most of the president's senior advisers, including McMaster, Tillerson, and Mattis, disagreed with the president on the advisability of seeking closer relations with Russia. Indeed, they strongly doubted that US and Russian interests were aligned in Syria, Ukraine, or elsewhere. In meetings with Trump, they advised against lifting sanctions absent concrete steps by Moscow to cease its efforts to destabilize Ukraine. And they urged appropriate skepticism of Putin's motives in seeking to improve relations with Washington.

There were also America's allies. They had lived with a revived Russian threat for three years and had coalesced around a view that there could be no business as usual as long as Russia continued to occupy Crimea and undermine Ukraine. In her first meeting with Trump, Theresa May pressed him to take a firm stance against Putin and align with Europe in keeping sanctions in place.[47] When Merkel came to the White House, she used her one-on-one meeting to show Trump a map of the former Soviet Union, overlaid with all of the independent countries Putin was now seeking to destabilize. "Putin is back to fighting the Cold War," Merkel told the new president.[48]

Although these obstacles made a precipitous move on Russia more difficult, neither Trump's view of Russia nor his desire for better relations ever really changed. "The whole Russian thing—that's a ruse," Trump said at his first press conference and in one form or another many times afterward. "And, by the way, it would be great if we could get along with Russia."[49] That was also Trump's attitude when he met Putin for the first time on the sidelines of the G-20 meeting. According to Tillerson, the only other American official to attend the two-hour meeting, the first part was devoted to the question of Russia's interference in the elections, with Trump asking Putin repeatedly whether he had ordered it. "He said absolutely not, twice," Trump later recalled. "What do you do? End up in a fistfight?"[50] So they moved on to other issues, including Syria and Ukraine. The two presidents agreed to establish a de-escalation zone and a ceasefire in southwest Syria, in what Tillerson characterized as the "first indication of the U.S. and Russia being able to work together in Syria." They also agreed to explore "a framework" for working together to deal with cyber threats, including preventing interference in "the internal affairs of countries." Overall, Tillerson said that "the meeting was very constructive," adding that "there was a very clear positive chemistry between the two." Neither wanted to relitigate the past, and both focused instead on making the relationship work. "We simply have to find a way to go forward."[51]

The positive chemistry was again on display over dinner later that evening. At one point, Trump walked over to the Russian president, who was seated next to the First Lady, and sat down for a conversation with Putin that lasted nearly an hour.[52] The only other person present was Putin's translator. In what was likely a first in modern great-power diplomacy, there was no official American record of the meeting between the two leaders. Whatever the issues that were discussed or the understandings that were reached during these informal talks, American officials had only Trump's recollection to go on. Trump later dismissed any such concern, saying that their lengthy conversation was all innocent small talk. It's doubtful that Putin, the former KGB man, was only interested in small talk. The larger point, though, was that everyone else at the dinner, including the leaders of America's closest and most important allies, noticed that the American president preferred to spend nearly an hour talking with Putin rather than with any of them. Trump seemingly put more stock in good relations with Moscow than in countering what they saw as Russia's destabilizing designs on European security and transatlantic unity.

Trump's apparent need to ingratiate himself with Putin remained one of the more puzzling elements of his tenure. Perhaps he really believed, as he frequently said, that having a good relationship with Putin was important because they could then tackle common challenges like Syria, Ukraine, and North Korea together. But this belief seemed to ignore that the United States and Russia had different interests in these cases that a close relationship between the two leaders could not by itself overcome. Perhaps Trump didn't see Moscow as a villain because Russia traded little with the United States and so hadn't been able to take advantage of America in the way he believed so many other countries had. Or perhaps there was something more nefarious that made Trump act in what looked like a subservient manner to the Russian president. Whatever the explanation, Trump treated Putin with a respect and deference that he frequently declined to extend to allied leaders.

DURING THE CAMPAIGN Trump argued that the United States needed to think outside the box and that better relations with Russia provided the best way to promote American interests, defeat the Islamic State, and end the civil war in Syria. Once he got in the room with Putin, Trump essentially bought into the Russian narrative. "I would tell you that, by and large, our objectives are exactly the same" on Syria, Tillerson said of the two countries. He even suggested that where the United States and Russia differed, "maybe they've got the right approach and we've got the wrong approach."[53] Of course, US and Russian objectives did differ in Syria. Moscow intervened to shore up Assad's hold on power and to secure a long-term military presence in the region. Washington still insisted that any lasting political solution would have to include Assad's departure. Its primary focus, moreover, was on defeating the Islamic State and minimizing the chances extremist forces could again take hold in the country.

Trump's chumminess with the Russian leader—and his refusal to accept the intelligence community's assessment on Russian interference in the 2016 elections—left many deeply concerned. Some Europeans spoke of a "Yalta 2.0"—a modern version of the United States and Russia dividing Europe. Merkel was especially worried that Trump's uncritical embrace of Putin would undermine her years-long efforts to ensure a united front against Russia over its destabilization of Ukraine. "The summit went very well for Russia," an internal German foreign ministry memo noted after the G-20 concluded. "As long as the US breaks rank, Russia can swim in the mainstream."[54] Even sympathetic lawmakers on Capitol Hill worried about Trump's refusal to respond forcefully to Russia's election interference. "When it comes to Russia, he's got a blind spot," Senator Lindsey Graham said after what he called Trump's "disastrous" meeting with the Russian leader. "To forgive and forget when it comes to Putin regarding cyber-attacks is to empower Putin and that's exactly what he's doing."[55]

In the weeks ahead, Congress moved swiftly to hem Trump in, passing new sanctions legislation by votes of 419–3 in the House and 98–2 in the Senate. The bill codified the sanctions Obama had placed on Russia for its interference in the elections and gave Congress the final say on whether and when any sanctions on Russia could be lifted. Trump was enraged by the bill's passage. He was only dissuaded from vetoing it because aides told him that he would look weak when his veto was overridden, as it surely would have been. Calling the bill "seriously flawed," the president nevertheless signed it on August 2, adding, "It represents the will of the American people to see Russia take steps to improve relations with the United States."[56] That was a serious misrepresentation. If anything, the bill and its overwhelming passage represented the view that Russia needed to be held to account for its actions during the 2016 elections—and that if the president wasn't willing to do so, Congress would.

Putin understood the true meaning of the new law. He ordered the closure of two American diplomatic posts and a 755-person cut in the US diplomatic presence in Russia even before Trump signed it. The State

Department followed suit a few weeks later by ordering the closure of another three Russian diplomatic sites in the United States. The tit-for-tat response shattered any hope for a quick improvement in relations. The American president, Putin declared a few days later, "is not my bride, and I am not his groom."[57]

After the new sanctions legislation and the back-and-forth response, the Trump administration, though not the president, increasingly spoke of Russia as a challenge rather than an opportunity. The new National Security Strategy, released in December 2017, labeled Russia (along with China) a strategic competitor. "Russia seeks to restore its great power status and establish spheres of influence near its borders," the strategy declared. "Russia aims to weaken U.S. influence in the world and divide us from our allies and partners."[58] In rolling out the new strategy, Trump acknowledged that Russia and China were "rival powers . . . that seek to challenge American influence, values, and wealth." But rather than gearing up for competition with these powers, his goal was "to build a great partnership" with both countries. And instead of detailing the many ways in which Russia was undermining American interests and values, he talked about a phone call he had received from Putin days earlier thanking him for information that helped thwart a terrorist attack. "That is the way it's supposed to work," he declared.[59] The president's new strategy could not paper over the essential division between Trump and his administration over Russia.

"AMERICA FIRST DOES not mean America alone," McMaster and Cohn proclaimed upon Trump's return to Washington after his first trip abroad.[60] It was a message Trump would repeat, somewhat less confidently, eight months later in his speech to the global elite gathered for the World Economic Forum in Davos.[61] Yet, in having to repeat the message, the administration only helped reinforce the reality that its America First policies meant that America was increasingly alone. That was true on issues like climate change and trade, where America's stance was shared by few if any other countries around the world. America's allies in Europe still desired a strong relationship with the United States—one built on a mutual commitment to the defense of shared interests and values—but an increasing number worried that Trump did not share that desire. Of course, America still had friends, and some of its friendships, notably those with Israel and Saudi Arabia, had been strengthened by Trump's overseas visits. And others, not least Vladimir Putin, still hoped that Trump's election would produce a stronger and better relationship with the United States.

Relations with critical countries around the world, notably with America's long-standing allies, had been frayed by the unpredictability of an administration in disarray, a president who spoke his mind and placed little value on past practices and considerations, and a set of policies that challenged the very foundation of allied relationships with the United States. Increasingly, countries that for decades had first looked to Washington for guidance and assistance began looking elsewhere to achieve their goals and objectives. If Washington was going to pursue a policy of America First, then it would have to do so on its own. And when the time came for Washington to turn to its allies, friends, or partners to achieve its goals—be it to pressure rogue actors like North Korea and Iran, help rebuild societies devastated by war and conflict in the Middle East, or negotiate new trading arrangements more favorable to American workers—it might find they were no longer there. America First could become America Alone.

8

Fire and Fury

"THE CHEAP 12 INCH sq. marble tiles behind speaker at UN always bothered me," Donald Trump tweeted in 2012. "I will replace with beautiful large marble slabs if they ask me."[1] His criticism of the United Nations didn't stop with what offended his real estate developer's eye. He was equally alarmed by what he saw as the UN's mix of anti-Americanism and ineffectiveness. "The United Nations is not a friend of democracy," he complained on the campaign trail. "It's not a friend to freedom, it's not a friend even to the United States of America."[2] Being elected president didn't improve his view. Three weeks before he took the oath of office, he tweeted, "The United Nations has such great potential but right now it is just a club for people to get together, talk and have a good time. So sad!"

Trump got his chance to tap the UN's great potential. On September 19, 2017, he took the podium in front of the cheap marble tiles he so disliked. He was there partly because of expectations. American presidents typically joined with other world leaders every September to address the opening session of the UN General Assembly. But Trump was in New York to do more than just uphold tradition. He was there to make the case that UN members had to rally against the threats that North Korea and Iran posed to American, and global, security.

Trump started his speech diplomatically, lauding the UN Security Council for unanimously passing two resolutions tightening sanctions on North Korea for its nuclear and ballistic missile tests. But he quickly cast aside diplomatic niceties and threw down the gauntlet. "The United States has great strength and patience," he warned, "but if it is forced to defend itself or its allies, we will have no choice but to totally destroy North Korea. Rocket man is on a suicide mission for himself and for his regime." He then turned to Iran and the nuclear deal that it had negotiated with the five permanent members of the UN Security Council plus Germany two years earlier. "The Iran Deal was one of the worst and most one-sided transactions the United States has ever entered into. Frankly, that deal is an embarrassment to the United States, and I don't think you've heard the last of it—believe me."[3]

Trump concluded his remarks to polite applause. Much of the media coverage of the speech debated whether White House Chief of Staff John Kelly had reacted to Trump's disparagement of North Korean leader Kim Jong-un as "rocket man" with a facepalm. The more consequential reactions, though, were in foreign capitals. A few world leaders applauded Trump for his clarity. "In over 30 years in my experience with the UN," Israeli Prime Minister Benjamin Netanyahu said, "I never heard a bolder or more courageous speech."[4] The spokesman for South Korean President Moon Jae-in praised Trump for his "firm and specific stance" while skillfully avoiding comment on his threat to "totally destroy" North Korea.[5]

Most reactions, however, were critical. "We don't talk about destroying countries," complained Federica Mogherini, the European Union's High Representative for Foreign Affairs and Security Policy. "We talk about finding peaceful solutions."[6] Swedish Foreign Minister Margot Wallstrom struck a similar note: "This was a bombastic, nationalist speech . . . at the wrong time to the wrong audience."[7] Iran's President Hassan Rouhani took the podium after Trump and warned that "it will be a great pity" if the Iran nuclear deal were "destroyed by rogue newcomers to the world of politics."[8] But the most pointed response came from Pyongyang. Two days after Trump spoke, Kim Jong-un delivered a televised rebuttal. Calling Trump a "mentally deranged U.S. dotard" and "a rogue and a gangster fond of playing with fire, rather than a politician," he warned that any US action against North Korea would be met with "the highest level of hard-line countermeasure."[9]

Trump's tough talk at the UN put the world firmly on notice that he intended to coerce North Korea and Iran into ending their nuclear and ballistic programs. But if tough talk had been enough to compel either country to capitulate, the problem would have been solved years earlier. As Trump's predecessors had discovered, it wasn't. Pyongyang and Tehran had shown time and again that they were willing and able to resist intense diplomatic and economic pressure. Meanwhile, as the North Korean and Iranian programs progressed, the range of possible

US diplomatic options shrank. Talk turned instead to the looming choice to be made between accepting the supposedly unacceptable or waging potentially catastrophic wars to prevent it. Not surprisingly given that context, Trump's tough talk alarmed many US friends and allies rather than rallied them behind his lead.

"IT'S VERY LATE," Trump complained in early February 2017, just after Kim Jong-un's regime tested a medium-range ballistic missile in violation of UN Security Council resolutions. "We're very angry at what he's done, and frankly this should have been taken care of during the Obama administration."[10] Trump's pique was understandable. North Korea was getting perilously close to being able to hit the United States with a nuclear-armed ballistic missile. But the problem long predated Obama. By the tail end of George H. W. Bush's presidency, it was evident that Pyongyang was developing nuclear weapons. Bush's three successors all tried to derail the program and failed.

That failure wasn't because Presidents Clinton, Bush, and Obama didn't grasp the consequences of what North Korea was seeking to do. They understood the risks well. Their fear wasn't so much that Pyongyang would launch a bolt-from-the-blue attack, though that prospect couldn't be ruled out if the North Korean regime believed its survival was threatened or if the regime crumbled and lost control of its weapons. Under most circumstances the prospect of devastating US retaliation should deter Pyongyang. What troubled Clinton, Bush, and Obama more was that a North Korea capable of hitting the United States with nuclear-armed missiles would throw into question America's security guarantees to Japan and South Korea. Pyongyang might doubt that the White House would risk the destruction of San Francisco to stop an attack on Seoul. If so, North Korea might act more aggressively, possibly triggering the very war the United States had for decades sought to prevent. This problem of extended deterrence, as foreign policy experts called it, wasn't new. The United States had confronted it throughout the Cold War with the Soviet threat to Europe. Then the question was whether presidents would risk Boston to save Bonn. The fact that extended deterrence hadn't failed in Europe didn't make the problem any less pressing in Northeast Asia.

Extended deterrence would cease to be a problem, of course, if Japan and South Korea acquired their own nuclear weapons. Trump had suggested as much during the campaign. Pyongyang wouldn't doubt that a nuclear-armed Tokyo and Seoul would retaliate if attacked. But the United States had worked for seventy years to prevent the spread of nuclear weapons, particularly by championing the Non-Proliferation Treaty. Japan and South Korea, along with 180 other countries, had signed it, agreeing never to develop or acquire nuclear weapons. Global nonproliferation efforts would be upended if Tokyo and Seoul reneged on their commitments. Other countries, including many hostile to the United States, would use the move to justify launching their own nuclear weapons programs. A South Korean or Japanese decision to become a nuclear weapons state would also threaten China, potentially setting off an arms race in Northeast Asia. So encouraging Seoul and Tokyo to acquire nuclear weapons might solve one problem but create a host of other, possibly worse, ones.

The failure to stop North Korea also wasn't for a lack of trying. Clinton, Bush, and Obama each took a different approach to the looming nuclear danger, trying a mix of strategies that eventually included threats, foreign aid, negotiations, ostracism, and during the latter years of the Obama administration, cyber-attacks.[11] Each president also insisted publicly that all options were on the table, but privately each recognized that the cost of ending North Korea's nuclear program by force would be high. Its army was one of the largest in the world, possessing both chemical and biological weapons. Seoul, a city of more than ten million, lay just thirty-five miles south of the demilitarized zone, well within reach of North Korean artillery and rocket fire. The potential price tag of a military strike jumped after 2006 when North Korea first tested a nuclear device. A war that might kill hundreds of thousands now could kill millions.

By the end of Obama's second term, it was clear that his policy of "strategic patience," which married tougher sanctions to a refusal to negotiate with North Korea until it first took steps to denuclearize, was failing. North Korea had built a stockpile of perhaps as many as sixty nuclear weapons. In September 2016 North Korea conducted its fifth nuclear test, which generated a blast greater than the bomb dropped on Hiroshima. Even more worrying was the progress North Korea was making in building long-range ballistic missiles and mastering the technology required to put nuclear warheads atop them. Faced with the likelihood that North Korea could hit South Korea with a nuclear-armed missile, the Obama administration in 2016 persuaded Seoul to deploy the US-built ballistic missile defense system known as Terminal High Altitude Area Defense (THAAD). Seoul took the step despite fierce opposition at home stemming from the belief that the move would provoke North Korea and China, which worried that THAAD might one day be expanded to undermine its nuclear deterrent.

Although North Korea still lacked the capability to hit the continental United States with a nuclear-armed missile as Obama's presidency ended, the trend was ominous. James Clapper, the director of national intelligence, acknowledged in late October 2016 that the American effort to convince North Korea to shutter its nuclear program was "probably a lost cause" because it was "their ticket to survival" and any discussion about ending their nuclear ambitions would be a "nonstarter."[12] Two weeks later Obama met with President-elect Trump in their first and only meeting before Inauguration Day. Once the pleasantries were completed, Obama offered his successor some advice: North Korea's nuclear weapons program would be the gravest and most immediate foreign policy threat Trump would face as president.

OBAMA'S WARNING HIT home. Trump had seldom mentioned North Korea or Kim Jong-un on the campaign trail. He had focused his ire instead on the Islamic State, free-loading allies, and bad trade deals. When he had spoken of North Korea, it had been to complain that "we get virtually nothing" for protecting Japan and South Korea and to argue that the United States should "let China solve that problem."[13] But three weeks before Inauguration Day, he put a bull's-eye squarely on Pyongyang. "North Korea just stated that it is in the final stages of developing a nuclear weapon capable of reaching parts of the U.S.," he tweeted. "It won't happen!"[14]

Trump had drawn a red line. Now he had to find a way to enforce it. The answer was what his aides called a strategy of "maximum pressure." The United States would squeeze North Korea harder and force it to cry uncle. Administration officials repeatedly said publicly that "all options are on the table" when it came to using military force. They even floated the possibility that the United States would strike North Korea first "if they elevate the threat of their weapons program."[15] But the most enthusiastic—and dramatic—in banging the war drum was Trump himself. In April he warned that "there is a chance that we could end up having a major, major conflict with North Korea."[16] He made the same point more colorfully in August during a photo opportunity at his Bedminster, New Jersey, golf course: "North Korea best not make any more threats to the United States. They will be met with fire and fury like the world has never seen."[17] Three days later he tweeted, "Military solutions are now fully in place, locked and loaded, should North Korea act unwisely. Hopefully Kim Jong Un will find another path!"[18]

The administration coupled its saber rattling with efforts to ratchet up economic pressure on Pyongyang. Critical to strangling the North Korean economy was getting the cooperation of China, which accounted for 90 percent of North Korea's trade. Trump made no secret of how he intended to get the Chinese to pitch in: he would hold off on his campaign promise to get tough with China on trade. "I explained to the President of China," he tweeted after Xi Jinping visited Trump's Florida home at Mar-a-Lago in April, "that a trade deal with the U.S. will be far better for them if they solve the North Korean problem!"[19] And if Beijing wasn't willing to cooperate, Trump would consider "stopping all trade with any country doing business with North Korea."[20]

Trump's tough talk and public tweets created the impression he had repudiated Obama's policy. But on close inspection the strategy of maximum pressure looked a lot like strategic patience—and it suffered from the same flaws. No amount of military exercises or intensified planning changed the fact that the likely price tag of a war in Korea remained grim—and got grimmer with every North Korean technological advance. It wouldn't just be Koreans who died if Trump's major war came. With nearly thirty thousand US troops and many of their families stationed in South Korea and tens of thousands of US businesspeople, students, and tourists in South Korea on any given day, large numbers of Americans would die as well, even if no missiles hit US soil.

Likewise, the Obama administration had tightened the economic vise on North Korea and sought to enlist China's cooperation to do it. Indeed, it had become a cottage industry for American officials and experts to travel to Beijing to lecture their Chinese counterparts on how it was in China's interest to rein in North Korea. But great powers seldom do favors for their rivals; they instead exploit their rivals' vulnerabilities. Even as Obama accused China in 2010 of "willful blindness" in overlooking Pyongyang's misdeeds, Beijing judged its interests differently.[21] A nuclear-armed North Korea might be undesirable, but it was preferable to a North Korean government that collapsed. That might generate chaos as North Koreans poured across the border into China. Perhaps worse, it might produce a unified Korean peninsula aligned with the United States. Thousands of Chinese had died fighting in the Korean War to prevent just that outcome. For Beijing, then, North Korea's nuclear weapons program was fundamentally an American problem and not a Chinese one.

The strategy of maximum pressure also didn't offer Pyongyang anything in the way of carrots. Trump occasionally flattered Kim Jong-un, at one point calling him a "pretty smart cookie."[22] And US officials repeatedly stated what the United States wouldn't do: it wouldn't seek to change the regime in Pyongyang, trigger its collapse, accelerate the reunification of the peninsula, or send the US military north of the 38th Parallel. But these so-called "four noes" were all negative; the Trump administration wasn't offering any rewards. Rather, North Korea was expected to trade something for nothing. Talks could only begin if North Korea agreed to an "immediate cessation of its provocative threats, nuclear tests, missile launches, and other weapons tests."[23] When Rex Tillerson suggested in late September 2017 that he was exploring possible talks, Trump publicly cut him off at the knees, tweeting that Tillerson "is wasting his time trying to negotiate with Little Rocket Man. . . . Save your energy Rex, we'll do what has to be done!"[24] When Tillerson floated the idea of talks again in December, the White House shot down the idea once more.[25] But if, as the US intelligence community had concluded, asking North Korea to give up its nuclear program was a nonstarter, the maximum pressure strategy guaranteed a stalemate.

Trump's tough line did yield some diplomatic successes in 2017. The UN Security Council voted three times to tighten sanctions on North Korea, and China reduced its shipments of coal and oil. These successes were far from complete, however. What China and Russia gave with one hand, they took back at least partly with the other. Trump himself repeatedly took to Twitter to highlight China's failed and faltering efforts, and he lamented that "Russia is not helping us at all with North Korea."[26] Even so, the tighter sanctions did begin to bite into the North Korean economy. In his 2018 New Year's Day Address, Kim noted that international pressure had created "difficult living conditions" in North Korea.[27]

The problem was that economic pain wasn't an end in and of itself. It was a means to force Pyongyang to cry uncle. And as 2017 closed, it wasn't flinching. Despite being subjected to "just about every lever you can use, short of starving the people of North Korea to death, to change their behavior," as US Homeland Security Adviser Thomas Bossert put it, North Korea doubled down, matching the United States threat for threat and insult for insult.[28] Most important, North Korea had moved perilously close to crossing Trump's red line: gaining the ability to hit the United States with a nuclear-armed missile. On July 4, North Korea conducted its first test of a missile theoretically capable of reaching North America, calling it "a package of gifts" to the "American bastards."[29] In September, North Korea conducted its sixth nuclear test, detonating a device that generated an explosive force ten times that of the bomb dropped on Hiroshima. In November, North Korea tested a more advanced intercontinental ballistic missile, crowing in the aftermath of the successful test that it "finally realized the great historic cause of completing the state nuclear force."[30]

Trump administration officials acknowledged the significance of the accomplishment. Yet they also stressed Trump's continued willingness to act. "Our president has been really clear," H. R. McMaster, the national security adviser, insisted. "He is not going to permit this rogue regime, Kim Jong-un, to threaten the United States with a nuclear weapon. And so, he is willing to do anything necessary to prevent that from happening."[31] That "anything" included preventive military action. The Pentagon was ordered to examine a range of military options, including possible strikes against North Korea's long-range missile launchers and production facilities. Sometimes referred to as the "bloody nose" strategy, the idea was that Kim Jong-un might abandon his effort to develop long-range missiles in the face of a limited US strike rather than doom his regime by escalating the fighting.[32] It was a high-risk option. North Korea might retaliate by attacking South Korea and Japan. Trump, it appeared, might be willing to take such a risk. "If thousands die, they're going to die over there. They're not going to die here," Senator Lindsey Graham said the president had told him.[33] It was a chilling reminder of how high the stakes had become.

THREATS OF WAR played a central role in the administration's strategy of maximum pressure. But although the intended audience was North Korea, America's allies were listening as well. Washington's challenge was to threaten Pyongyang without scaring Seoul and Tokyo into going their own way. If the unified front among the three countries collapsed, so too would the maximum pressure. The success of the administration's policy, then, depended on keeping Seoul and Tokyo firmly behind it.

Japan was the easier relationship to manage. Tokyo applauded Trump's early calls for tough action on North Korea. Prime Minister Shinzo Abe, a conservative politician who had long favored a more assertive Japanese foreign policy, was more in tune with Trump on foreign policy than he had been with Obama. Abe worried about the growing threat that North Korea posed to Japan, and he had chafed at Obama's reluctance to take a harder line with Pyongyang. Abe's greater fear, however, was a rising China. Anti-Japanese sentiment ran deep in China; memories of Japan's brutal World War II occupation remained fresh for many Chinese.

World War II had two other lasting consequences for Japan. One was a constitution, which the occupying American forces helped write, that barred it from using force to settle disputes. That provision had long been interpreted as limiting the size and reach of Japan's military. The other was the deep aversion of the Japanese public, given the horrors of Hiroshima and Nagasaki, to the idea of acquiring nuclear weapons. Left to itself, then, Japan would face Chinese domination and intimidation; it could counter its far larger neighbor only with the help of the United States. The lesson for Abe's government was clear: whatever reservations it might have about the Trump presidency, and there were many, maintaining close ties with Washington was essential. So Abe made it a point to cultivate good relations with Trump.

Japanese officials worried, however, that sticking close to the United States would be easier said than done. One fear was that Trump would make an issue of Japan's persistent trade surplus with the United States, which would roil Japanese domestic politics. Abe had no interest in the sort of bilateral deals that Trump favored. He had championed the Trans-Pacific Partnership, and he still hoped that he might persuade Trump to reconsider his opposition. Although Trump refrained from pushing the trade issue during his first year in office, he turned to it with a vengeance in 2018. In March, he imposed steep tariffs on steel and aluminum imports into the United States from Japan and other countries (though he temporarily exempted other US allies).

Another Japanese fear was of entrapment: Trump's brinkmanship might trigger a war that Japan didn't want. At a minimum, if Trump didn't "act on North Korea in concert with the UN, that would be controversial" with the Japanese public, as one senior Japanese official dryly put it.[34] But Japan's greatest fear was of abandonment. Trump's skepticism about the value of America's alliances and his preference for a transactional foreign policy were clear. That raised the possibility, as one retired Japanese diplomat noted in late 2017, that he might "sacrifice the region for America First" by striking a deal with North Korea or China that served US interests but damaged Japan's—for example, by focusing only on the long-range missile threat while leaving the North's short- and medium-range missiles in place.[35] Tokyo's best hope to avoid that outcome was to stick close to the Trump administration and quietly work to derail any deal that did not take Japan's interests into account.

South Korea presented a different, and more complex, challenge for Trump. North Korea had been an existential threat to its southern neighbor since the two countries came into existence, and South Koreans had lived with the possibility of a North Korean nuclear attack since 2006. Like Japan, South Korea's security policy rested on its military alliance with the United States. But South Korean attitudes toward the United States, China, and North Korea were more varied than in Japan. South Korea harbored a strong strain of anti-Americanism, a legacy of Washington's support for the authoritarian presidents who ran the country until the late 1980s. There was no equivalent anti-Chinese sentiment; many South Koreans saw China more as a friend and trading partner than as a potential overlord. The biggest split in South Korean foreign policy was over whether North Korea was best dealt with through a closed fist or an open hand. Conservatives called for meeting the North Korean threat with might and determination, and they saw a strong alliance with the United States as critical. Liberals argued that North Korea was best dealt with through economic and diplomatic engagement, the so-called Sunshine policy that South Korean President Kim Dae-jung had championed in the 1990s.

The election of Moon Jae-in as South Korea's president in May 2017 brought these issues to the fore. The left-leaning former special forces soldier, human rights lawyer, and son of North Korean refugees was Trump's opposite in most ways. He had campaigned on a pledge to revive the Sunshine policy that South Korea's previous two conservative presidents had abandoned. He had criticized what he saw as the rushed move to deploy THAAD and promised to review the decision once in office. He repeatedly spoke of deepening South Korea's ties to China. Most important, he stressed that he wouldn't blindly follow Washington's lead. Where Trump championed "America First," Moon championed a South Korean counterpart, "National Interest First." It stressed preserving South Korea's freedom to act as it saw fit. "I'm pro-US," he wrote in a campaign book, "but now South Korea should adopt diplomacy in which it can discuss a US request and say no to the Americans."[36] He insisted that Seoul and not Washington should "take the lead on matters on the Korean Peninsula."[37] That was particularly the case on matters of war. "I want to say it sternly," he wrote a month before his election. "Military action on the Korea peninsula cannot happen without Korea's consent."[38] Entrapment, not abandonment, was his main fear.

Moon initially trod carefully in his dealings with Trump. He recognized that if he wanted to avoid rupturing the US-South Korean alliance—and likely forfeiting any opportunity to influence US policy— he needed to avoid a rift with Washington. Although he kept his campaign promise to suspend further deployments of THAAD, he sidelined the campaign talk about reopening an inter-Korean dialogue and reaching out to China. He traveled to Washington in late June for his first meeting with Trump. As the two stood side by side in the Rose Garden, Trump declared that "the era of strategic patience with the North Korean regime has failed." Moon quickly echoed his comments, saying that "threats and provocations from the North will be met with a stern response."[39] In the wake of North Korea's September nuclear test, Moon reversed himself on THAAD and allowed deployment to resume.

Moon had not, however, accepted the wisdom of the US strategy for dealing with North Korea. The United States had, as one of his senior advisers argued, simply shifted "from strategic patience to strategic confusion" without achieving "strategic coherence."[40] Moon continued to believe, as another of his advisers put it, that "it is more effective to engage North Korea and to lead them where we want to go."[41] Moon and his advisers were "alarmed" by Trump's tough talk and the suggestion that military strikes were a possible option.[42] Such bluster, in their view, simply incited more North Korean provocations, which in turn closed off opportunities to engage Pyongyang.

Besides the differences over policy, Trump's refusal to acknowledge Moon's domestic political situation rankled the South Korean president. Moon had promised his supporters that he would open a dialogue with North Korea, place South Korea's interests before America's, and reach out to China. He had slow played all those initiatives at a political cost to himself in order to maintain good relations with the White House. Trump nonetheless talked blithely about initiating a war, and after North Korea's September nuclear test, he took to Twitter to say that South Korea's "talk of appeasement with North Korea will not work, they only understand one thing!"[43] Further compounding matters, Trump demanded that Seoul renegotiate the terms of the 2011 US-Korea Free Trade Agreement. Moon eventually agreed to revise the deal, at the risk of antagonizing his supporters who thought he had already been too accommodating to Washington.

Even as Moon worked to keep close to Washington, his focus remained on finding a way to engage North Korea. The opening came two months later with Kim's traditional New Year's Day address to the North Korean people. Trump seized on the fact that Kim said that "a nuclear button is always on the desk of my office."[44] Trump responded that his nuclear button was "much bigger" and "more powerful."[45] Moon, however, disregarded Kim's belligerent rhetoric; South Koreans had heard it for years. He fixed instead on Kim's statement that North Korea would consider participating in the Winter Olympics that were to be held in South Korea two months later. Within twenty-four hours, and without consulting Washington, Moon proposed talks with North Korea to explore the idea. The two sides quickly reached an agreement to form a combined Korean team at Pyeongchang and to walk together under a common flag at the opening ceremony.

The Olympics proved a turning point. Kim sent his sister to the games with an invitation to Moon for a summit meeting in Pyongyang. Within weeks, a senior delegation from Seoul met with the North Korean leader to prepare the meeting. In two days of detailed talks, Kim not only agreed to hold the summit by the end of April in the demilitarized zone but also suggested that he was willing to negotiate with the United States on denuclearizing the Korean Peninsula. Kim added that he would freeze any missile and nuclear testing when talks began.[46]

Moon had risked a major breach with the United States in pursuing talks with the North. Trump had consistently denounced negotiations as useless and only months earlier had accused him of appeasement. But Moon's gamble paid off. Instead of blocking inter-Korea discussions, Trump claimed credit for them, tweeting in the wake of the initial decision to hold talks: "Does anybody really believe that talks and dialogue would be going on between North and South Korea right now if

I wasn't firm, strong and willing to commit our total 'might' against the North."[47] Pleasantly surprised by Trump's willingness to encourage talks and determined to keep him on the diplomatic path, Moon stressed that South Korea remained committed to the maximum pressure strategy. He also played to Trump's ego, saying publicly, "I am giving a lot of credit to President Trump" for making inter-Korean dialogue possible.[48] Having jump-started negotiations, Moon faced a critical question: How far was Trump willing to go?

The answer turned out to be surprisingly far. A few days after the meeting in Pyongyang, the South Korean officials who had met with Kim traveled to Washington to brief the administration on the talks. They brought with them an invitation from Kim to meet with Trump as well. To the astonishment of the South Koreans—and his senior national security advisers, who were not asked for their advice—Trump immediately said yes.[49] The president, who only weeks earlier had threatened war, now embraced the prospect of peace. "The deal with North Korea is very much in the making and will be, if completed, a very good one for the World," Trump tweeted.[50]

"To jaw, jaw is always better than to war, war," as Winston Churchill famously said. But the decision to enter a dialogue with Kim hardly resolved the underlying issues. An immediate question was why Kim had extended his olive branch. Trump credited his maximum pressure strategy. Equally plausible, however, was that Kim came to the bargaining table because he believed he could negotiate from a position of strength, given the progress North Korea's nuclear and missile programs had made. The risk also remained that Kim was playing both Trump and Moon. Kim's so-called smile diplomacy, with its ill-defined promises of denuclearization, might have been a ruse to buy time for his regime, gain sanctions relief, and drive a wedge between South Korea and the United States. Pyongyang had agreed several times before to dismantle its nuclear program in exchange for economic benefits, only to work clandestinely to keep it alive. As the title of one skeptical op-ed put it, "North Korea Might Negotiate in Good Faith This Time but It Would Be the First Time."[51]

The summit almost did not happen. In late May, Trump called it off in response to a series of harsh statements from Pyongyang that culminated in a senior North Korean official calling Vice President Mike Pence a "political dummy."[52] The cancellation came without any consultation with Moon, who said upon learning the news, "I am embarrassed."[53] Trump, however, left the door open to reversing his decision, writing to Kim that "I very much look forward to meeting you" should North Korea abandon its "tremendous anger and open hostility."[54] A flurry of diplomatic exchanges ensued, including an unscheduled second meeting between Kim and Moon. A week after canceling the summit, Trump announced that it was back on. "We're getting along," Trump said after meeting Kim's envoy in the White House, adding, "It's not a question of maximum pressure. It's staying essentially the way it is."[55] In Trump's mind, the relationship had moved from the brink of nuclear war to the brink of a historic peace.

When Trump and Kim shook hands in Singapore in June, it was indeed historic. But the reason why had yet to be determined. Unlike most summits, the two sides had not agreed in advance on a detailed plan for their two leaders to bless. Indeed, in the run-up to the meeting, Washington and Pyongyang talked past each other. US officials spoke repeatedly of seeking North Korea's "complete, verifiable, and irreversible" nuclear disarmament. North Korean officials, however, carefully avoided making any such commitment, only repeating long-standing promises to "denuclearize the Korean Peninsula." Pyongyang did take a few steps, such as blowing up tunnels to its nuclear testing site, that seemed to signal it was charting a new course. It was far from clear, however, whether those steps were either meaningful or irreversible.

The summit itself lasted just five hours and produced a four-hundred-word communiqué that was as remarkable for its lack of specifics as it was for its brevity. Kim "reaffirmed his firm and unwavering commitment to complete denuclearization of the Korean Peninsula," and Trump "committed to provide security guarantees" to North Korea. But the joint statement was silent on what denuclearization meant, what the timeline for implementation would be, or how it would be comprehensive, verifiable, and irreversible. The communiqué did obligate North Korea and the United States "to hold follow-on negotiations," but it neither offered a deadline for completing such talks nor specified what tangible goals they should achieve beyond finding ways "to implement the outcomes" of the summit.[56]

The lack of specifics didn't matter to Trump. The meeting was a victory. "Our whole relationship with North Korea and the Korean Peninsula is going to be a very much different situation than it has in the past," he declared at the summit's conclusion.[57] He then went well beyond what the communiqué said, announcing he was suspending joint US military exercises with South Korea. He complained strenuously about the "tremendously expensive" cost of these "war games," denigrating them as "very provocative"—language that before then had come from Pyongyang and not from Washington. Trump announced the suspension of military exercises without having first consulted with Seoul—or the Pentagon. He also said he wanted "to bring our soldiers back home," signaling to Pyongyang that this was a concession he was prepared to make down the road.[58] It was another potential move that he hadn't discussed with South Korea, Japan, or the US military.

At a minimum, the Singapore summit diminished the threat of war on the Korean Peninsula in the short term. Talk of "fire and fury" and "nuclear buttons" gave way to diplomatic negotiations. That was no small feat. But the essential problem remained: the threat posed by North Korea's nuclear arsenal. Trump tweeted as Air Force One landed at Andrews Air Force Base that "there is no longer a Nuclear Threat from North Korea."[59] But the Singapore summit hadn't ended the North Korean threat—nuclear or otherwise. All of the issues that had stymied previous negotiations with Pyongyang remained—starting with deep uncertainty that Kim was willing to give up his country's nuclear weapons. In his eagerness to claim a win, Trump glossed over all these realities. He instead told Americans to "sleep well tonight!"[60] But in suspending exercises and calling into question the longevity of the US military presence in South Korea, Trump had conceded a lot and gotten very little in return.

IRAN'S NUCLEAR PROGRAM lagged far behind North Korea's. Iran had no nuclear weapons when Trump assumed office. That would not change during his presidency if the 2015 Iran nuclear deal held. Formally known as the Joint Comprehensive Plan of Action (JCPOA), it was the result of years of negotiations between Iran and the so-called P5+1, the five permanent members of the UN Security Council plus Germany. The complicated agreement required Iran to give up virtually all of its stockpile of low-enriched uranium (a critical element to building a bomb), accept significant restrictions on the nuclear activities it could conduct, allow intrusive international inspections to verify its compliance, and recommit to never developing or acquiring nuclear weapons. In exchange, Iran received relief from nuclear-related sanctions that the United States, the European Union, and the UN Security Council had imposed. In all, it was a deal that stretched the likely breakout time before Iran could build a nuclear weapon from two months to a year or more.

It was also an agreement that candidate Trump assailed as the "dumbest deal perhaps I've ever seen in the history of deal-making."[61] Some of Trump's pique over the deal reflected his habit of attacking any agreement he hadn't crafted as the "worst deal ever." He repeatedly riffed on how he would have negotiated with the Iranians and why he would have gotten a far better deal. That hubris aside, many of Trump's substantive criticisms, although frequently overstated and laced with misinformation, raised issues that concerned even the deal's supporters. The restrictions on Iran's nuclear activities weren't permanent; some provisions would lapse in 2026, and others would be lifted in 2031. The inspection protocols, although highly intrusive and permanent, weren't foolproof. Iran's ballistic missile program, which was covered by separate UN Security Council resolutions and US sanctions, wasn't part of the deal. Sanctions relief would energize the beleaguered Iranian economy as Iran resumed normal trade relations and regained access to overseas accounts that had been frozen. The regime could use this influx of funds, the size of which Trump regularly exaggerated, to finance its long-standing efforts to destabilize its neighbors and extend its influence in the region. And contrary to the hopes of many of the deal's supporters, Tehran hadn't responded to the deal by moderating its behavior. It had instead moved more aggressively to press its interests in the region.

Whether Obama could have negotiated a better deal was a question for debating societies by the time Trump took office. The choice he faced was what to do about the deal that existed. He had considerable freedom to decide how to act. Obama had not designated the JCPOA a treaty because he knew he could not win the necessary support of two-thirds of the Republican-controlled Senate. He instead treated it as an executive agreement, which the Constitution empowers presidents to approve on their own authority. But executive agreements signed with one president's pen can be undone by another's. As a candidate Trump initially said he would enforce the deal rather than rip it up, because although "we have a horrible contract . . . we do have a contract."[62] He eventually shifted gears, however, and pledged that his "number one priority is to dismantle the disastrous deal with Iran."[63]

Trump could have scuttled the agreement simply by reimposing the sanctions Obama had waived once the Iran deal was signed. US law required that such waivers be renewed every four months. That simple solution, however, came with two substantial disadvantages. The first was that it would trigger a diplomatic row with the other members of the P5+1. They adamantly opposed upending the deal, arguing that Iran was complying with the agreement and that no better deal could be had. None of them was likely to follow Trump's lead if he did torpedo the agreement, creating the almost unthinkable situation in which Iran and US negotiating partners would be lined up against the United States. The second problem was even more troubling. If the United States reimposed sanctions without persuasive evidence that Iran had violated the deal, Tehran would be free to resume the prohibited nuclear activities, and its ability to become a nuclear weapons power would be constrained only by its willingness to abide by its commitment never to do so. If Tehran cast that commitment aside, the United States might confront the prospect of a nuclear Iran not in 2031 but in a matter of months. That possibility meant that leaving the deal, to borrow the words of Otto von Bismarck, could be like committing suicide out of fear of death.

Unwilling to trigger a crisis he wasn't prepared to handle, Trump put aside the campaign talk about ripping up the deal while signaling that he would pursue a hard line on Iran. After Tehran tested a medium-range ballistic missile in January 2017, Trump sent his national security adviser into the White House briefing room to denounce Iran for its "destabilizing behavior across the Middle East."[64] Whether the tests violated Iran's obligations was debatable; the nuclear deal had relaxed previous prohibitions on ballistic missile testing and only barred Iran from "activity related to ballistic missiles designed to be capable of delivering nuclear weapons."[65] The administration nonetheless sanctioned several Iranian officials and groups for seeking to procure ballistic missile testing materials.

The administration's attention quickly turned toward a looming April deadline. In a tussle with the Obama administration in 2015, Congress had passed a law requiring the president to certify every ninety days that Iran was fully complying with the terms of the JCPOA *and* that it was in America's vital interest to adhere to the deal. Refusing to certify would not by itself kill the agreement. The certification was a purely internal

American arrangement. It had no effect on the actions of the other parties to the deal. A refusal to certify would not automatically reimpose
sanctions. The whole process was more about politics than about policy.
Congress wrote the provision expecting it would be facing a president
eager to proceed with the deal. The certification process would provide
members a convenient way to hold his or, perhaps more accurately, her
feet to the fire.

The April deadline provided the first evidence of the division between
Trump and his advisers. The White House rejected the State Department's initial draft letter to Congress providing the necessary certification. The disagreement wasn't over whether to certify—even the president
agreed the administration should—but rather over how to describe the
decision to honor a deal Trump had repeatedly denounced. The letter
that finally went to Congress incorporated Trump's preferred tougher
line. It noted that Iran had complied with the letter of the agreement
but had violated its spirit with its continued support for international
terrorism. As a result, the administration had ordered an interagency
review to determine whether maintaining sanctions relief for Iran was in
America's national security interests.[66] In a further sign of the administration's "get-tough" policy, the Pentagon announced that it would step
up its efforts to challenge Iranian naval activities in the Persian Gulf.

The decision to certify the Iran deal kicked the can down the road
for another ninety days. Trump hadn't answered the core question of
whether the United States should abide by it. A week before the July
deadline, McMaster, Tillerson, Secretary of Defense James Mattis, and
General Joseph Dunford, the chair of the Joint Chiefs of Staff, assembled in the White House to brief the president. They unanimously recommended that he certify the deal once again. Trump pushed back hard.
His advisers had failed to deliver what he had requested back in April:
a new strategy for countering Iran. He continued to resist their recommendation over the next week and relented only hours before the
deadline.[67] But he extracted a price for his consent. The United States
would impose new sanctions on Iran for its ballistic missile activities and
its support for international terrorism.[68] Just as important, Trump took
the certification portfolio away from the State Department. He instead
directed White House staffers to generate plans that would give him
the option of decertifying Iran when the next deadline rolled around in
October.[69]

Trump made no attempt to hide where he intended to go next. A week after the decision to recertify, he told the *Wall Street Journal* that although he had "great respect for my people," he would have declared Iran "noncompliant 180 days ago." When asked if that meant he expected to decertify Iran at the next deadline, he answered simply, "Personally, I do. I do."[70] The only questions, then, seemed to be what US actions would accompany the inevitable decertification and how the world would react.

THE RESPONSE WAS swift in coming. Abroad, France, Germany, and the United Kingdom closely coordinated their efforts. French President Emmanuel Macron used his speech to the UN General Assembly to argue that "terminating" the Iran deal, "without anything to replace it, would be a grave mistake," a point he also made privately to Trump.[71] So did British Prime Minister Theresa May, who told him of Britain's "strong commitment to the deal, saying it was vitally important for regional security."[72] When May asked Trump directly if he intended to leave the deal, he refused to answer her.[73] "Logical arguments did not work," a senior British official later observed. "For Trump this is an emotional issue. It's just the worst deal ever. The word that comes to mind is 'petulance.'"[74]

Trump's national security team likewise worked to persuade him to stick with the deal. Tillerson publicly acknowledged that he and Trump had "differences of views on things like the JCPOA and how we should use it," and that he felt "quite comfortable telling him my views."[75] So, apparently, was Mattis. Even knowing full well the president's stance on the issue, Mattis told the Senate Armed Services Committee two weeks after Trump's UN speech that "absent indications to the contrary," the Iran nuclear deal "is something that the president should consider staying with." When a senator asked Mattis point-blank whether he thought the deal was in the US national interest, Mattis replied, "I do."[76] The Republican chair of the House Foreign Affairs Committee also weighed in, saying, "As flawed as the deal is, I believe we must now enforce the hell out of it."[77]

None of these pleadings moved Trump. He had said what he meant and meant what he said: the Iran deal was a bad agreement, and he would force negotiations on a better deal. On October 13, he announced that he would no longer certify that the deal served American interests.

"We will not continue down a path whose predictable conclusion is more violence." He called on "Congress and our allies to address the deal's many serious flaws so that the Iranian regime can never threaten the world with nuclear weapons."[78]

The other parties to the deal criticized Trump's decision. Iranian President Hassan Rouhani complained that Trump "has not studied international law. . . . Apparently, he doesn't know that this agreement is not a bilateral agreement solely between Iran and the United States."[79] China reiterated its view that the deal was "a model of peacefully resolving [an] international hot-spot issue through political and diplomatic means on the part of the international community."[80] Russia denounced Trump's "aggressive and threatening rhetoric" and said his decision "will not have a direct effect on the progress of implementation of the agreements."[81] Most important, Macron, May, and German Chancellor Angela Merkel issued a joint statement reaffirming that they "stand committed" to the nuclear deal, adding that "preserving the JCPOA is in our shared national security interest."[82]

The swift condemnations hid what was in fact a deep sigh of relief in most foreign capitals—Trump hadn't upended the JCPOA by revoking his waiver of the nuclear-related sanctions or asking Congress to reimpose them for him. The decertification merely triggered a provision in US law giving congressional leaders sixty days to introduce legislation reimposing US sanctions on Iran. Any motion they introduced during the window would receive expedited consideration, meaning that the legislative maneuvers that lawmakers typically invoked to delay or block legislation could not be used.

Trump's decision to pass the baton to Congress would have been significant if congressional leaders were ready to act. But they weren't. Members of Congress were accustomed to criticizing White House decisions rather than driving them, and they recognized that if they did act, they, not Trump, would shoulder the blame for triggering a diplomatic crisis. The reluctance to act was reinforced by the fact that McMaster, Mattis, and Tillerson all favored the status quo; they weren't pushing Congress to take actions that they had urged Trump to avoid. From their point of view, the point of the decertification gambit was to allow the president to vent his anger with the Iran deal without actually derailing it. Doing otherwise would have moved the potential showdown with Iran from the 2030s to the here and now. With a major confrontation with North

Korea already looming, Trump's national security team didn't see the value of picking a fight that could be left for later.

With no one pushing congressional leaders to pick up the baton that Trump had handed them, Congress did what it did best—nothing. The closing of the sixty-day window on December 13, and with it the opportunity for congressional leaders to bypass the numerous ways that small groups of members could derail the legislative process, passed with little comment. Congress could now direct Trump on how to act only if its members decided to put aside the other issues bidding for its attention and were in sufficient agreement to steamroll their opponents. Given the political realities on Capitol Hill, that meant Congress was effectively a bystander to events.

But if Congress wasn't ready to act, Trump was. On January 12, 2018, he announced that he would waive nuclear-related sanctions on Iran one more time. But he added an important caveat: "I am waiving the application of certain nuclear sanctions, but only in order to secure our European allies' agreement to fix the terrible flaws of the Iran nuclear deal. This is a last chance. In the absence of such an agreement, the United States will not again waive sanctions in order to stay in the Iran nuclear deal."[83] Trump had had enough. Regardless of what America's closest allies and his own national security team said, he would no longer live with the "horrible" deal that he was convinced could and should be made better. If it weren't revised to his satisfaction, he would end it.

What followed was a concerted European effort to find a way to keep the United States in the deal. In the climate change dispute, Berlin, London, and Paris had exhorted Trump to stay with the Paris Agreement but offered no tangible concessions to keep him on board. In contrast, on Iran they sought to address his three most significant concerns with the deal: it did not cover Tehran's ballistic missile program or its regional behavior, and some of the main limits on Iran's nuclear program expired over time. Britain, France, and Germany all agreed to impose sanctions in response to Iran's continued missile testing. They also agreed to take stronger steps to curtail Tehran's support for terrorists and other radical forces in Iraq, Lebanon, Syria, and Yemen. They were even willing to consider enacting new sanctions after the deal's original limits expired if the "breakout time" Iran needed to build nuclear weapons was judged to have fallen to less than a year. What the Europeans weren't willing to do, however, was to jettison the deal itself. It, they argued, remained "the best way of neutralising the threat of a nuclear-armed Iran."[84] Leaving the deal would simply pick a fight they judged could not be won at an acceptable cost.

Macron, Merkel, and British Foreign Minister Boris Johnson made separate visits to the White House to make the case for the plan they had negotiated with administration officials. It wasn't enough. In May, Trump announced that he was withdrawing the United States from the nuclear deal. The fact that the International Atomic Energy Agency, the UN watchdog agency responsible for verifying the JCPOA, had issued ten reports stating that Iran had complied with its terms—a conclusion that the US intelligence community shared—was beside the point. For Trump, the agreement was "defective at its core."[85] He ordered US sanctions reimposed on Iran. Just as important, he signaled that Washington would punish any countries or foreign companies that sought to continue doing business with Tehran.

Israel and Saudi Arabia praised the decision. But few other countries joined them. Britain, France, and Germany issued a joint statement expressing "regret and concern" over the United States' departure from the deal.[86] China and Russia did much the same. American allies like Australia and Japan announced that they continued to support the JCPOA and urged all parties to it to show restraint. At least initially, Tehran did just that. Iranian officials denounced Trump but continued to abide by the terms of the agreement.

Trump's decision set the United States on a collision course not just with Tehran but with many other countries as well. The renewed sanctions applied not just to US firms but to any companies or countries that did business with Iran. In essence, Trump was threatening to use the reach of US law to punish anyone who abided by a deal that Iran hadn't violated but that the United States now had. And that was the point. Trump was betting that companies and countries would stop selling goods to Iran and buying its oil in the face of US sanctions, thereby ratcheting up economic pressure that would either break the Iranian regime or compel it to negotiate on his terms.

That approach carried significant risks. Countries could refuse to buckle under US pressure and dare Trump to carry through on his threat to punish them. China and Russia topped the list of countries likely to push back. They saw his decision to withdraw from the JCPOA as an opportunity to deepen their relations with Tehran, and they were better placed than most countries to avoid US economic pressure. Chinese and Russian companies often operated outside the US financial system; indeed, many Russian businesses had been forced to do so because of US sanctions aimed at Russia. And both Beijing and Moscow could potentially retaliate against US economic pressure by obstructing US policy on security issues. But China and Russia weren't alone in ignoring Trump's threat. India, which had long-standing political ties with Iran and which was a major customer for Iranian oil, announced that it would not observe US sanctions because it "follows only U.N. sanctions, and not unilateral sanctions by any country."[87] New Delhi's decision reflected not just principle but a reasoned calculation that Trump would not want to jeopardize a relationship he was hoping to develop.

Many of America's friends and allies were likely to comply with US policy, however, even as they bridled at the prospect. They weren't in a position to retaliate against Washington on unrelated matters, and their companies and economies were simply too intertwined with the US financial system. Even if these governments defied Washington, companies in their countries would probably decline to jeopardize their substantial interests in the United States over far smaller stakes in Iran. Indeed, while European governments struggled in the first two months after the US withdrawal from the JCPOA to develop a policy to shield their companies from US sanctions, major European corporations such as BP, Peugeot, and Total announced that they were halting their business operations in Iran.

Trump's decision posed a larger challenge for Europe beyond the loss of possible exports to Iran and bans on investments in the Iranian oil industry. Britain, France, and Germany had gone a long way toward meeting Trump's concerns about the deal. He brushed away their advice, however, and not for the first time. He hadn't even bothered to convene his national security team to debate the merits of what they had put on the table or to lay out a strategy for how he intended to proceed.[88] When "we asked what is Plan B, what will be the next step," said one European official, "the answer was we have not had time to prepare Plan B because of the change of people at the National Security Council," referring to the appointment of John Bolton as national security adviser days earlier.[89] Trump had seemingly decided that he was going to leave the deal no matter what they did, and he believed that if he pushed them harder, he would get even more.

By taking this maximalist line, however, Trump risked making the perfect the enemy of the good. The conclusion many Europeans drew from his decision was that he wasn't a reliable partner and had no interest in being one. He was instead turning his back on America's friends "with a ferocity that can only surprise us," as European Commission President Jean-Claude Juncker put it, and signaling that the United States "no longer wants to cooperate with other parts in the world."[90] *Der Spiegel,* one of Europe's leading publications, went even further: "The West as we once knew it no longer exists." Trump had left Europe with only one option: "Resistance against America."[91]

WITH HIS MOVES on North Korea and Iran, Trump showed his appetite for big gambles—and his disdain for conventional wisdom. He believed that his maximalist demands, belligerent rhetoric, and petty insults had forced Pyongyang to the bargaining table. He believed that he could do the same with Iran. Allies and advisers alike warned him of the complexities he faced, the risks he ran, and the dangers he might unleash. He was undeterred. These were the same people who in his view had created the problems he had inherited. He was comfortable with his diplomatic rolls of the dice. And he cared little that allies might be discarded in the process. He was looking for wins, to do what no other president had done before. It was far from clear, however, that his gambles would turn out in his—or America's—favor.

9

Trade Wars Are Good, and Easy to Win

Reporters entered the Cabinet Room for President Trump's meeting with steel and aluminum company executives on March 1, 2018, not knowing what to expect. The *Washington Post* had reported the night before that he would use the meeting to announce major new tariffs—that is, taxes—on imported steel and aluminum. The announcement was the result of a process that had begun ten months earlier when Trump ordered his commerce secretary to invoke a seldom-used provision of US trade law to investigate whether steel and aluminum imports endangered US national security. Wilbur Ross came back in January 2018 with the answer that Trump had given repeatedly on the campaign trail: they did. But many senior administration officials disagreed. Secretary of Defense James Mattis argued that "U.S. military requirements for steel and aluminum each only represent about three percent of U.S. production" and therefore did not "impact the ability of DoD programs to acquire the steel or aluminum necessary to meet national defense requirements."[1] Stiff opposition within the administration to tariffs was thought to be why White House officials suddenly announced that morning that the meeting with the steel and aluminum executives would just be a "listening session."

The invited reporters watched Trump do what he had done many times before: rail about how American steel and aluminum companies had "been very unfairly treated by bad policy, by bad trade deals, by other countries."[2] At Trump's behest, several of the executives detailed what unfair competition had done to their companies. Not mentioned in the discussion was the fact that American steel and aluminum companies were doing well. Nucor, America's largest steel producer, had earned a

$1.3 billion profit in 2017. The conversation also didn't mention technology's contribution to the massive job losses both industries had suffered over the previous forty years; simply put, far fewer workers were needed to produce a ton of steel or aluminum.[3] Trump dwelled instead on how both industries had been done in by trade. Then he announced his solution: "We'll be imposing tariffs on steel imports, and tariffs on aluminum imports. And you're going to see a lot of good things happen."[4]

The reaction abroad to Trump's announcement was swift and negative. Prime Minister Justin Trudeau of Canada, the largest exporter of steel to the United States, said it was an "absolutely unacceptable" decision that "makes no sense."[5] British Prime Minister Theresa May called Trump to express her "deep concern" about his decision."[6] French President Emmanuel Macron urged the European Union (EU) to react "swiftly and proportionately" to the US move.[7] "If you put tariffs against your allies," the head of the European Central Bank mused, "one wonders who the enemies are."[8] The head of the World Trade Organization (WTO), noting the potential for retaliation, warned that "a trade war is in no one's interests."[9] Most governments understood that retaliation could take the world economy down a perilous path. They also understood that doing nothing would allow Washington to steal jobs from their citizens. European Commission President Jean-Claude Juncker put the problem bluntly: "This is basically a stupid process, the fact that we have to do this. But we have to do it. We will now impose tariffs on motorcycles, Harley Davidson, on blue jeans, Levis, on bourbon. We can also do stupid."[10]

In keeping with his lifelong philosophy that it is best to always "fight back very hard," Trump responded to his foreign critics by upping the stakes rather than backing down.[11] He took to Twitter to argue that "trade wars are good, and easy to win."[12] Angered by the talk that Europe would retaliate, he vowed to "simply apply a Tax on their Cars which freely pour into the U.S."[13] He took similar aim at Canada and Mexico. "Tariffs on Steel and Aluminum will only come off if new & fair NAFTA agreement is signed," he tweeted.[14] In linking his decision to impose tariffs to his overall frustration with foreign trade practices, Trump undercut his argument that national security considerations had driven his decision.

A week after Trump's announcement, the White House rolled out an executive order formally imposing the tariffs. It exempted Canada and Mexico, at least temporarily, pending the outcome of the testy talks already under way on the renegotiation of the North American Free Trade Agreement (NAFTA). The directive also gave European and other countries fifteen days—a deadline that was subsequently extended twice—to avoid the tariffs by proposing mutually agreeable "alternative ways to address the threatened impairment of the national security caused by imports from that country."[15] The temporary exemptions did little to mollify America's friends. Canada and Mexico both said they would not be bullied into conceding to US demands on NAFTA. German Chancellor Angela Merkel said that "the best thing would be if we [the EU] could be excluded." She added, however, that if the talks failed, "we, in Europe, can of course also react."[16]

On the same day that Trump was giving America's allies their fifteen-day notice, trade officials from Australia, Canada, Japan, Mexico, and seven other Pacific Rim countries gathered five thousand miles away in Santiago, Chile, to make history. They were there to sign the Comprehensive and Progressive Agreement for Trans-Pacific Partnership (CPTPP), better known as TPP-11. It was the successor to the Trans-Pacific Partnership (TPP), the sweeping, twelve-nation trade deal that Barack Obama had championed as a counterweight to rising Chinese power. Trump had withdrawn the United States from the deal at the start of his presidency. The agreement hadn't died, however. Instead, the eleven other countries remained committed to the idea that lower tariffs and clearer trade rules promoted economic growth, and they worked to salvage the deal. "Now in some parts of the world, there is a move toward protectionism," Japan's economic revitalization minister had said when the deal on CPTPP was struck six weeks earlier, "and I think the TPP-11 is a major engine to overcome such a phenomenon."[17]

The message of March 8, 2018, was clear: Donald Trump was leading the United States in one direction on trade. America's friends and allies were headed in another.

HOSTILITY TOWARD US trade policy formed a core part of Trump's campaign message. He insisted that trade was impoverishing Americans, not enriching them. He focused his ire particularly on how in his view trade had hollowed out American manufacturing. Economists pointed to technology as the main culprit in the roughly one-third decline in the number of manufacturing jobs since the Clinton administration. Trump, however, ignored technology's role in job loss. He instead blamed elites who he said put global interests ahead of American interests. "Our politicians," he told workers in Pennsylvania in 2016, "have aggressively pursued a policy of globalization—moving our jobs, our wealth and our factories to Mexico and overseas." He heaped scorn on the decisions to sign NAFTA, which he called "the worst trade deal in history," and to admit China into the WTO in 2001, which he said "enabled the greatest jobs theft in history."[18]

A specific complaint Trump leveled against US trade deals was that they weren't "reciprocal"—that is, they did not guarantee US exporters the same access to overseas markets that foreign competitors had to the US market. The point was politically powerful. Like many of his criticisms, however, it obscured more than it revealed. US tariffs rates on average are lower than those of most other countries, but by no means all. Britain, France, and Germany, for example, all have the same average tariff rate as the United States, and Canada's and Japan's are slightly lower.[19] And in the case of some individual products, US tariffs are actually higher than those of its trading partners. So Trump repeatedly complained that the EU imposed a 10 percent tariff on imported cars, compared to the 2.5 percent tariff the United States imposed. He never mentioned, however, that imported pickup trucks face a 25 percent tariff entering the US market, more than double the EU's 10 percent tariff. That is a considerable trade barrier given that every year, Americans buy more pickup trucks than cars. Likewise, the United States used tariffs and quotas to shelter agricultural products such as asparagus, peanuts, sugar, and tobacco from foreign competition. Trump also failed to acknowledge that US trade negotiators over the decades had used the openness of the US economy to persuade other countries to lower their tariffs and reduce or eliminate other trade barriers. TPP, for example, would have lowered or ended eighteen thousand tariffs on US goods, without requiring equivalent cuts by the United States, because US tariffs were already so low.

Overall, Trump's indictment of US trade policy had an element of Queen of Hearts jurisprudence to it: verdict first, trial second. He had been leveling the same complaints since at least his 1987 open letter "To the American People," before many of the specific agreements he denounced in the 2016 presidential campaign had been envisioned, let alone negotiated. He stuck to his complaints regardless of which party held the White House or what they did. His criticisms always focused on what trade cost Americans, never on how it benefited them. And he ignored the fact that Americans wanted to buy imported goods. When Trump railed about all the Mercedes and BMWs that were coming into the country, he failed to acknowledge that these were cars Americans wanted to drive. Indeed, he himself had a nice collection of foreign cars, including three Mercedes.[20]

Of course, trade inevitably creates losers—a reality that pro-trade politicians often gloss over—even as it creates winners. Whereas some industries and companies buckle in the face of foreign competition, others prosper as they gain access to new markets. (Consumers also benefit from lower prices as more companies, foreign and domestic, compete for their dollars.) Because trade typically creates jobs as well as destroys them, and because the size of the US economy usually dwarfs that of its trading partners, trade deals typically have a small impact on overall US employment even as they make the country as a whole wealthier.

The great exception to the rule, however, was China. Here Trump was right, though the story was once again more complicated than the one he told. The rise of the Chinese economy, which predated its entry into the WTO, was unprecedented in its speed and scope. Between 1980 and 2010, China's share of global manufacturing increased twenty-fold. US manufacturers were hit hard as a result. The so-called China Shock may have accounted for as much as 40 percent of the decline in US manufacturing jobs between 2000 and 2007—or about one million jobs in total. (Economists debate the exact numbers, which don't examine any nonmanufacturing jobs created by US-China trade.)[21] This disruption disproportionately affected the Midwest, where much of America's manufacturing capacity is concentrated. As workers in Indiana, Michigan, Ohio, and elsewhere lost their jobs, they found it hard to find new ones because so many other local employers had either gone out of business or moved production overseas. When they did find new work, it typically paid far less than before. China's rapid rise was owed in part to its much lower labor costs and sound government policies. But it also reflected the country's lax health, safety, and environmental regulations and Beijing's ability and willingness to exploit global trading rules or even ignore them entirely.

Trump's blistering attacks on Chinese trade practices helped him win Midwestern states like Michigan and Wisconsin that had voted consistently for Democratic presidential candidates over the previous quarter century. But by 2016 the economic and social damage to these states had been done and would not be easily reversed. China had also changed several of its specific trade practices (though it continued to exploit global trading rules). That threw into question some of Trump's proposed solutions. The problem with his prescriptions was clearest with his vow to punish China for manipulating its currency to boost its exports. In the first decade of the twenty-first century, Beijing had depressed the value of its currency. That made Chinese goods less expensive for Americans to buy and harder for US companies to compete against. By 2014, however, Beijing decided that its economic and political interests had changed and began propping up the value of its currency. The decision made it harder for Chinese companies to compete in the US market and slowed the rise in the bilateral trade deficit.

The broader problem was that Trump didn't have a strategy for avoiding the many and well-known dangers of the protectionist trade policies he favored. The most immediate danger is that tariffs, quotas, and other measures to curtail imports drive up costs for American companies and consumers. Compounding the problem is the fact that modern manufacturing relies heavily on regional and global supply chains that use parts made abroad to build things at home. Roughly half of all US imports are for so-called intermediate goods that go into making other products. So even a narrowly targeted restriction can have potentially broad ripple effects across industries. Meanwhile, any steps Washington takes to protect US companies invites retaliation from trading partners against American exports, hurting companies and workers in those sectors and making them less competitive in global markets.

At its worst, protectionism can escalate in a tit-for-tat fashion as countries seek to take jobs from their trading partners while trying to protect jobs at home. Such trade wars can leave all countries worse off and potentially sow the seeds for conflict. Such a dynamic is not idle conjecture but lived experience. The US decision to impose the Smoot-Hawley tariffs in 1930 intensified the Great Depression globally and facilitated the rise of fascism in Europe. It was precisely the memory of that experience that drove subsequent generations of American policy makers to embrace the trade approach that Trump so disliked. Trade was not just about promoting narrow economic interests; it was about creating conditions that diminished the chances for conflict and enhanced security. Sacrificing an immediate economic advantage was worth it if it made Americans safer.

Even when protectionism doesn't lead to trade wars, it frequently fails to deliver lasting benefits. This is especially true when the goal is to rejuvenate declining industries facing foreign competition, as Trump proposed to do with steel. Rather than gaining time to become more competitive, protected companies often come to depend on protection to stay in business. The US steel industry provides a textbook case. From the 1960s through the 1980s, administrations sheltered steel companies from foreign competition with a variety of protectionist measures. The tactics seldom worked as advertised, and new protectionist schemes were adopted. Even with help from Washington, many US steel companies went out of business. Protectionism can also backfire. The quotas that Washington imposed in the 1980s to protect sugar farmers drove sugar prices so high that American candy makers either moved production (and jobs) abroad or went out of business. By one official estimate, three jobs in the candy-making business were lost for every sugar-farming job that was saved.[22]

The lesson from these and other protectionist initiatives is that Washington would be wiser to focus on investing in the industries of tomorrow, creating the conditions that enable American companies to flourish, and doing more to help workers whose lives are disrupted by trade while helping all Americans gain the skills needed to succeed in a fiercely competitive global economy.[23] But that approach did not resonate with Trump, who instead insisted on blaming foreign countries for America's economic plight.

THREE DAYS INTO his presidency, Trump began making good on his vow to do things differently on trade. With the stroke of a pen, he withdrew the United States from participating in TPP. His comment as he signed the executive order terminating US participation summarized his objective: "We're going to have trade but we're going to have it one-on-one, and if somebody misbehaves, we're going to send them a letter of termination, 30 days, and they'll either straighten it out or we're gone. Not one of those deals where we can't get out of them. It's a disaster."[24] Trump's tough talk didn't persuade America's trading partners. Australian Prime Minister Malcolm Turnbull admitted that "losing the United States from the TPP is a big loss." But, he added, "we are not about to walk away" from the agreement.[25] To underscore that point, within hours of Trump's decision, Turnbull called the prime ministers of Japan, New Zealand, and Singapore to discuss how they might proceed without the United States. Chile's foreign minister invited fellow TPP signatories to begin talks on a new TPP, citing Santiago's determination "to persist in the opening up of the world" to trade.[26] None, moreover, showed any interest in Trump's call to negotiate bilateral trade deals. "If you ask me today," said New Zealand Prime Minister Bill English, "I'd think there's a pretty low chance of that happening in a form we'd find satisfactory."[27]

Countries that weren't party to TPP saw Trump's decision as an opportunity. "If Mr. Trump starts a trade war with Asia and South America," Germany's economic minister said, "it will open opportunities for us."[28] Beijing felt similarly. "If it's necessary for China to play the role of leader," a senior official in the Chinese foreign ministry noted, "then China must take on this responsibility."[29] Indeed, three days before Trump took office, President Xi Jinping cast his country as the new, and somewhat improbable, defender of open trade. Mixing a variety of Chinese proverbs in a speech at Davos and never mentioning Trump by name, he spoke of having "the courage to swim in the vast ocean of the global market."[30] His audience got his message. "There is a vacuum when it comes to global economic leadership," a former Swedish prime minister tweeted, "and Xi Jinping is clearly aiming to fill it. With some success."[31]

The reactions in foreign capitals had no effect on Trump. To the contrary, administration officials vowed to press ahead with a hard line on trade. "You have to think about it this way," Ross explained. "We are in a trade war. We have been for decades. The only difference is that our troops are finally coming to the rampart."[32]

The challenge was finding the right adversary to engage on the rampart. China was the obvious target. It accounted for roughly two-thirds of the overall US trade deficit. But Trump quickly abandoned his plans to impose tariffs on China and declare it a currency manipulator. Although he had repeatedly complained that his predecessors had sacrificed America's economic interests to advance its geopolitical interests, he made exactly that same calculation. He judged that he needed Beijing to pressure North Korea to abandon its nuclear weapons program, and he knew Beijing wouldn't if he pressed it on trade. Trump was open about his calculus. "Why would I call China a currency manipulator when they are working with us on the North Korean problem?" he tweeted after hosting Xi at Mar-a-Lago in April. "We will see what happens!"[33]

With China on the sidelines, the bull's-eye naturally gravitated to NAFTA. Trump attacked the trade agreement continually on the campaign trail, though he never offered evidence substantiating his claims that it had hollowed out the American middle class. NAFTA had hurt some companies and workers, but it also had benefited many others. Instinct, however, mattered more than evidence to Trump. He wanted NAFTA gone. He hoped to repeat what he had done with TPP and simply end America's participation. In April he nearly did just that. White House staff drafted the order necessary to put a US withdrawal in motion. The decision was to be announced on his hundredth day in office to highlight that he had delivered on his campaign promises. "You know," Trump said later, "I was really ready and psyched to terminate NAFTA."[34]

But he didn't. His about-face partly reflected the diplomatic skills of Trudeau and Mexican President Enrique Peña Nieto. Both men called Trump just hours before he was set to announce his decision. They made the case that it would be better to try to renegotiate NAFTA than to kill it outright. Trump himself played up this explanation—and his own generosity—saying that he had "a very good relationship" with Trudeau and Peña Nieto. "It's very hard when you have a relationship" to rip up NAFTA. That's "very much something that would not be a nice act."[35]

A bigger factor in Trump's reversal was the political cost of getting out. Unlike TPP, NAFTA had been in place for more than twenty years. Exiting it would create chaos. US corn and soybeans, which under NAFTA entered Mexico tariff-free, for example, would potentially face tariffs of as much as 37 and 33 percent respectively, making them far less competitive. Ford, General Motors, and Fiat Chrysler risked the upending of their carefully constructed supply chains, in which parts typically crossed borders multiple times before ending up in a finished car or truck. Not surprisingly, they and others similarly affected pressed the White House and Congress to shelve the termination order. Most of Trump's senior advisers saw the looming costs and warned him against withdrawing. Agriculture Secretary Sonny Perdue made the biggest impact. He brought to the Oval Office a map showing who would be hardest hit by NAFTA's demise. The biggest losers were located squarely in "Trump country," those states that had propelled Trump to his upset presidential victory.

Trump's reversal was perhaps unsurprising. During his real estate days, he had often made outlandish demands as a way to drive harder bargains. "My style of deal-making is quite simple and straightforward," he wrote in *The Art of the Deal*. "I aim very high, and then I just keep pushing and pushing and pushing to get what I'm after. Sometimes I settle for less than I sought, but in most cases I still end up with what I want."[36] In backing down from his threat to withdraw unilaterally from NAFTA, he had gotten something he wanted: Canada's and Mexico's agreement to renegotiate the deal. He had also gained negotiating leverage by suggesting that only diplomatic decorum had held him back from doing what had previously been unthinkable. He now had the opportunity to give the world a master class in the art of the deal. He just had to do something that he had so far failed to do: decide what a great deal looked like.

BOTH CANADA AND Mexico had their own reasons to want to renegotiate NAFTA. It had been written in the early 1990s, long before the rise of digital trade and heightened concerns about labor rights and protecting the environment, and many of its provisions needed updating. Indeed, NAFTA had been implicitly modernized once already because Canada, Mexico, and the United States were all parties to TPP. Ottawa and Mexico City also had good reason to want the negotiations to go quickly. As long as NAFTA's fate was in limbo, companies would be hesitant to invest. A decision to open a new factory that made sense under the original NAFTA might become a disaster under an overhauled NAFTA or no NAFTA at all. But if companies sat on the sidelines, economic growth would slow, and potential jobs would be lost.

The fact that the three countries had already settled many issues during the TPP negotiations simplified things somewhat for Robert Lighthizer, the new US trade representative. To the extent that those changes didn't rankle Trump, they could easily be folded into a revised NAFTA. But those changes had been negotiated with an eye toward writing rules that eased the passage of goods across borders. Trump, however, wasn't focused on creating a better process. He wanted rules that generated a specific outcome: smaller US trade deficits—and ideally, trade surpluses—with both Canada and Mexico.

Trump's fixation with bilateral trade deficits drove economists to distraction. They pointed out that bilateral deficits are meaningless numbers in a global economy; a deficit with one country can be balanced with a surplus with another. When countries consistently run trade deficits with the rest of the world, as the United States did, that reflects broader national decisions on savings and consumption. Simply put, Americans saved too little and consumed too much. Unless a deal curtailed trade— and thereby killed the domestic jobs that depended on the ability to export—it wouldn't shrink the overall US trade deficit much, if at all. It would simply change which countries the United States ran a deficit with. In that respect using trade agreements to solve bilateral deficits would be much like squeezing a balloon. Pressing at one point would merely cause it to bulge at another point. Press too hard, and all would be ruined.

Just as vexing to economists was Trump's fixation on deficits in the trade of goods rather than on the broader measure of trade in goods and services. Consulting, financial services, entertainment, education, tourism, and other services overtook manufacturing as the largest component of the US economy decades earlier and by 2018 accounted for six times as many private sector jobs as manufacturing.[37] Services also constitute an increasing share of America's exports, leading Trump's own Council of Economic Advisers to conclude that "focusing only on the trade in goods alone ignores the Unites States' comparative advantage in services."[38] Whether services are counted or not can give a different picture of who is "winning" and who is "losing." Trump, for instance, could say that the United States ran a $17.5 billion goods deficit with Canada in 2017. Trudeau could counter that the United States ran an $8.4 billion good and services surplus with Canada.[39] Both were right.

In trying to push Canada and Mexico to accept a revised NAFTA that would shrink America's goods deficit and do so quickly, Lighthizer had the threat of withdrawal as leverage. But that bargaining chip was far smaller than the great disparity in the size of the three economies suggested. Ottawa and Mexico City both knew that NAFTA's demise would hurt American companies and farms as much or more than their own. Canada was America's largest export market; Mexico was its second. Each country bought more US products than China, Japan, and Brazil combined. Because of other trade arrangements, as much as 40 percent of each country's exports entered the United States outside of NAFTA rules.[40] Many Canadian and Mexican exporters judged that the costs of satisfying NAFTA rules negated any savings achieved by avoiding tariffs. If Trump ripped up NAFTA, both Canada and Mexico would fall back on these other deals. Much of the US trade within North America, and with Mexico in particular, was in agriculture, which didn't get the same special treatment, in good part because Washington had long protected American farmers from foreign competition. Canadian and Mexican officials reminded American businesses, farmers, and trade groups, along with US governors and members of Congress, at every chance that they would lose a lot if NAFTA ended.

When the first round of NAFTA talks opened at a Washington hotel in August, it immediately became clear that these bargaining realities had not deterred Trump. Canada's Foreign Minister Chrystia Freeland spoke first. Holding aloft photos of Americans and Canadians fighting a fire together as a symbol of the "deep friendship" the two countries shared, she called Canada's trade with the United States "balanced and mutually beneficial."[41] Mexico's Economy Minister Ildefonso Guajardo followed in a similarly cordial vein. "NAFTA has been more than a trade agreement," he said. "It has made us think of ourselves as a region." He also pledged that "Mexico is committed to obtaining a win, win, win for all three countries."[42] Lighthizer threw cold water on these diplomatic pleasantries. While acknowledging that "many Americans have benefited from NAFTA," he argued that "for countless Americans, this agreement has failed." As a result, the Trump administration was "not interested in a mere tweaking of a few provisions." It wanted wholesale change; achieving that outcome would be "a very difficult" task.[43]

The maximalist proposals that Lighthizer put on the table as the negotiating rounds proceeded matched his tough talk—and alarmed Canada and Mexico. "They do not come to the table—our counterparts—with a lot of flexibility," Canada's chief trade negotiator complained.[44] And it wasn't just Canadians and Mexicans who feared that the US negotiating strategy was designed to get to no rather than to yes. The head of the US Chamber of Commerce objected to the "poison pill proposals still on the table that could doom the entire deal."[45] Administration officials occasionally acknowledged that they were offering Canada and Mexico lots of vinegar and little honey. "We're asking two countries to give up some privileges that they have enjoyed for 22 years," Ross admitted. "And we are not in a position to offer anything in return. So that's a tough sell."[46]

Not surprisingly, the talks quickly deadlocked. The hope had been that they could be wrapped up in a few months. Mexicans would be voting for a new president and Congress in July 2018. If it took too long to strike a deal, the new Mexican government might repudiate whatever agreement was reached, sending all three countries back to square one. Even if that problem could be avoided, a deal that was reached late would become caught up in the 2018 US midterm elections. But despite five formal rounds of negotiations, 2017 ended without any significant progress beyond agreement over elements that had been settled as part of TPP. With NAFTA still in limbo and the electoral calendar looking increasingly unfriendly, Trump appeared to have violated one of his cardinal rules for deal making: don't take your negotiating partners "beyond their breaking point."[47]

WHEN TRUMP SET off in November 2017 for his first Asia trip, trade was very much on his mind. More than nine months into his presidency, he had yet to make much progress in enacting his nationalist trade agenda. Besides forcing NAFTA renegotiations, he had pressed an extremely reluctant South Korea into agreeing to discuss amending the US-Korea Free Trade Agreement. The deal, better known as KORUS, was negotiated by the George W. Bush administration and had gone into effect during Obama's first term. Trump had called it "a horrible deal" that had "destroyed" the United States because the US trade-in-goods deficit increased after its enactment.[48] Trump had also imposed a 20 percent tariff on Canadian softwood lumber, a long-standing source of tensions in US-Canadian trade relations.

Beyond these actions, however, Trump had no trade wins to point to by the fall. Several factors explained his failure to get the quick results he had promised. One was the slowness in staffing his administration. His general trade objectives had to be translated into specific and detailed trade proposals. But he failed to move quickly to nominate many of the senior positions in the Office of the US Trade Representative, which negotiated trade agreements and pursued enforcement actions at the WTO. Those positions wouldn't be filled until 2018. Another obstacle was that Trump now had to confront the trade-offs he had brushed away on the campaign trail. He wanted to punish China and South Korea on trade, but he also wanted their cooperation in dealing with North Korea. He could have one but not both. Likewise, he couldn't, as he often suggested, make trade policy as he saw fit. The US Constitution had lodged the power to regulate foreign commerce with Congress. Over the years, lawmakers had delegated considerable trade authorities to the White House. In doing so, however, they created an elaborate system of notifications, reviews, and waiting periods that the executive branch had to follow. Even a president who saw himself as a disruptor couldn't ignore these rules.

The biggest obstacle to Trump's ability to upend US trade policy, though, was opposition within the administration. His trade advisers, including Lighthizer, Ross, and Peter Navarro, who had come to the White House to run the new National Trade Council, all shared his protectionist instincts. They wanted the United States to worry less about opening up foreign markets to American exports and worry more about discouraging imports. Those with broader responsibilities on Trump's senior team—like Gary Cohn, the head of the National Economic Council; Treasury Secretary Steven Mnuchin; and Secretary of State Rex Tillerson—all saw the trade policies that Trump favored as the road to economic ruin. The pro-trade members of the administration used a variety of bureaucratic tricks to keep protectionist trade recommendations from making it to the Oval Office. Navarro, for instance, saw his National Trade Council folded into the National Economic Council. He was required to report to Cohn, who excluded him from meetings with Trump.[49]

Trump understood that many of his senior advisers opposed the protectionist measures he wanted. During a meeting in July to review possible trade actions against China, he told his new chief of staff, John Kelly, of his frustrations. "John," Trump said, "you haven't been in a trade discussion before, so I want to share with you my views. For the last six months, this same group of geniuses comes in here all the time and I tell them, 'Tariffs. I want tariffs.'" No tariffs came, however. "John, let me tell you why they didn't bring me any tariffs," Trump went on. "I know there are some people in the room right now that are upset. I know there are some globalists in the room right now. And they don't want them, John, they don't want the tariffs. But I'm telling you, I want tariffs."[50]

Despite his frustration, Trump declined during his first year in office to overrule his advisers. The Asia trip, however, gave him the opportunity to take his grievances directly to three countries in his crosshairs: China, Japan, and South Korea. Trump hit the ground running on his first stop, Tokyo. "We want fair and open trade," he told US service members assembled to greet him. "But right now, our trade with Japan is not fair and it's not open."[51] Trump repeated his arguments in meetings with Japanese officials. Prime Minister Shinzo Abe deftly deflected Trump's trade pressure by shifting the conversation to the North Korean threat whenever possible. Despite predictions that Abe would unveil new Japanese investments in the United States, he mentioned only deals that had been previously announced.[52] That fact didn't dent Trump's willingness to declare a win. It was sufficient that Abe had said he planned to beef up Japan's military forces by buying US weapons. "My visit to Japan and friendship with PM Abe will yield many benefits, for our great Country," he tweeted. "Massive military & energy orders happening+++!"[53] Trump received a similar reception in Seoul, where President Moon Jae-in also said he favored more military spending. Trump eagerly claimed credit. "South Korea will be ordering billions of dollars of that equipment, which, frankly, for them makes a lot of sense," he said at a joint press conference with Moon. "And for us, it means jobs; it means reducing our trade deficit with South Korea."[54]

Beijing, however, was not to be outdone by its neighbors in playing to Trump's vanity and giving him deals he could tout as wins. It rolled out the red carpet, making him the first American president to be hosted at a state dinner in the Forbidden City, the former palace of the Chinese emperors. The decision to offer Trump "state-visit-plus" treatment paid off. Although he pressed President Xi in private to reduce China's trade surplus with the United States, he was on his best behavior in public. Gone was talk about China "raping" America. Instead, he said he didn't blame China for running up large trade surpluses. "After all, who can blame a country for being able to take advantage of another country for the benefit of its citizens?" The blame instead lay with past US "administrations for allowing this out-of-control trade deficit to take place and to grow."[55] Trump and Xi concluded their meetings by announcing roughly $250 billion in deals between Chinese and American companies.[56] Although Trump touted his deal-making prowess, the deals would unfold over years and, as a result, could be canceled if political winds changed. Tillerson dismissed what had been accomplished, saying the deals were "small in the grand scheme of things" given a trade deficit of more than $300 billion a year.[57]

What Trump wasn't willing to say publicly in Beijing, he said at his next stop, the annual Asia-Pacific Economic Cooperation meeting, held in Da Nang, Vietnam. Speaking to delegates from the twenty-one Pacific

Rim member countries, he took aim at China's "unfair trade practices," which he called "unacceptable." He insisted, "From this day forward, we will compete on a fair and equal basis. We are not going to let the United States be taken advantage of anymore." What he was offering others was a willingness to "make bilateral trade agreements with any Indo-Pacific nation that wants to be our partner and that will abide by the principles of fair and reciprocal trade. What we will no longer do is enter into large agreements that tie our hands, surrender our sovereignty, and make meaningful enforcement practically impossible."[58] Behind the scenes, US officials fought to keep any mention of "multilateralism" out of the meeting's final communiqué. In doing so, they squared off against Australian diplomats, who pushed hard for language endorsing the existing rules-based order. Most of the other countries at the negotiations were stunned to see the United States fighting with one of its closest allies.[59] The Australians, backed up by most of the other delegates, carried the day.[60]

On the flight back to the United States, Trump boasted about the wins he had scored on his visits. He was "very proud" of what he had accomplished "from a standpoint of security and safety, military—very proud—and trade." Better yet, he had "sold $300 billion worth of equipment and other things. And I think that number is going to be quadrupled very quickly. So that's over a trillion dollars' worth of stuff."[61] Trump continued to give himself an A+ for what he accomplished on the trip once he was back in the White House. "Our great country is respected again in Asia," he tweeted. "You will see the fruits of our long but successful trip for many years to come!"[62]

Many experts, however, read the results of Trump's visit, and his first year more generally, for US trade policy differently. "His bark is worse than his bite," was how a former British ambassador to the United States put it.[63] True, Trump had withdrawn from TPP, but that's where his disruption ended. He had repeatedly threatened to withdraw the United States from NAFTA and KORUS, but he had always found reasons not to follow through. He had threatened to impose tariffs on countries he deemed to be cheating the United States, but he had actually done so only against Canada on softwood lumber. That dispute had such a long history that it hardly counted to many trade experts.

Trump likewise had railed against China's predatory practices but done little about them. Most notably, he hadn't filed any cases at the WTO challenging Beijing's trade behavior; in contrast, Obama had initiated four such suits during his final year in office. That discrepancy reflected more than a desire to enlist Beijing's cooperation in dealing with North Korea. The United States had championed the creation of the WTO, which began operating in 1995, to help ensure that countries followed global trade rules. It established courts that were empowered to hand down binding decisions on trade disputes. Trump, however, saw that power as a threat, not a benefit. "The WTO was set up for the benefit [of] everybody but us," he claimed. "We lose the lawsuits, almost all of the lawsuits in the WTO."[64] The United States did indeed lose the vast majority of cases brought against it at the WTO. But it also won the vast majority of cases it filed. Its win-loss rates mirrored those of most other countries, which reflected the fact that countries generally filed cases only when they were certain they would win.[65] (China was an exception: its win-loss rates were well below average.)[66] The problem for Trump was that the WTO courts had consistently ruled against the sorts of protectionist policies he favored. And turning to the WTO to pressure China would potentially concede the principle he contested—that a foreign body could rule US trade practices illegal and authorize other WTO members to impose retaliatory tariffs.

The most significant development on the trade front during Trump's first year in office, though, was that not a single country had signed up to negotiate a new bilateral trade deal with the United States. Even Abe, the foreign leader who went the furthest to cultivate relations with Trump, had rebuffed his calls for a bilateral deal. Abe had instead fought to keep TPP-11 alive and struck a major trade deal with the EU. Other countries continued to conduct business as usual, even with the United States headed for the sidelines, and none had paid a price for it. The trade superstorm that many experts had feared Trump would trigger when he took the oath of office had seemingly passed.

IN RETROSPECT, 2017 turned out to be the calm before the storm. The new year brought with it what Trump had long craved—tariffs. In January, the White House imposed tariffs on imported solar panels and a mix of tariffs and quotas on imported washing machines. The decisions were the first sign of what was to come. By March, Trump had announced the steel and aluminum tariffs. The move to protect American solar and washing machine manufacturers had produced limited grumbling in foreign capitals, in good part because they did not affect most of America's closest trading partners. The steel and aluminum tariffs were the opposite; they targeted America's allies and friends specifically. Opposition to the tariffs was further fueled by the national security argument that Trump used to justify them. For better or worse, the solar panel and washing machine tariffs were based on a market-disruption argument that was broadly recognized as legitimate under WTO rules, even if in specific cases the WTO ruled they had been enacted improperly. Trump's national security justification, in contrast, threatened to set a new precedent that would blow a hole in the effort to root global trade in a clear set of enforceable rules.[67] Although WTO rules contained a national security exception, it had seldom been used and never by the United States. The reason was simple: any country could find a national security pretext for imposing tariffs or other protectionist measures. Trump justified that fear two months later when he directed the Commerce Department to investigate whether imports of foreign-made cars threatened US national security.

The anger abroad over the steel and aluminum tariffs also reflected the widespread belief that they would disrupt global trade without accomplishing Trump's goal of creating more American jobs. Protection would enable American steel and aluminum companies to charge higher prices, and as a result they might add workers at mills and smelters already in operation and even reopen ones that had been shuttered. But higher prices also meant higher costs for automakers, beer companies, and a host of other steel- and aluminum-using industries that employed far more workers. These higher costs in turn meant lower profits or fewer workers, or possibly both. It wasn't a theoretical concern. Sixteen years earlier George W. Bush had imposed tariffs to stop a surge in steel imports. The number of jobs created in the steel industry was swamped by the number of jobs lost in steel-using industries.[68]

At its root, however, the anger in foreign capitals at Trump's decision reflected frustration that it put the global trading system at risk while failing to target the source of pressure on steel and aluminum companies in the United States and many other Western countries—China. Beijing had overinvested in both industries and had flooded the world market as a result; China had gone from producing a third of the world's steel to producing half in just over a decade. Little of that steel made it to the United States; just 2 percent of US steel imports came directly from China. That was no accident. The United States had placed more than two dozen tariffs on Chinese steel products over the years.[69] The EU had been pressing Beijing hard to curtail the dumping of steel on the world market, and it was scheduled to meet in mid-March with US and Japanese officials to discuss possible joint action.[70] Trump hadn't waited to see how those talks played out or whether a cooperative approach with allies might prove more effective. Instead, he imposed tariffs on America's closest partners—including formal allies such as Canada, Germany, Japan, and South Korea—and on national security grounds, no less. It was unsurprising, then, that China's most senior officials refrained from publicly criticizing Trump's initial tariff announcement, even though it affected Chinese steel exports. Beijing was following Napoleon's maxim: "Never interrupt your enemy when he is making a mistake." Once the decision was formally implemented, though, China promptly retaliated by placing tariffs as high as 25 percent on 128 different US exports, including on fruit, pork, and wine.

WHEN TRUMP FIRST announced the steel and aluminum tariffs, White House officials insisted they would apply across the board. "As soon as he exempts one country," noted Navarro, whom Trump had rescued from the bureaucratic wilderness, "his phone starts ringing with the heads of state of other countries."[71] Exemptions also would mean less protection for US steel and aluminum producers and less pressure on overseas producers, defeating the purpose of imposing tariffs. Yet Trump initially approved temporary exemptions for Australia, Canada, the EU, Mexico, South Korea, and several other countries. Japan, a treaty ally and the seventh largest exporter of steel to the United States, notably didn't receive an exemption. The White House hoped the move would pressure Tokyo to agree to negotiate a bilateral trade deal. "I'll talk to Prime Minister Abe of Japan and others," Trump said, "and there will be a little smile on their face. And the smile is, 'I can't believe we've been able to take advantage of the United States for so long.' So those days are over."[72] In April, Abe grudgingly agreed to begin a "free, fair and reciprocal" dialogue with the United States on trade, though he stopped short of agreeing to bilateral negotiations.[73]

Australia quickly won permanent exemptions from both the steel and aluminum tariffs without making any trade concessions. The other US treaty ally to receive a permanent exemption from the steel (but not the aluminum) tariffs was South Korea. The move came as the result of a deal that US and South Korean negotiators struck in late March to amend KORUS. Seoul agreed to cut its steel exports to the United States by 30 percent, though the measure likely violated WTO rules, which prohibit such quotas. The other provisions the two sides agreed to either were symbolic or were minor variations on the existing agreement. For instance, the amended deal doubled the quota on the number of cars each American manufacturer could sell annually without satisfying South Korean safety regulations, from twenty-five thousand to fifty thousand. No American car manufacturer, however, sold more than eleven thousand cars a year in South Korea. That didn't stop Trump from claiming credit for a big win. The old deal had been "a horror show"; his modest changes had transformed it into "a wonderful deal."[74]

Discussions with Canada, Mexico, and the EU didn't produce similar breakthroughs. At the end of May, the Trump administration announced that it would not renew the temporary exemptions the three had received and that the steel and aluminum tariffs would go into effect on June 1. The announcement came against the backdrop of Trump's decision a week earlier to order an investigation in whether foreign auto imports posed a national-security risk to the United States and thereby justified the imposition of additional tariffs. US allies knew that the investigation targeted them—Canada, the EU, Japan, Mexico, and South Korea accounted for 98 percent of the foreign cars sold in the United States.[75] Anger at the White House boiled over with the news the exemptions would not be renewed. Trudeau noted that Canadians imported more steel from the United States than they exported and dismissed the idea that Canada was "somehow a national security threat to the United States" as "insulting and unacceptable."[76] Merkel called the decision to implement steel and aluminum tariffs a "mistake" and warned that "the measures carry the threat of a spiral of escalation that will result in damaging everyone."[77] Juncker blasted the metals tariffs as "protectionism pure and simple."[78] In keeping with Juncker's vow that America's trading partners could also "do stupid," the EU, Canada and Mexico all announced retaliatory tariffs on US exports.

The escalating row over tariffs effectively derailed the annual G-7 summit meeting, held in Quebec in June. Macron tweeted on the eve of the meeting that "the American President may not mind being isolated, but neither do we mind signing a 6 country agreement if need be," thereby encouraging talk that the G-7 had become the G-6+1.[79] Trump responded in kind, tweeting that he was "looking forward to straightening out unfair Trade Deals with the G-7 countries," but adding that "if it doesn't happen, we come out even better!"[80] The summit's public events proceeded cordially, but Trump made no effort to mollify Macron or anyone else. He used the private sessions to criticize the other G-7 countries for treating the United States unfairly. To drive home that point, he vowed at a concluding press conference that America's trading partners would be "making a mistake" if they retaliated against his tariff decisions and he warned that if other countries like India didn't reduce their tariffs "we'll stop trading with them."[81] Although the G-7 leaders had agreed to paper over their differences with Trump in a final communiqué, he balked after Trudeau said in his own press conference that he would stand up for Canada's interests. Trump, who had left the meeting hours earlier than scheduled, tweeted from Air Force One that he wouldn't sign the communiqué after all.[82] His decision left America isolated among its traditional allies and put the future of the G-7—the body that had coordinated Western policy for four decades—into doubt.

TRUMP'S IMPOSITION OF steel and aluminum tariffs was just the opening salvo to remake US trade policy. He also wanted to target China directly, and in late March he declared that he would impose a 25 percent tariff on $50 billion of Chinese goods. The move was to retaliate against Beijing for forcing American companies to surrender their trade secrets as a price of doing business in China or for stealing those secrets outright. The administration's calculus was that the United States had more leverage precisely because it was running a trade deficit. "Let's remember: We buy five times more goods than they buy from us," Navarro explained. "They have a lot more to lose in any escalation of this matter."[83] Trump was pithier: "When you're already $500 Billion DOWN, you can't lose!"[84]

Trade wars, however, typically turn less on how much pain a country can inflict and more on how much pain it can tolerate. When the White House at the start of April unveiled the list of Chinese goods it was proposing to hit with tariffs, Beijing responded immediately with a list of American products it would hit in retaliation. The news alarmed American farmers and manufacturers and sent stock markets plunging. The administration responded to these fears in two divergent ways. Trump immediately upped the pressure, announcing that he would impose tariffs on another $100 billion of Chinese imports. Leading administration officials, however, did the opposite, taking to the airwaves to reassure Americans that they did not face tough economic times ahead. "Even shooting wars end with negotiations," Ross said, and "it wouldn't be surprising at all if the net outcome of all this is some sort of negotiation."[85] Larry Kudlow, who in March 2018 replaced Cohn as Trump's national economic adviser, had an even sunnier outlook, predicting that the trade fight would eventually produce a "pot of gold."[86]

The threat of tariffs did generate negotiations, and Trump began the talks by playing hardball. In early May, he sent his entire economic and trade team to China with what amounted to a call for Beijing's unconditional surrender. A four-page proposal to "rebalance" trade demanded that China cut its annual trade surplus with the United States by $200 billion by the end of 2020 and cancel its Made in China 2025 industrial plan, by which Beijing hoped to become a leader in critical new technologies like robotics and artificial intelligence. The proposal made a host of other demands on China, including eliminating a range of tariff and nontariff barriers, treating US service providers the same way it did Chinese providers, and agreeing not to challenge any of the US demands at the WTO.[87] The Chinese were in no mood to negotiate. The delegation's planned meeting with President Xi Jinping never materialized, and Beijing responded with a list of its own demands, including dropping restrictions that barred Chinese companies from buying sophisticated electronics and other high-tech products that had potential military applications. The US delegation left Beijing empty handed.

The two sides met twice more over the next month. In the wake of talks in Washington in mid-May, US and Chinese negotiators announced that "both sides agreed on meaningful increases in United States agriculture and energy exports" to China, and that a US team would head to Beijing "to work out the details."[88] Treasury Secretary Mnuchin in turn declared "the trade war on hold."[89] In what looked to be a goodwill gesture, Beijing quickly announced it would go forward with previously announced plans to cut its tariffs on imported cars and auto parts, though the lower tariff rates remained well above the equivalent US rates. As tentative as these moves were, Trump nonetheless declared victory: "On China, Barriers and Tariffs to come down for first time."[90]

The emerging deal, however, drew more jeers than cheers on Capitol Hill and among US trade experts. An immediate problem was confusion over its size. The administration suggested that China had agreed to buy as much as $200 billion in US goods by 2020.[91] Beijing, however, denied making any such offer.[92] The broader problem was that in offering to buy more US farm products and natural gas, Beijing was agreeing to purchase things it planned to buy in any event to feed its people and fuel its growing economy. The deal that administration officials sketched also wouldn't address the Chinese trade practices that had prompted the tariff threat in the first place. That criticism took on special weight given that the week before the meeting, Trump had overturned a Commerce Department order banning the Chinese telecommunications firm ZTE from purchasing critical US technology products for seven years. The ban, which was imposed because ZTE had been caught multiple times selling telecommunications equipment to Iran and North Korea in violation of US sanctions, would have put the firm out of business. Trump, in the view of his critics, was giving Beijing a substantial concession while getting nothing in return.

US and Chinese trade negotiators met for a third time in early June. The talks ended after two days without any breakthrough. The discussions had proceeded under the shadow of a White House announcement a week earlier that, contrary to Mnuchin's talk of a trade truce, the United States planned to move ahead with imposing 25 percent tariffs on $50 billion of Chinese exports and that it would announce the list of targeted goods by June 15.[93] Beijing immediately accused the administration of reneging on "the consensus that China and the U.S. reached not long ago in Washington" to continue negotiating and vowed that it had "the confidence, the capacity and the experience to defend the interests of the Chinese people."[94] When the White House unveiled the list of targeted imports and the timetable for implementing the tariffs as promised in mid-June, China responded within hours. Undeterred by Trump's previous threat to impose additional tariffs if it retaliated against US exporters, Beijing announced that it would "immediately introduce taxation measures of the same scale and the same strength" as the US had and that "all the economic and trade achievements previously reached" with the United States "will no longer be valid."[95] Trump in turn responded by directing US trade officials to identify $200 billion in additional Chinese goods that could be hit with a 10 percent tariff and threatening to target another $200 billion worth of imports if necessary to force China to capitulate. Washington and Beijing were now nose to nose in a contest of economic brinkmanship. The question was, who would blink first?

TRUMP INSISTED THAT his tough trade actions would ultimately convince America's trading partners to "like us better" and "respect us much more."[96] Little evidence, however, indicated that he was right. Eighteen months into his presidency, he had few wins to show for the fire and fury he had unleashed. The overall US trade deficit had jumped nearly 13 percent, and the bilateral trade deficit with China had hit a record high.[97] The NAFTA renegotiation had deadlocked. Canada, China, and Europe had all retaliated against his tariffs. Although he backed off his threat to impose new tariffs on imported European cars as part of a July 2018 deal with the EU to begin trade talks, it was unclear the truce would last, let alone produce an agreement. The future didn't promise better results, with economists warning that his tax cuts and increased federal spending would drive the deficit higher by fueling domestic demand.[98]

Trump had achieved the worst of both worlds. He had upended relations with major trading partners, undermined international trade rules, and spurred others to cut trade deals without the United States. But he had generated few trade breakthroughs that benefited American companies or workers. His strategy seemingly ignored the advice he gave in *The Art of the Deal:* "The key" to striking a smart deal, he wrote back then, "was to find a mutual interest. Deals work best when each side gets something it wants from the other."[99] America's friends and partners saw little for them in what Trump was offering. And they were no longer afraid to look for alternatives that excluded the United States.

10

Winning Again

D onald Trump was pleased as Air Force One climbed into the
sky over Helsinki on July 16, 2018. He had just concluded
what he saw as a successful six-day trip to Europe. His final
meeting was a two-hour one-on-one with Russian President Vladimir
Putin, which he believed had put US-Russia relations on a positive footing thanks to "a direct, open, deeply productive dialogue."[1] The Helsinki
meeting had come just days after a NATO summit in Brussels, where
Trump thought his tough talk had compelled other NATO members to
spend more on defense. In between Brussels and Helsinki, he had traveled to Britain where he was the first president to be hosted for a state
dinner at Blenheim Palace, the birthplace of Winston Churchill. Trump
felt satisfied that his busy week had delivered on the promise he had
made in his inaugural address that "America will start winning again,
winning like never before."[2]

By the time Air Force One landed back in the United States, however,
it was clear that Trump was nearly alone in thinking his trip had been a big
win. While he was in the air, Republicans had joined with Democrats in
criticizing his press conference in Helsinki, where he stood next to Putin
and seemingly accepted the Russian leader's denial that Moscow had
interfered in the 2016 US presidential election. Senate Majority Leader
Mitch McConnell and Speaker of the House Paul Ryan both dismissed
the idea that Russia was a friend of the United States and endorsed the
unanimous assessment of the US intelligence community that Russia
had interfered in the election. Other critics went further. The Helsinki
press conference was "one of the most disgraceful performances by an
American president in memory," Senator John McCain said. "President
Trump proved not only unable, but unwilling to stand up to Putin."[3]
Former CIA Director John Brennan called Trump's comments "nothing

short of treasonous."[4] And Dan Coats, Trump's own director of national intelligence, issued a statement to "correct the record," saying, "We have been clear in our assessments of Russian meddling in the 2016 election and their ongoing, pervasive efforts to undermine our democracy."[5]

The controversy over the Helsinki press conference overshadowed the turmoil Trump had caused at his previous stops. He had kicked off the NATO summit by attacking German Chancellor Angela Merkel, whom he accused of being "totally controlled" by and "captive to Russia" because Germany was building a pipeline to import Russian natural gas.[6] He then threw the second day of meetings into an uproar by demanding an emergency session so he could press NATO members to spend more on defense. If they declined to increase defense spending, Trump warned, he would "do his own thing," which other leaders took as a threat to leave NATO.[7] Although Trump later claimed he forced NATO members "to substantially up their commitment [to] levels that they've never thought of before," the allies merely reaffirmed their pledge, first made in 2014, to spend 2 percent of their GDP on defense by 2024.[8]

Trump's bull-in-china-shop ways continued when he reached Britain, where he avoided London because large numbers of demonstrators had gathered to protest his visit. As his dinner with British Prime Minister Theresa May at Blenheim Palace was concluding, a London newspaper released an interview in which he criticized her for ignoring his advice on how to negotiate Britain's exit from the European Union (EU). In the interview, he also suggested that Boris Johnson, who days earlier had resigned from May's cabinet because of her handling of Brexit, would make "a great Prime Minister."[9] Trump ended his weekend stay in Britain by calling the EU "a foe" because of how it treated the United States on trade. He tellingly added that "Russia is a foe in certain respects."[10] Trump amended that assessment in Helsinki, saying that Putin was a "good competitor" and that he viewed the word "competitor" as "a compliment."[11]

Faced with the barrage of criticism, Trump did what he hated to do: he walked back his Helsinki remarks on Russia and the election. He insisted that the controversy had been triggered by a slip of the tongue on his part, adding, "I accept our intelligence community's conclusion that Russia's meddling in the 2016 election took place." But he immediately began retracting his concession, noting that "other people also" could have interfered.[12] And he declined to temper his criticisms of the

EU or NATO, even after the release of an interview, conducted in Helsinki but not aired until he returned to Washington, in which he again threw into doubt his commitment to defending America's allies. When asked why Americans should be prepared to defend a NATO member like Montenegro, Trump responded, "I understand what you're saying. I've asked the same question." He went on to complain that Montenegro, a small Balkan country of some six hundred thousand inhabitants that had more troops per capita in Afghanistan than the United States did, was "very aggressive" and might cause World War III.[13]

The outcry that followed Trump's return from Europe in July 2018 was in a way surprising. What he said in Brussels, Britain, and Helsinki he had said many times before. And that was the trip's real lesson. The 2016 presidential campaign had generated talk that reporters took Trump literally but not seriously, while voters took him seriously but not literally.[14] The European trip showed that on foreign policy he should be taken literally *and* seriously. Experts had continually wondered what his true foreign policy views were and when his advisers would persuade him to chart a more traditional course abroad. But much like Edgar Allan Poe's purloined letter, Trump's foreign policy views, and how he intended to implement them, had been hidden in plain sight all along. He made clear in Europe what he argued for decades—that US foreign policy had been misguided with its focus on friends and allies, who were only interested in taking advantage of America's generosity, and that he had no intention of deferring to the recommendations of experts, even ones he picked to staff his own administration. He wasn't looking to lead. He was looking to win.

EVERY AMERICAN PRESIDENT since Franklin Delano Roosevelt sought to lead globally—and to do so by promoting cooperation for mutual gain. They didn't choose this path out of altruism or naïveté. They chose it out of self-interest and hard-headed calculation. World War II had shaped their choice. It had taught them that the United States could not escape perils overseas by retreating to Fortress America, as the original American Firsters had promised. The perils came anyway. Retreat only meant facing them alone. The Greatest Generation instead looked to work with others, organizing collective security, opening up markets, and promoting democracy, human rights, and the rule of law. The strategy calculated that creating the space for other countries to flourish would enable the United

States to flourish as well. It assumed that by leading abroad, America could win at home. It succeeded beyond anyone's wildest dreams.

It was not, however, a strategy that Donald Trump ever embraced. From the first moment he burst into the public eye in the 1980s, he championed the return to the older logic of competition and domination. He argued that the United States should use its preponderant power to dictate to others. Cooperation and multilateralism were fool's errands. America's friends and allies weren't looking to cooperate but to get a free ride on its security guarantees and to pick its pockets on trade deals. All that losing was going to stop once he reached the White House. America was going to win again.

Did Trump produce the foreign policy wins he had promised? He certainly had no doubt: "I would give myself an A+," he told interviewers on *Fox & Friends* in April 2018.[15] He had kept the promises he had made on the campaign trail. He had left the Trans-Pacific Partnership (TPP), begun the process of withdrawing from the Paris Agreement on climate change, moved the US embassy to Jerusalem, imposed tariffs on unfair trading partners, walked away from the Iran nuclear deal, became the first US president to meet with North Korea's leader, and restarted a dialogue with Russian President Vladimir Putin. Each of these moves was a win on Trump's scorecard.

Presidents aren't ultimately judged on whether they keep their campaign promises, however. They are judged by whether their choices make Americans safer and more prosperous. Eighteen months into his presidency, Trump had surprisingly few "wins" to show for his disruptive decisions. He had tightened controls on illegal immigration and had all but stopped the admission of refugees. But the much-ballyhooed wall with Mexico remained unbuilt, Mexico still refused to pay for it, and the number of migrants illegally crossing the southern border surged in 2018 after falling sharply following his inauguration. The missile strikes he had ordered against Syria in April 2017 failed to deter Syrian strongman Bashar al-Assad from using chemical weapons again in 2018. American airpower and special forces helped Iraqi and other local forces dislodge the Islamic State from Iraq and much of Syria. But Trump had no diplomatic strategy for securing the peace, and his promise in April 2018 that US troops would leave Syria "very soon" undermined any long-term effort to stabilize the country.[16] Despite his praise for Saudi Arabia, the United Arab Emirates, and Egypt, Arab nations ignored his call to deploy their own troops to Syria and to spend massively on reconstructing the war-torn country. Trump reversed course on his campaign pledge to withdraw from Afghanistan and said that the United States would "fight to win."[17] But the security situation continued to deteriorate during the first half of 2018, and the White House began exploring a diplomatic course to end the war instead.

Things looked much the same on trade policy. Trump won at best modest adjustments in the US-Korea Free Trade Agreement. And he sidelined, at least temporarily, a budding trade war he had started with the EU by agreeing to begin new talks on reducing trade barriers on most industrial goods. Beyond that, his tough line with America's trading partners yielded few results, other than to jeopardize US exports. Canada and Mexico dug in their heels when it came to his demand that they rewrite NAFTA to guarantee better results for the United States. Japan, Australia, and the other nine signatories to the Trans-Pacific Partnership ignored his efforts to torpedo the deal and instead negotiated a revised agreement that left the United States on the outside looking in. Country after country rebuffed his demands to negotiate bilateral deals. Instead, major trading partners such as Canada, Europe, Japan, and Mexico opted to go around Washington, seeking to make themselves less reliant on the US market by negotiating new deals among themselves and with other countries.

In the spring of 2018, Trump made big rolls of the dice on North Korea, Iran, and trade. It would take months, if not years, to get a final accounting on each. The Singapore Summit with Kim Jong-un may have jump-started a negotiating process, but it hardly guaranteed that the two sides would make quick progress in their talks or even that they had agreed on the specific goal the talks were designed to achieve. In withdrawing from the Iran nuclear deal, Trump gambled that he could either break the mullahs' hold on power or force them to negotiate on his terms. But without the broad international support Obama had secured previously, the unilateral reimposition of sanctions set the stage for a crisis in transatlantic relations and created an opening for Russia and China to solidify their trade ties with Tehran. Transatlantic unity was further undermined by Trump's decision to impose tariffs on the import of steel and aluminum from Europe and Canada, as well as by his threats to impose tariffs on automobiles. Similarly, the tariffs Trump slapped on Chinese imports in June 2018 did little to force China to revamp its predatory economic policies. Achieving that goal would have required enlisting America's allies in the effort. Trump hailed his tariffs as wins to reset unfair balances of trade. But they were more likely to generate a trade war that would leave everyone worse off.

Trump also did little in his first eighteen months in office to set America up for future wins and plenty to leave it vulnerable to painful reverses. The massive tax cuts he signed into law in December 2017, followed by large spending increases approved in early 2018, deepened America's fiscal woes. The Congressional Budget Office projected that the US federal budget deficit would nearly double by 2020, with the US government spending $1 trillion more per year than it would receive in taxes.[18] Washington was projected to spend more than $600 million a year by 2022 in interest on the national debt, or about as much as it spent annually on the Pentagon.[19] The national debt was on a path to surpass $28 trillion by 2028, or 96 percent of total US annual economic output.[20] That number was larger than at any point since just after World War II. The soaring deficit and debt also meant Washington would have little to spend on new domestic or national security programs and would be hard-pressed to weather a major economic recession.

Running large fiscal deficits can be justified when spending is channeled into productive investments that offer the promise of bigger payoffs down the road. Americans follow that logic every day when they take out loans to pay for college or vocational training. But Trump was doing just the opposite. The first two budgets he submitted to Congress proposed slashing the federal government's overall spending on research and development by some 20 percent.[21] Congress refused to go along, leaving spending roughly level with that of the Obama years. That was a victory only if one ignored the billions of dollars China and others were pouring into quantum computing, robotics, artificial intelligence, synthetic biology, and renewable energy in a bid to dominate these and other technologies of the future.

Trump similarly ignored the pressing need to rebuild America's dilapidated infrastructure, despite its potential to fuel future economic growth. He rightly argued on the campaign trail that "our roads and bridges are falling apart. Our airports are Third World condition." But rather than following through on his vow to spend $1 trillion to "build the roads, highways, bridges, tunnels, airports and the railways of tomorrow," the White House admitted in May 2018 that he was unlikely to push, let alone sign, an infrastructure bill any time soon.[22] American businesses were left to hope that a few more years could be squeezed out of the country's aging ports, freight lines, and roadways.

Most important, Trump did little for the forgotten men and women he had championed on the campaign trail and who were to be the main beneficiaries of his America First foreign policy. His economic vision was fundamentally backward looking. He trumpeted what his bluster and tariffs would do for the workers who had lost their jobs in the coal and steel industries. He ignored the fact that far more Americans worked in industries that would be hurt by higher coal and steel prices. He similarly ignored the fact that the loss of steel jobs resulted largely from big leaps in productivity and that the decline of the coal industry owed less to government regulation or Obama's so-called war on coal than it did to American ingenuity. The wildcatters who pioneered hydraulic fracturing or "fracking" had unlocked vast quantities of cleaner natural gas that could power America's economy at substantially lower costs. And major investments in renewables had reduced the price of wind and solar power to competitive levels. Trump likewise did little to help Americans face a future in which advances in artificial intelligence, robotics, and related technologies would put pressure on jobs and wages. Trump's policies emphasized theatrics. They ignored fundamentals.

TRUMP'S SHORTAGE OF wins partly reflected his own shortcomings as president—his ignorance on many issues, his unwillingness to take advice from others, his impulsiveness, and his lack of strategic thinking. He had insisted during the campaign that he knew the issues better than the experts and that even if he didn't, he would master them quickly and easily. Once he was in office, neither turned out to be true. He was remarkably incurious, often declining to read the briefings papers his advisers prepared for him and repeating urban legends as gospel truths. So he announced the US withdrawal from the Paris climate agreement because he rejected the science of climate change—wrongly claiming that the North Pole ice cap was at record high levels.[23] And he refused to delve into the details of uranium enrichment, plutonium reprocessing, and nuclear weapons and missile production in preparation for his summit with Kim Jong-un.[24] "I don't think I have to prepare very much," he said days before he flew to Singapore. "It's about the attitude. It's about willingness to get things done."[25] He took the same approach to his June

2018 meeting with Putin, preferring two rounds of golf in Scotland to preparing for his one-on-one with the wily Russian leader.

All presidents know less than they need to about the policy challenges they face. That is why it is critical they appoint a team of seasoned advisers and create a process that enables them to work through complicated issues. Trump had promised on the campaign trail that he would pick the "best people." And he did pick many eminently qualified people to staff his cabinet. But in office he repeatedly ignored their advice or didn't even bother to solicit it. He made the critical decisions to meet with Kim Jung-un and to reject a European proposal to toughen sanctions on Iran without convening his national security team to evaluate the pros and cons. He frequently announced his decisions on important policy matters through tweets that came as much as a surprise to his advisers as they did to everyone else. Trump himself made clear how little stock he put in advice and advisers when he dismissed concerns about his failure to fully staff the State Department by declaring, "I'm the only one that matters."[26]

Trump compounded the chaotic nature of his administration's decision making with his impulsiveness. He frequently trumpeted the virtue of being unpredictable. Unpredictability can put adversaries on their back feet and potentially create new diplomatic openings. Kim Jong-un's decision to open up a diplomatic path rather than continuing to escalate the confrontation with the United States and others may have been a case in point. But like cayenne pepper, unpredictability is not suited for all occasions and is best used judiciously when it is. Friends, allies, and trading partners in particular need and prefer dependability and predictability, not surprises. Trump, however, careened so frequently from position to position that it appeared he had no coherent alternative in mind. He repeatedly praised China, then challenged it, and then discarded the challenge. He hailed the potential for US-Russian cooperation while his own National Security Strategy called Russia a rival power "attempting to erode American security and prosperity."[27] He offered to negotiate a trade deal with the European Union, then called it a "foe" and imposed tariffs, then committed to pursue talks to build "strong trade relations in which both of us will win."[28] He denounced TPP, suggested the United States might rejoin it, and then denounced it again. Friends and foes alike suffered whiplash trying to determine what precisely he wanted.

"The indispensable power," complained one European ambassador in Washington, "has become the unpredictable power."[29]

Trump's inflated sense of his own knowledge, his reluctance to solicit and take advice, and his tendency to pursue disruption for disruption's sake fueled his administration's inability to generate and execute a sustainable foreign policy strategy. In violation of the old military adage—and common sense—to avoid waging two-front wars, he picked fights on multiple issues with multiple countries all at the same time. He wanted China's help in pressing North Korea to give up its nuclear weapons and Iran to accept more restrictions on its behavior while at the same time demanding major changes in China's trade and economic policy. It was hardly a surprise that Beijing balked. He needed US allies in Asia, Europe, and North America to contain Iran, constrain North Korea, and counter China and Russia. But instead of leading them in a common cause, he targeted them with trade sanctions, insulted them in tweets and interviews, and ignored their pleas for common action.

Most important, winning strategies answer the critical question: What next? Trump seldom had a ready answer on that score. When he pulled the United States out of TPP, he didn't have an alternative for forging better trade rules for the Asia-Pacific region or blunting growing Chinese power—even though his own administration viewed Beijing as America's main strategic competitor. He walked away from the Paris climate agreement promising to negotiate a better deal but offered neither ideas for how to mitigate climate change nor a strategy for getting all the other countries that were sticking with Paris on board. He ordered the US embassy moved to Jerusalem without devising a diplomatic plan to address Palestinian anger or keep the peace process from being derailed. He withdrew the United States from the Iran agreement but outlined no strategy for getting a better deal or for preventing Iran from restarting its nuclear weapons program. His answer to "What next?" was usually "We'll see what happens."[30] It was a disquieting response. And it showed that the man who had written *The Art of the Deal* was a better deal breaker than deal maker.

THE BIGGER PROBLEM with Trump's foreign policy was his abdication of American global leadership. He saw little value in friends and allies, and he showed no interest in leading them. They were instead foes to be bullied into complying with his demands. His hostility to America's traditional leadership role was clear to those who had long been accustomed to being led. "The fact that our friend and ally has come to question the very worth of its mantle of global leadership puts in sharper focus the need for the rest of us to set our own clear and sovereign course," said Chrystia Freeland, Canada's foreign minister, five months into Trump's presidency. "To say this is not controversial: It is a fact."[31]

To be sure, American allies had complained about Washington's flagging leadership before. French President Jacques Chirac famously grumbled that "the position of leader of the Free World is vacant" when Bill Clinton hesitated to stop ethnic cleansing in Bosnia.[32] Obama was criticized for initially refusing to support military action against Muammar Gaddafi in Libya and then reversing course on using force to oust Bashar al-Assad from power in Syria. But these were all complaints about America's failure on specific issues. They were not fears that the United States was turning it back on its friends and allies more broadly. Conversely, many American allies bitterly opposed George W. Bush's unilateral decision to invade Iraq. But they weren't attacking the idea of US leadership. They were warning, rightly as it turned out, that Bush was plunging the world into a maelstrom he could not control. Trump's approach to foreign policy felt—and was—different. America wasn't leading anymore. It wasn't even trying.

Trump's supporters insisted the allies had it all wrong, that he was leading. "In almost every area, in his own way, with his own rhetoric, he has reasserted American leadership," Sen. Tom Cotton claimed.[33] But true leadership isn't so much about who is behind the wheel as how many others come along for the ride. And Trump's greatest flaw was that he not only failed to persuade others to follow his chosen course but in many instances even failed to try. When he announced he was withdrawing the United States from the Paris climate agreement, no other country joined him in exiting. Indeed, Nicaragua and Syria, the only two countries that had not yet signed the accord, did so after he opted out. "Whatever leadership is," a senior French diplomat said at the G-20 meeting that reaffirmed support for the climate agreement, "it is not being outvoted, 19 to 1."[34] The same dynamic repeated itself with his decisions to leave TPP, to move the US embassy to Jerusalem, to withdraw from the Iran nuclear deal, to take America out of UNESCO, and to walk away from global negotiations on a UN Compact on Migration. Trump went one way. America's friends and allies went another.

Trump and his advisers dismissed the complaints from America's friends. "What's good for the US is what's good for the rest of the world,"Treasury Secretary Steven Mnuchin argued.[35] But few of America's allies agreed. Aside from a few friends, like Israel and Saudi Arabia, who applauded Trump's choices because he gave them what they wanted and asked for nothing in return, most allies saw his decisions as straining and potentially rupturing their ties with the United States. Mexicans elected a president hostile to America. Canadians openly discussed how to diversify their foreign policy portfolio so they could rely less on the United States. Japanese worried that the United States would soon abandon them. Australians wondered what an inward looking and more nationalist and transactional America would mean for their future.

But the sentiment that something fundamental had changed in relations with the United States was felt most strongly in Europe. "We have experienced a break in German-American, in European-American relations," Merkel said after Trump withdrew from the Iran nuclear deal.[36] Donald Tusk, president of the European Council and the former prime minister of Poland, went further: "Looking at the latest decisions of Donald Trump, someone could even think: With friends like that who needs enemies."[37] And Jean-Claude Juncker, the president of the European Commission, pointedly noted, "At this point, we have to replace the United States, which as an international actor has lost vigor, and because of it, in the long term, influence."[38] These views were echoed widely across the continent, with newspapers running stories declaring the transatlantic alliance, a foundational pillar of American and European foreign policy for more than seventy years, at an end. Even Europeans not ready to give up on Washington were asking the question a former French ambassador to the United States posed: "How do we make" our relations with America "work with a US leadership that doesn't want to play the role of leader?"[39]

The questions in friendly capitals about the future of their relations with the United States highlighted an important lesson. Far more than Trump realized, America's friends and allies had choices about their future, including the choice to work without, or around, the United States. If he wanted to be transactional, they could be as well. The willingness of allies to chart their own course was most obvious on trade. When Trump slapped tariffs on their imports, they responded in kind. And rather than signing up to the bilateral deals he wanted, they looked elsewhere to strike new deals. Canada, Japan, and Mexico—three of America's top four trading partners—struck or extended free-trade agreements with the EU and worked with the other TPP signatory countries to create the TPP-11. Contrary to what Trump and his advisers insisted, America First increasingly looked like America Alone.

The instinct of allied leaders to chart a different path was reinforced by the plunging faith that their publics had in Trump. The Pew Research Center found in 2017 that confidence in the US president to do the right thing in world affairs fell in thirty-five of the thirty-seven countries it surveyed. In thirty-one of them, it fell by double digits, and it dropped by fifty points or more in major allied countries, including Britain, France, Germany, Australia, and Japan. Even more troubling, more people around the world had faith in Xi Jinping (28 percent) than in Trump (22 percent) to do the right thing in world affairs.[40] Surveys that Gallup released in early 2018 from 134 countries showed a similar pattern. The United States had the highest global leadership approval ratings by a comfortable margin at the end of Obama's presidency. A year later, the United States had fallen to third place, well behind Germany, slightly behind China, and only a few percentage points ahead of Russia.[41]

Leaders listen to what citizens think. And the message that publics around the world were sending in 2018 was not good news for the United States. They were losing trust in Washington. As with the loss of trust caused by infidelity in a marriage, it will likely be difficult to restore. American global leadership benefited enormously from the political capital the United States built up defeating Nazi Germany and fending off the Soviet Union. For decades Washington often got the benefit of the doubt or quick forgiveness for policy choices others opposed. But the number of people who grew up in the shadow of World War II and during the Cold War is shrinking. Instead, more and more people around the world know the United States as the country that invaded Iraq, waterboarded prisoners, nearly wrecked the global economy with subprime mortgages, and turned hostile toward immigrants and refugees. Trump's insistence that the United States was like every other country, free to pursue its narrow interests and not obligated to pursue a common good, only encouraged skepticism that America represented broader interests and values. As a result, foreign publics were less likely to forgive and forget and more open to their governments working without, or even against, the United States.

DID IT MATTER that so many of America's friends and allies opposed and even resisted Trump's policies? In the short term, the answer was no. Countries seldom change their security and economic policies overnight. Throughout 2017 and into 2018, many US partners held out hope that Trump might eventually be persuaded to return to a traditional American foreign policy even as they criticized the choices he made. Their guiding principle, as one Washington foreign policy analyst put it, was, "Don't isolate him. Don't give into him. Don't give up on him."[42] And countries like Japan, Mexico, and South Korea found it hard to break quickly with Washington. Their security and prosperity were too heavily tied to America's to make it easy to chart an entirely new course.

But foreign policy decisions aren't felt only in the moment. They also play out over time. And the fact that in the summer of 2018 so many American friends and allies were seriously discussing giving up on Trump and beginning to edge away from Washington could have enormous consequences for the United States. French President Emmanuel Macron highlighted the dynamic to reporters during his April 2018 visit to Washington. Trump's abandonment of global leadership "can work in the short term," he noted, "but it's very insane in the medium to long term."[43] And the reason was the long-term damage caused by loss of trust. Trump's conduct, German Foreign Minister Heiko Maas noted after the disastrous G-7 meeting in Quebec, "shakes the certainty that we and the US are allies in the fight for multilateralism and a rules-based world. And this certainty has unfortunately already been shaken so badly that it is bound to go beyond Trump's presidency."[44]

The costs of Trump's America First foreign policy were most immediately apparent in the economic realm. Americans have a tremendous stake in global trade. Exports support nearly eleven million American jobs.[45] Sales abroad account for more than 40 percent of the revenues for S&P 500 firms.[46] TPP would have slashed thousands of tariffs on US exports—many of them far higher than the tariffs the United States placed on equivalent imports. With Trump's decision to pull the United States out of the agreement while the other signatories moved ahead with TPP-11 and other trade deals, American firms and farms swung from potentially being more competitive in TPP markets to suddenly being far less competitive. So American agriculture, to take one example, went from gaining long-desired access to the relatively closed Japanese market to seeing that competitive advantage shift to their European rivals when Japan gave the EU essentially the same deal the United States would have received under TPP.[47] Likewise, Trump's tariffs helped the American steel and aluminum industries but at the cost of hurting the far greater number of firms that used steel and aluminum in making their products.

Trump's decision to abandon the Paris Agreement had similarly significant economic consequences. The market for clean energy products like wind and solar power in 2017 topped $300 billion globally and was set to grow rapidly. Walking away from Paris left other countries to set the global technical standards and market rules for new climate-friendly technologies. Given the competitive nature of the industry, with many countries hoping to dominate the technology of tomorrow, they had few incentives to accommodate US interests or American companies.

The consequences of Trump's skepticism of US alliance commitments and his dismissal of efforts to promote democracy, the rule of law, and human rights were harder to measure but potentially no less important. By questioning the value of alliances, Trump raised doubts in the minds of allies and adversaries alike about whether he would honor America's security commitments. That had the perverse effect of potentially emboldening adversaries while encouraging friends to hedge their bets in dealing with other great powers for fear that Washington would abandon them. Thus, Japan, faced with questions about the durability of the American troop presence on its territory, sought more cooperative relations with China, just in case. "I want to lift up the Japan-China relationship to a new stage," Japanese Prime Minister Shinzo Abe said after meeting with Chinese Premier Li Keqiang for the first time in May 2018. The meeting, he noted, represented "an important first step toward a dramatic improvement" in relations.[48] In Europe, the unified front against Russia that emerged in the wake of Moscow's invasion of Ukraine was starting to unravel as more and more countries sought to end Russia's isolation and improve bilateral relations.

Similarly, Trump's praise for autocrats; his lack of interest in challenging human rights abuses outside of a few countries like Iran and Venezuela; and his attacks on journalists at home weakened the forces abroad that shared America's values. Autocrats around the globe used Trump's attacks on journalists to justify their decisions to suppress their critics. So the Chinese state news media dismissed reports that a human rights activist had been tortured as "fake news," and Syrian President Assad did the same in response to reports that thousands had been killed in Syrian prisons.[49] It all damaged America's image abroad. "In Latin America, the relationship with the U.S. has gone from the aspirational to the transactional," lamented Jorge Gujardo, a retired Mexican diplomat. "There's this idea that the States is just like the rest of us. That's the saddest thing to me."[50]

EVEN MORE IMPORTANT than Trump's decisions on specific issues was their cumulative effect. The rules-based order that shaped world politics created after World War II was neither inevitable nor necessarily permanent. It resulted from conscious American leadership. Trump's abdication of that leadership raised two possible future scenarios, neither of them reassuring.

One is a world in which no one leads. That might mean a return to the world of the late nineteenth century, with great powers carving out spheres of influence that they can dominate.[51] Or it could mean a world of ever-growing disarray as no single or combination of powers has the capacity or the will to maintain international order.[52] Either version of a world with no leader would leave the United States poorer and less secure than if it continued to lead globally. Too many of today's problems spill across borders. Climate change, nuclear proliferation, terrorism, just to name a few pressing problems, won't be solved by one or even a few countries acting alone. Active leadership is required to marshal effective global responses to these cross-border challenges. At the same time, retreating to regional spheres of influence or within one's own borders would inhibit the global trade on which so much of today's prosperity depends. And it would offer the prospect of a return to the very instability and great-power wars that America's post–World War II leadership sought to prevent. To be sure, the United States would likely fare better than most other countries in such a world. But that is not the same as doing well.

The alternative outcome is that another country fills the leadership vacuum Trump's abdication created. The best outcome would be if one or more of America's allies took the baton of global leadership. But none of America's allies or friends is up to the task. Europe is consumed with growing populism and nationalism, continued economic and financial woes, and Brexit. Japan and India both lack the power and the will to be more than regional powers. As for America's adversaries, Russia has the will but lacks the economic power and political appeal to create what its foreign minister, Sergei Lavrov, called a "post-West world order."[53]

China, though, is another matter. President Xi Jinping has abandoned the time-tested strategy, first embraced by Deng Xiaoping in the 1980s, to "hide your strength, bide your time, and never take the lead." Instead, he is reasserting China's greatness, and Trump's election provided a grand strategic opportunity. That became clear in October 2017, during the 19th Communist Party Congress. In a path-breaking address, Xi warned that "no country alone can address the many challenges facing mankind; no country can afford to retreat into self-isolation." But if America were to do so, then a newly confident China was more than happy to take its place. Xi declared the arrival of a "new era" for China, one that would see it "moving closer to center stage and making greater contributions to mankind." And he offered "a new option for other countries," an alternative that was based on "Chinese wisdom and a Chinese approach to solving the problems facing mankind."[54] Xi's challenge to America wasn't just economic but ideological as well.

"As the U.S. retreats globally," Chinese Major General Jin Yinan noted gleefully, "China shows up."[55] And China was showing up everywhere—with checkbook in hand. Its ambitious One Belt, One Road initiative, a $1 trillion investment in ports and overland routes in more than sixty countries, created new bonds across south and central Asia, all the way to Europe and North Africa. It invested large sums in Africa and Latin America, opening new markets and creating new dependencies. With decades of double-digit growth in defense spending, China had built a conventional military force that was second in size and capability only to the United States. Long focused on territorial defense, China now projected military power well beyond its shores, creating an intimidating presence in the disputed islands chains of the South China Sea, opening its first foreign military base in Djibouti, and conducting naval exercises with Russia in the Mediterranean and Baltic Seas. Beijing also set up a host of new multilateral institutions, including the Asian Infrastructure Investment Bank, the New Development Bank, the Asian Regional Comprehensive Economic Partnership, the 16+1 framework between China and East and Central European countries, and the Shanghai Cooperation Organization. Common to all these initiatives was that Beijing stood at the center—and the United States was excluded from all.

A Chinese-dominated world would not be friendly to the United States. Beijing has little incentive to resolve security crises to Washington's satisfaction. It did nothing to persuade Washington to stick with the Iran nuclear deal, seeing America's withdrawal as an opportunity to strengthen its ties with Tehran. And while Beijing did pressure North Korea, its own security interests differ from Washington's, thus complicating any negotiations on a deal with Pyongyang. As for trade, Beijing has no interest in writing trade rules that favor American firms. And Xi's China would surely be the last country to champion democracy, human rights, and the rule of law. Indeed, China's foreign policy has sought to expand Beijing's options overseas at Washington's expense. That's what great powers do. Trump's abdication of America's global leadership role has made this challenge possible far sooner than would otherwise be the case.

China's ascendance to global leader is by no means guaranteed. It faces numerous internal challenges, including an aging workforce, deep regional and economic inequalities, and a potentially brittle political system. Just as important, China has few friends. Other countries certainly envy China's rapid growth, but "no one wants to be China," as one Asian diplomat put it.[56] The reason is straightforward. They fear that China seeks domination and not cooperation. "China uses its money to buy off many leaders," one senior Vietnamese general noted, "but none of the countries that are its close allies, like North Korea, Pakistan or Cambodia, have done well. Countries that are close to America have done much better."[57]

Even so, with the United States abdicating its longstanding global leadership role, America was finding it increasingly difficult to dissuade countries from following Beijing's lead. In early 2018, Secretary of State Rex Tillerson warned African and Latin American leaders not to be taken in by "new imperial powers that seek only to benefit their own people."[58] But his words had little effect. "I think that with this attitude the United States is leaving a void, and that void may be filled by China," President Sebastián Piñera of Chile responded.[59] Moussa Faki Mahamat, chairman of the African Union Commission, said much the same thing: "I think Africans are mature enough to engage in partnerships of their own volition."[60] Besides, in cutting back on foreign aid and closing markets to foreign products, the United States offered little incentive to follow its lead. "If you are not there," Singapore's Prime Minister Lee Hsieng Loong explained, "then everybody else in the world will look around and say, I want to be friends with both the U.S. and the Chinese—and the Chinese are ready, and I'll start with them."[61]

THE TRAGEDY OF America's abdication of global leadership is that it was unnecessary. The United States was not the pitiful, wounded giant Trump repeatedly described, the victim of carnage inflicted by greedy friends and uncaring elites. It remained the world's largest and most vibrant economy, accounting for one-quarter of the world's economic output. Its military dwarfed that of every other country, with Washington continuing to spend more than the next ten countries, including all its potential foes or rivals, combined.[62] Its values resonated around the globe.

Likewise, the foreign policies Trump's predecessors pursued weren't the unmitigated disaster he portrayed them to be. For all the missteps and mistakes the United States made abroad, global leadership had served its—and the world's—interests for more than seven decades. And the grave foreign policy errors the United States made in places like Vietnam and Iraq were not pushed on it by the demands of global leadership but rather were self-inflicted wounds, typically incurred over the objections and counsel of its closest friends. Had Trump been more willing to listen and learn, he might have fashioned a foreign policy that addressed the real problems he had inveighed against for three decades. That would have meant not repelling friends and allies but rallying them in a common cause.

"Nothing is possible without allies and partners," Rex Tillerson noted in his parting remarks to reporters after being fired as secretary of state.[63] Indeed, friends and allies are one of the keys to America's global power and success. It is what separates the United States from strategic competitors like China and Russia. Washington has fifty-five formal allies all across the world and many others like Israel, Saudi Arabia, and the United Arab Emirates that are effectively allies. In contrast, Moscow has five formal allies (stalwarts like Armenia, Belarus, Kazakhstan, Kyrgyzstan, and Tajikistan), and Beijing has just one (North Korea). And whereas Russian and Chinese allies are clients that must heed their far more powerful patrons, America's are friends. And they are powerful friends. Six of the top ten economies are American allies; together they nearly equal the US economy in size.[64] And five of the top ten military spenders in the world are treaty allies who together spend more on defense than China and Russia combined.[65]

The potential still exists to reinvigorate American global leadership. Trump unintentionally has set the grounds for such a renewal. Much as oxygen goes unnoticed until it's gone, his refusal to lead showed allies how much they had invested in the international order—and how essential American leadership was to maintaining it. Their concerted efforts to find ways to work with Trump—despite deep-seated difference over issues such as climate change, trade, and Iran, and despite his frequent use of ham-handed tactics and petty insults—showed that they understood that the underlying bargain between leader and followers needed to be revised. They looked for ways to take on more of the burden of collective defense, to make the rules of international trade more effective and more congenial to the United States, and to otherwise do more to take a greater role in helping to solve some of the world's greatest challenges. As Macron put it: "The United States is the premier power; it is our most important partner in multilateral endeavors; it's our first partner in the fight against terrorism; it is important for collective security. We can be angry with the United States, we may disagree about the methods as we do on Iran, but at the end, we are in agreement."[66] America's allies still needed it to lead the Free World.

At the same time, Trump's foreign policy choices also reminded Americans of the benefits of global leadership. Trump's election spurred much talk about how Americans had turned inward, disillusioned by the costs of overseas interventions and the weight of global responsibilities. But that was and remains a minority view in the United States. A majority of Americans have consistently favored American engagement abroad and seen alliances as one of the most effective means by which the United States can advance its interests in the world. And on issues such as the importance of defending allies for American security and the domestic economic benefits of trade, public support actually increased after Trump took office.[67] Americans, too, seemingly gained a greater appreciation of the costs of America First. And while shifting opinions hardly constituted a public demand for a course shift, they signaled that Americans were prepared to support one—if somebody led the way.

Renewing American global leadership and deepening the partnership with friends and allies will not be easy, and they will not wait indefinitely for the United States to return to its cooperative ways. Washington will need to avoid the hubris of Clinton's and Bush's indispensable nation and the reluctance of Obama to flex America's muscles. Nor will reasserting American leadership miraculously sweep away the challenges facing the United States. American power is in relative decline as China's power rises. Russia remains dedicated to restoring its dominance in its neighborhood and dividing the Western alliance. Europe continues to struggle with anemic economic growth, swelling national debts, a rising tide of nationalism and populism, and debates about the EU's very purpose and future. Emerging powers like Brazil and India are more interested in the perks of great-power status than its responsibilities. Globalization continues to generate new and messy problems, ranging from infectious diseases to financial contagions to nuclear proliferation and terrorism.

But all these trends will continue if the United States stays on the path of America First. Indeed, by running roughshod over friends and allies, Trump was adding to America's burdens rather than reducing them and making the challenges it faced larger and harder to address. As much as he berated them for not carrying their weight and for taking advantage of the United States, they were force multipliers for American power and American values. In fact, they were essential to competing effectively with China and securing many of the goals Trump had set—including a freer and fairer trade regime, a stronger response to terrorism, and an end to the nuclear threat from North Korea and Iran. The observation one Asian diplomat made was inescapable: "America is stronger and greater with friends."[68] The key to winning again, to put it in Trumpian terms, is by leading again.

THAT WAS THE point that Secretary of Defense James Mattis tried to make to the US president on that July day in the Tank. Trump didn't listen then, and he didn't later, even as criticisms of his decisions mounted and one policy initiative after another foundered. He instead doubled down on his commitment to America First. Many of the advisers who attended the meeting in the Tank and who sought to tame his foreign policy instincts were fired or resigned. In their place, Trump surrounded himself with advisers like National Security Adviser John Bolton and

Secretary of State Mike Pompeo, who were more inclined to confirm his beliefs than to challenge them.

The July 2018 trip to Europe showed Trump acting on his America First vision. He was convinced that global leadership had hurt rather than helped the United States, and he intended to set things right. He would no longer allow countries to take advantage of America by calling themselves friends and allies. "It's not going to be that way anymore," he insisted in Helsinki. "You've got to pay up. You've got to pay up. You got to pay more."[69] Other countries weren't potential partners that could help advance American interests. They were instead competitors he planned to beat. He wanted to win because there is "nothing like winning, you got to win."[70] What Trump didn't recognize was that the price for winning rather than leading will be large—a world in greater disarray and an America that is less prosperous, less secure, and perhaps even less free.

Acknowledgments

Every book is to some extent a collaboration. This one started in many ways more than fifteen years ago, when, as senior fellows at the Brookings Institution, we began to examine the course and consequences of George W. Bush's foreign policy. That collaboration led to our first coauthored book, *America Unbound: The Bush Revolution in Foreign Affairs*. But it also laid the seeds for this second collaborative effort. Shortly after Donald Trump's election in November 2016, we talked about the need for a book to explain Trump's approach to foreign policy, and what it would mean for America and the world. *The Empty Throne* is the result of those first conversations.

Along the way of writing this book, we benefitted from the help and insight of many. First and most important is our publisher, Clive Priddle, who from the beginning encouraged us to write a book explaining what Trump meant for the world. Our telephone conversations, his keen eye for making an argument, and his belief in the importance of what we had to say helped make this book possible.

We owe a deep debt of gratitude to Richard Haass, and not just for his incisive comments on an early version of *The Empty Throne*. Two decades ago Richard recruited both of us into the think tank world. He pushed us to ask big questions, to provide rigorous analyses, and above all to write clearly. It is a standard he has met time and again in his own writings, and we are both better scholars because of his guidance and example.

We also benefited greatly from the comments and suggestions of friends and colleagues who read early drafts, including Edward Alden, James Goldgeier, Philip Gordon, Richard Longworth, and Paul Stares. Their questions and criticisms made *The Empty Throne* a better book. Carla Anne Robbins not only read the manuscript and gave critical comments, but improved it greatly with her masterly editorial suggestions.

Corey Cooper and John Richard Cookson helped with the research, tracking down sources and suggesting interesting quotes and articles to read. Isabella Javadin, Rodolfo Martinez-Don, Patrice Narasimhan, Angela Peterson, Madison Phillips, and Benjamin Shaver helped make sure our citations and quotations were accurate and provided additional research support. We are grateful to all of them.

We owe a special thanks to Amy Baker and Honore Raz for helping to make sure we had the time to focus on research and writing the book. Athena Bryan, Megan Daley, Patricia Dorff, Evan Fazio, Jamie Leifer, Aliya Medetbekova, Lisa Park, Melissa Raymond, Megan Schindele, Angelique Dunn, Anya Schmemann, and Sam Skinner all helped to turn the manuscript into a finished book and to share it with the world.

Over the course of the past eighteen months, we talked to many foreign government officials. They freely shared their views of the Trump administration's policies and provided important insight into the workings of a president and administration that differed so much from what had come before. While we can't list them here given that they spoke in confidence, they know who they are, and we want them to know how grateful we are for their help. We share their great concern that the United States' abdication of its global leadership role will harm not just its friends and allies, but America and Americans as well.

Last, but certainly not least, we owe so much to our spouses, Elisa and Marci, who have stood by and supported us unwaveringly as we wrote and revised the manuscript over weekends, long evenings, and even on vacations. Our thanks for this and for so much more.

Of course, we alone are responsible for any mistakes that remain.

Notes

Chapter 1—The Empty Throne

1. See Eliana Johnson, "Why Trump Hasn't Fired Mattis," *Politico Magazine*, March 23, 2018, https://www.politico.com/magazine/story/2018/03/23/james-mattis-defense-secretary-how-to-succeed-in-trump-cabinet-without-getting-fired-217699; Courtney Kube, Kristen Welker, Carol E. Lee, and Savannah Guthrie, "Trump Wanted Tenfold Increase in Nuclear Arsenal, Surprising Military," NBC News, October 11, 2017, https://www.nbcnews.com/news/all/trump-wanted-dramatic-increase-nuclear-arsenal-meeting-military-leaders-n809701; Mark Landler, "Trump, the Insurgent, Breaks with 70 Years of American Foreign Policy," *New York Times*, December 28, 2017, https://nytimes.com/2017/12/28/us/politics/trump-world-diplomacy.html; Matthew Lee and Jonathan Lemire, "How Trump's Advisers Schooled Him on Globalism," Associated Press, September 18, 2017, https://apnews.com/4cef63caf6b34cb796bc4c196d47c143; Kevin Liptak, Dan Merica, Jeff Zeleny, and Elise Labbott, "Tense and Difficult Meeting Preceded Tillerson's 'Moron' Comment," CNN, October 12, 2017, https://edition.cnn.com/2017/10/11/politics/tillerson-moron-comment/index.html; Jamie McIntyre, "Trump Briefed on Hot Spots at Pentagon Session," *Washington Examiner*, July 20, 2017, http://www.washingtonexaminer.com/trump-briefed-on-world-hot-spots-at-pentagon-session/article/2629271; Ali Vitali, "Trump at Pentagon: ISIS Is 'Falling Fast,'" NBC News, July 20, 2017, https://www.nbcnews.com/politics/white-house/trump-pentagon-isis-falling-fast-n784841; and Robert Worth, "Can Jim Mattis Hold the Line in Trump's 'War Cabinet'?" *New York Times Magazine*, March 26, 2018, https://www.nytimes.com/2018/03/26/magazine/can-jim-mattis-hold-the-line-in-trumps-war-cabinet.html.

2. Quoted in Landler, "Trump, the Insurgent, Breaks with 70 Years of American Foreign Policy."

3. Quoted in Worth, "Can Jim Mattis Hold the Line in Trump's 'War Cabinet'?"

4. Quoted in Johnson, "Why Trump Hasn't Fired Mattis."

5. "President Trump Remarks on ISIS Strategy," CSPAN, July 20, 2017, https://www.c-span.org/video/?431598-1/president-speaks-isis-strategy.

6. Quoted in Landler, "Trump, the Insurgent, Breaks with 70 Years of American Foreign Policy."

7. See, for example, Ashley Parker and John Wagner, "Trump Says 'I Inherited a Mess,' Blasts Media and Detractors at Combative News Conference," *Washington Post*, February 16, 2017, https://www.washingtonpost.com/news/post-politics/wp/2017/02/16/trump-says-he-inherited-a-mess-blasts-media-and-detractors-for-treatment-of-his-administration/?utm_term=.f1bef5ad6432.

8. Dwight D. Eisenhower, "Special Message to the Congress on the Mutual Security Program," March 13, 1959, http://www.presidency.ucsb.edu/ws/?pid=11680.

9. Francis Fukuyama, *The End of History and the Last Man* (New York: Free Press, 1992).

10. Richard Haass, *A World in Disarray: American Foreign Policy and the Crisis of the Old Order* (New York: Penguin Books, 2017).

11. Fareed Zakaria, *The Post-American World* (New York: Norton, 2009).

12. Robert Zoellick, "Whither China? From Membership to Responsibility," Remarks to the National Committee on U.S.-China Relations, New York, September 21, 2005, https://www.ncuscr.org/sites/default/files/migration/Zoellick_remarks_notes06_winter_spring.pdf.

13. Letter from Barack Obama to Donald J. Trump, reproduced in Kevin Liptak, "Exclusive: Read the Inauguration Day Letter Obama Left for Trump," CNN, September 5, 2017, http://www.cnn.com/2017/09/03/politics/obama-trump-letter-inauguration-day/index.html.

14. "A Transcript of Donald Trump's Meeting with The *Washington Post* Editorial Board," *Washington Post*, March 21, 2016, https://www.washingtonpost.com/blogs/post-partisan/wp/2016/03/21/a-transcript-of-donald-trumps-meeting-with-the-washington-post-editorial-board/?utm_term=.d1e2ad91e4cb.

15. Donald J. Trump, "Remarks at McGlohon Theatre at Spirit Square in Charlotte, North Carolina," October 26, 2016, http://www.presidency.ucsb.edu/ws/?pid=119188.

16. Donald J. Trump, "The Inaugural Address," January 20, 2017, https://www.whitehouse.gov/briefings-statements/the-inaugural-address/.

17. "Transcript: Donald Trump's Foreign Policy Speech," *New York Times*, April 27, 2016, https://www.nytimes.com/2016/04/28/us/politics/transcript-trump-foreign-policy.html?_r=0.

18. "Transcript: Trump on NATO, Turkey's Coup Attempt, and the World," *New York Times*, July 21, 2016, https://www.nytimes.com/2016/07/22/us/politics/donald-trump-foreign-policy-interview.html.

19. Ibid.

20. Quoted in Jim VandeHei and Mike Allen, "Reality Bites: Trump's Wake Up Call," Axios, January 18, 2017, https://www.axios.com/reality-bites-trumps-wake-up-call-1513299979-3bd3a708-26be-4232-8faa-6970e65c6cf1.html.

21. Quoted in Landler, "Trump, the Insurgent, Breaks with 70 Years of American Foreign Policy."

22. "Full Transcript of Donald Trump's Acceptance Speech at RNC," *Vox*, July 21, 2017, https://www.vox.com/2016/7/21/12253426/donald-trump-acceptance-speech-transcript-republican-nomination-transcript.

23. Donald J. Trump and Bill Zanker, *Think Big: Make It Happen in Business and Life* (New York: Harper Collins, 2008), p. 35.

24. Donald J. Trump, "Remarks to the 72nd Session of the United Nations General Assembly," New York, September 19, 2017, https://www.whitehouse.gov/briefings-statements/remarks-president-trump-72nd-session-united-nations-general-assembly/.

25. Interview, Tokyo, October 23, 2017.

26. Robert Kagan, *The World America Made* (New York: Alfred Knopf, 2012).

27. Major General Jin Yinan and Jia Qingguo, quoted in Evan Osnos, "Making China Great Again: How Beijing Learned to Use Trump to Its Advantage," *New Yorker*, January 8, 2018, https://www.newyorker.com/magazine/2018/01/08/making-china-great-again.

28. "CPC Newspaper Says China Should 'Grasp Historic Opportunity,'" Xinhuanet, January 15, 2018, http://www.xinhuanet.com/english/2018-01/15/c_136897189.htm?utm_source=newsletter&utm_medium=email&utm_campaign=&stream=top-stories.

29. Quoted in Peter Baker and Maggie Haberman, "Trump, Defending His Mental Fitness, Says He's a 'Very Stable Genius,'" *New York Times*, January 6, 2018, https://www.nytimes.com/2018/01/06/us/politics/trump-genius-mental-health.html.

30. Quoted in "Read President Trump's Interview with *Time* on Truth and Falsehoods," *Time*, March 22, 2017, http://time.com/4710456/donald-trump-time-interview-truth-falsehood/?xid=homepage.

31. Quoted in Peter Coy, "After Defeating Cohn, Trump's Trade Warrior Is on the Rise Again," Bloomberg, March 8, 2018, https://www.bloomberg.com/news/articles/2018-03-08/after-defeating-cohn-trump-s-trade-warrior-is-on-the-rise-again.

Chapter 2—Present at the Creation

1. Franklin Delano Roosevelt, "January 6, 1941: State of the Union (Four Freedoms)," https://millercenter.org/the-presidency/presidential-speeches/january-6-1941-state-union-four-freedoms.

2. Woodrow Wilson, "Address to Congress Requesting a Declaration of War Against Germany," April 2, 1917, https://millercenter.org/the-presidency/presidential-speeches/april-2-1917-address-congress-requesting-declaration-war.

3. Ibid.

4. Dean Acheson, *Present at the Creation: My Years in the State Department* (New York: W. W. Norton, 1969).

5. Thomas Paine, *Common Sense* (1776; repr. New York: G. P. Putnam's Sons Knickerbocker Press, 1894), https://www.law.gmu.edu/assets/files/academics/founders/Paine_CommonSense.pdf.

6. *The Writings of George Washington*, vol. 35, ed. John C. Fitzpatrick (Washington, DC: Government Printing Office, 1940), p. 234.

7. Wilson, "Address to Congress Requesting a Declaration of War Against Germany."

8. "President Woodrow Wilson's Fourteen Points," January 8, 1918, http://avalon.law.yale.edu/20th_century/wilson14.asp.

9. "The Covenant of the League of Nations," June 28, 1919, http://avalon.law.yale.edu/imt/parti.asp.

10. Franklin Delano Roosevelt, "Address to the White House Correspondents Association," February 12, 1943, http://www.presidency.ucsb.edu/ws/?pid=16360.

11. Quoted in Benn Steil, *The Battle of Bretton Woods: John Maynard Keynes, Harry Dexter White, and the Making of a New World Order* (Princeton: Princeton University Press, 2013), p. 13.

12. Quoted in Stephen Schlesinger, "FDR's Five Policemen: Creating the United Nations," *World Policy Journal* 11 (Fall 1994): 88.

13. Quoted in Thomas G. Patterson, J. Garry Clifford, and Kenneth J. Hagan, *American Foreign Relations: A History Since 1895*, vol. 2, 4th ed. (Lexington, MA: D.C. Heath, 1995), p. 28.

14. *Public Papers of the Presidents of the United States: Harry S. Truman, 1947* (Washington, DC: Government Printing Office, 1963), pp. 178–179.

15. The term was coined by French Foreign Minister Hubert Védrine. "To Paris, US Looks like a 'Hyperpower,'" *New York Times*, February 5, 1999, https://www.nytimes.com/1999/02/05/news/to-paris-us-looks-like-a-hyperpower.html.

16. George H. W. Bush, "Address Before a Joint Session of the Congress on the State of the Union," January 29, 1991, http://www.presidency.ucsb.edu/ws/?pid=19253.

17. *National Security Strategy of the United States* (Washington, DC: National Security Strategy Archive, 1991), p. v, http://nssarchive.us/NSSR/1991.pdf.

18. William J. Clinton, "Remarks at the University of Nebraska at Kearney, Nebraska," December 8, 2000, http://www.presidency.ucsb.edu/ws/?pid=957.

19. Quoted in Elizabeth Drew, *On the Edge: The Clinton Presidency* (New York: Simon and Schuster, 1994), p. 138.

20. See Ivo H. Daalder, *Getting to Dayton: The Making of America's Bosnia Policy* (Washington, DC: Brookings Institution Press, 2000).

21. "Statement by Kofi Annan on the Kosovo Crisis," Press Release SG/SM/6997, May 18, 1999, https://www.globalpolicy.org/component/content/article/190/38833.html.

22. Quoted in Stephen Sestanovich, *Maximalist: America in the World from Truman to Obama* (New York: Knopf, 2014), p. 270.

23. William J. Clinton, "Remarks on the House of Representatives Action on Permanent Normal Trade Relations with China," May 24, 2000, in *Public Papers of the Presidents of the United States: William J. Clinton* (Washington, DC: US Government Printing Office, 2001), p. 1019.

24. Anthony Lake, "From Containment to Enlargement," US Department of State Dispatch, September 27, 1993, p. 659.

25. Quoted in Alison Mitchell, "Clinton Urges NATO Expansion in 1999," *New York Times*, October 23, 1996, http://www.nytimes.com/1996/10/23/us/clinton-urges-nato-expansion-in-1999.html.

26. Lake, "From Containment to Enlargement," p. 659.

27. William J. Clinton, "Remarks at Georgetown University," November 8, 1999, http://www.presidency.ucsb.edu/ws/?pid=56892.

28. George W. Bush, "A Distinctly American Internationalism," Ronald Reagan Library, Simi Valley California, November 19, 1999, https://www.mtholyoke.edu/acad/intrel/bush/wspeech.htm.

29. See Ivo H. Daalder and James M. Lindsay, *America Unbound: The Bush Revolution in Foreign Policy* (Washington, DC: Brookings Institution Press, 2003).

30. George W. Bush, "Address Accepting the Presidential Nomination at the Republican National Convention in Philadelphia," August 3, 2000, http://www.presidency.ucsb.edu/ws/index.php?pid=25954.

31. George W. Bush, "The President's News Conference with President Jiang Zemin of China in Shanghai, China," October 19, 2001, http://www.presidency.ucsb.edu/ws/index.php?pid=64116.

32. The term is credited to Robert Zoellick, "Whither China? From Membership to Responsibility."

33. "Second Inaugural Address of George W. Bush," January 20, 2005, http://avalon.law.yale.edu/21st_century/gbush2.asp.

34. "Obama's Speech Against the Iraq War," October 2, 2002, Chicago, https://www.npr.org/templates/story/story.php?storyId=99591469.

35. "Iraq," Gallup, http://news.gallup.com/poll/1633/iraq.aspx.

36. Barack Obama, "Remarks to the Chicago Council on Global Affairs," April 23, 2007, http://www.presidency.ucsb.edu/ws/index.php?pid=77043.

37. Barack Obama, "Remarks in Des Moines, Iowa: Lessons from Iraq," October 12, 2007, http://www.presidency.ucsb.edu/ws/index.php?pid=76989.

38. David Brooks, "Obama Admires Bush," *New York Times*, May 16, 2008, http://www.nytimes.com/2008/05/16/opinion/16brooks.html.

39. Derek Chollet, *The Long Game: How Obama Defied Washington and Redefined America's Role in the World* (New York: PublicAffairs, 2016).

40. "Obama's Speech in Berlin," *New York Times*, July 24, 2008, http://www.nytimes.com/2008/07/24/us/politics/24text-obama.html.

41. Barack Obama, "Remarks in Washington, DC: 'The War We Need to Win,'" August 1, 2007, http://www.presidency.ucsb.edu/ws/index.php?pid=77040.

42. "Obama's Remarks on Iraq and Afghanistan," *New York Times*, July 15, 2008, http://www.nytimes.com/2008/07/15/us/politics/15text-obama.html.

43. "President Obama: 'The Future of Syria Must Be Determined by Its People, but President Bashar al-Assad Is Standing in Their Way," August 18, 2011, https://obamawhitehouse.archives.gov/blog/2011/08/18/president-obama-future-syria-must-be-determined-its-people-president-bashar-al-assad.

44. Quoted in Ryan Lizza, "The Consequentialist," *New Yorker*, May 2, 2011, https://www.newyorker.com/magazine/2011/05/02/the-consequentialist.

45. Karen De Young and Greg Jaffe, "NATO Runs Short on Some Munitions in Libya," *Washington Post*, April 15, 2011, https://www.washingtonpost.com/world/nato-runs-short-on-some-munitions-in-libya/2011/04/15/AF3O7EID_story.html.

46. Quoted in Jeffrey Goldberg, "The Obama Doctrine: The U.S. President Talks Through His Hardest Decisions About America's Role in the World," *Atlantic*, April 2016, https://www.theatlantic.com/magazine/archive/2016/04/the-obama-doctrine/471525/.

47. "Transcript: Obama's Remarks on Russia, NSA at the Hague on March 25," *Washington Post*, March 25, 2014, https://www.washingtonpost.com/world/national-security/transcript-obamas-remarks-on-russia-nsa-at-the-hague-on-march-25/2014/03/25/412950ca-b445-11e3-8cb6-284052554d74_story.html?utm_term=.1865132a6b7c; and "Full Transcript: President Obama's Final End of Year Press

Conference," Politico, December 16, 2016, https://www.politico.com/story/2016/12/obama-press-conference-transcript-232763.

Chapter 3—America First

1. John Shanahan, "Trump: U.S. Should Stop Paying to Defend Countries That Can Protect Selves," Associated Press, September 1, 1987, http://www.apnewsarchive.com/1987/Trump-U-S-Should-Stop-Paying-To-Defend-Countries-that-Can-Protect-Selves/id-05133dbe63ace98766527ec7d16ede08.

2. "Here's Donald Trump's Presidential Announcement Speech," *Time*, June 16, 2015, http://time.com/3923128/donald-trump-announcement-speech/.

3. Bush, "A Distinctly American Internationalism."

4. "Remarks by the President in State of the Union Address," White House, January 24, 2012, https://obamawhitehouse.archives.gov/the-press-office/2012/01/24/remarks-president-state-union-address.

5. Bush, "A Distinctly American Internationalism."

6. "Transcript: Donald Trump Foreign Policy Speech," *New York Times*, April 27, 2017, https://www.nytimes.com/2016/04/28/us/politics/transcript-trump-foreign-policy.html?_r=0.

7. "Transcript: Donald Trump Expounds on His Foreign Policy Views," *New York Times*, March 26, 2016, https://www.nytimes.com/2016/03/27/us/politics/donald-trump-transcript.html.

8. "A Transcript of Donald Trump's Meeting with The *Washington Post* Editorial Board."

9. "Transcript: Donald Trump Expounds on His Foreign Policy Views"; and Ashley Parker, "Donald Trump Says NATO Is 'Obsolete,' UN Is a Political Game," *New York Times*, April 2, 2016, https://www.nytimes.com/politics/first-draft/2016/04/02/donald-trump-tells-crowd-hed-be-fine-if-nato-broke-up/?_r=0.

10. "Transcript: Trump on NATO, Turkey's Coup Attempt, and the World," and "Transcript: Donald Trump Expounds on His Foreign Policy Views."

11. "Transcript: Donald Trump Expounds on His Foreign Policy Views."

12. Donald Trump, *Great Again: How to Fix Our Crippled America* (New York: Threshold Editions, 2015), p. 32.

13. Quoted in Nick Gass, "Trump: We Can't Allow China to Rape Our Country," Politico, May 2, 2016, https://www.politico.com/blogs/2016-gop-primary-live-updates-and-results/2016/05/trump-china-rape-america-222689.

14. "Transcript: Trump on NATO, Turkey's Coup Attempt, and the World."

15. Quoted in Cristiano Lima, "Trump Calls Trade Deal a 'Rape of Our Country,'" Politico, June 28, 2016, https://www.politico.com/story/2016/06/donald-trump-trans-pacific-partnership-224916.

16. "Full Text: Donald Trump 2016 RNC Draft Speech Transcript," Politico, July 21, 2016, https://www.politico.com/story/2016/07/full-transcript-donald-trump-nomination-acceptance-speech-at-rnc-225974.

17. Quoted in Jenna Johnson and Abigail Hauslohner, "'I Think Islam Hates Us': A Timeline of Trump's Comments About Islam and Muslims," May 20, 2017, *Washington Post*,

https://www.washingtonpost.com/news/post-politics/wp/2017/05/20/i-think-islam
-hates-us-a-timeline-of-trumps-comments-about-islam-and-muslims/?utm_term
=.55087149991f; Lauren Carroll, "In Context: Donald Trump's Comments on a Data-
base of American Muslims," PolitiFact, November 24, 2015, http://www.politifact
.com/truth-o-meter/article/2015/nov/24/donald-trumps-comments-database-american
-muslims/; and Jenna Johnson and David Weigel, "Donald Trump Calls for 'Total' Ban
on Muslims Entering United States," *Washington Post*, December 8, 2015, https://www
.washingtonpost.com/politics/2015/12/07/e56266f6-9d2b-11e5-8728-1af6af208198
_story.html?utm_term=.11a61b7278c5.

18. Quoted in Tal Kopan, "Donald Trump: Syrian Refugees a 'Trojan Horse,'" CNN,
November 16, 2015, http://www.cnn.com/2015/11/16/politics/donald-trump-syrian
-refugees/index.html; and Ali Vitali, "'The Snake': Trump Poetry Slams Syrian Refugees with Allegorical Song," NBC News, January 12, 2016, https://www.nbcnews
.com/politics/2016-election/snake-trump-poetry-slams-syrian-refugees-allegorical
-song-n495311.

19. "Transcript: Donald Trump's Foreign Policy Speech."

20. "Presidential Candidate Donald Trump Campaign Rally in Greenville, North
Carolina," CSPAN, September 6, 2016, https://www.c-span.org/video/?414823-1/donald
-trump-campaigns-greenville-north-carolina.

21. "Transcript: Trump on NATO, Turkey's Coup Attempt, and the World."

22. "Here's Donald Trump's Presidential Announcement Speech."

23. Quoted in Jeremy Diamond, "Trump: World Would Be 100% Better with
Hussein, Gadhafi in Power," CNN, October 25, 2017, http://www.cnn.com/2015/10/25
/politics/donald-trump-moammar-gadhafi-saddam-hussein/index.html.

24. Quoted in Evan McMurry, "Trump on North Korean Leader Kim Jong-un: 'You
Gotta Give Him Credit,'" ABC News, January 10, 2016, http://abcnews.go.com/Politics
/trump-north-korean-leader-kim-jong-gotta-give/story?id=36198345.

25. Quoted in Cristiano Lima, "Trump Praises Egypt's al-Sisi: 'He's a Fantastic
Guy,'" Politico, September 22, 2016, https://www.politico.com/story/2016/09/trump
-praises-egypts-al-sisi-hes-a-fantastic-guy-228560.

26. Quoted in Jeremy Diamond, "Timeline: Donald Trump's Praise for Vladimir
Putin," CNN, July 29, 2016, http://www.cnn.com/2016/07/28/politics/donald
-trump-vladimir-putin-quotes/index.html.

27. Quoted in "Donald Trump: Putin Outsmarted Obama and the U.S.," *Politicking
with Larry King*, Ora TV, October 3, 2013, https://www.youtube.com/watch?v
=J2nAk5mhnIE.

28. Quoted in Christopher Massie and Andrew Kaczynski, "Trump Called Russia's
Invasion of Ukraine 'So Smart' in 2014," BuzzFeed, August 1, 2016, https://www.buzzfeed
.com/christophermassie/trump-called-russias-invasion-of-ukraine-so-smart-in
-2014?utm_term=.helO8NeJM#.kk75L729o.

29. Quoted in Colin Campbell, "Donald Trump Left Joe Scarborough Stunned After
Being Asked About Vladimir Putin Killing Journalists," *Business Insider*, December 18,
2015, http://www.businessinsider.com/donald-trump-vladimir-putin-joe-scarborough
-2015-12.

30. Quoted in Diamond, "Timeline: Donald Trump's Praise for Vladimir Putin."

31. "Transcript of the First Debate," *New York Times*, September 27, 2016, https://www.nytimes.com/2016/09/27/us/politics/transcript-debate.html.

32. "Transcript: Donald Trump Expounds on His Foreign Policy Views."

33. "Transcript: Trump on NATO, Turkey's Coup Attempt, and the World."

34. Among others, see "Public Uncertain, Divided Over America's Place in the World," Pew Research Center, May 5, 2016, http://www.people-press.org/2016/05/05/1-americas-global-role-u-s-superpower-status/; and Dina Smeltz, Ivo Daalder, Karl Friedhoff, and Craig Kafura, *What Americans Think About America First* (Chicago: Chicago Council on Global Affairs, 2017), https://www.thechicagocouncil.org/sites/default/files/ccgasurvey 2017_what_americans_think_about_america_first.pdf.

35. Secretary of Defense Robert Gates, quoted in Thom Shanker, "Defense Secretary Warns NATO of 'Dim' Future," *New York Times*, June 10, 2011, http://www.nytimes.com/2011/06/11/world/europe/11gates.html.

36. Quoted in Goldberg, "The Obama Doctrine."

37. Mark J. Perry, "The U.S. Produces 40% More Factory Output Today vs. 20 Years Ago with 5m Fewer Workers. Technology Job Theft?" AEIdeas, July 24, 2017, http://www.aei.org/publication/the-us-produces-40-more-factory-output-today-vs-20-years-ago-with-5m-fewer-workers-technology-job-theft/.

38. See David H. Autor, David Corn, and Gordon H. Hanson, "The China Shock: Learning from Labor Market Adjustment to Large Changes in Trade," NBER Working Paper 21906, January 2016, http://nber.org/papers/w21906.

39. For an assessment of Trump's claims on the Iraq War, see Eugene Kiely, "Donald Trump and the Iraq War," FactCheck.org, February 19, 2016, https://www.factcheck.org/2016/02/donald-trump-and-the-iraq-war/. On Trump's insistence that he had predicted "very strongly" that the Iraq War was a mistake, see "Transcript: Republican Presidential Debate," *New York Times*, December 15, 2015, https://www.nytimes.com/2015/12/16/us/politics/transcript-main-republican-presidential-debate.html.

40. "Here's Donald Trump's Presidential Announcement Speech."

41. Quoted in Tara Golshan, "Donald Trump Doesn't Care About Trade Wars, and It's Probably Keeping Economists Up at Night," *Vox*, May 20, 2016, https://www.vox.com/2016/5/20/11719594/donald-trump-trade-wars.

42. Quoted in Kurtis Lee, "Here Is Who Donald Trump Is Taking Advice From," *Los Angeles Times*, April 7, 2016, http://www.latimes.com/nation/politics/la-na-trump-foreign-policy-team-20160407-htmlstory.html.

43. Winston Churchill, "Blood, Toil, Tears and Sweat," Speech to the House of Commons, May 13, 1940, https://www.americanrhetoric.com/speeches/winstonchurchill bloodtoiltearssweat.htm.

44. David E. Sanger and Maggie Haberman, "In Donald Trump's Worldview, America Comes First, and Everybody Else Pays," *New York Times*, March 26, 2016, https://www.nytimes.com/2016/03/27/us/politics/donald-trump-foreign-policy.html.

45. Stephen Sestanovich, "The Brilliant Incoherence of Trump's Foreign Policy," *Atlantic*, May 2017, https://www.theatlantic.com/magazine/archive/2017/05/the-brilliant-incoherence-of-trumps-foreign-policy/521430/.

46. Quoted in Ian Schwartz, "Trump: 'We Will Have So Much Winning If I Get Elected That You May Get Bored With Winning,'" RealClearPolitics, September 9, 2015, https://www.realclearpolitics.com/video/2015/09/09/trump_we_will_have_so_much _winning_if_i_get_elected_that_you_may_get_bored_with_winning.html.

47. "Transcript: Donald Trump Expounds on His Foreign Policy Views."

48. Quoted in David Shefinksi, "Trump: 'I'd Bomb the Hell out of the Oil Fields,'" *Washington Times*, July 9, 2015, https://www.washingtontimes.com/news/2015/jul/9 /donald-trump-id-bomb-hell-out-oil-fields/.

49. Quoted in Eric Bradner and Tal Kopan, "Trump: I'd Declare War on ISIS, Send 'Very Few' Troops," CNN, July 17, 2016, http://www.cnn.com/2016/07/17/politics /donald-trump-mike-pence-60-minutes-interview/index.html.

50. "Transcript of the Republican Presidential Debate in Florida," *New York Times*, March 11, 2016, https://www.nytimes.com/2016/03/11/us/politics/transcript-of-the -republican-presidential-debate-in-florida.html?_r=0.

51. Quoted in Andrew Kaczynski and Christopher Massie, "Trump Claims He Didn't Support Libyan Intervention—But He Did, on Video," BuzzFeed, February 25, 2016, https://www.buzzfeed.com/andrewkaczynski/trump-claims-he-didnt-support -libya-intervention-but-he-did?utm_term=.kc4o45YAw#.axmwl5GLA; and Donald J. Trump (@realDonaldTrump), Twitter, June 15, 2013, https://twitter.com/realdon-aldtrump/status/346063000056254464.

52. Eduardo Porter, "Trump Isn't Wrong on China Currency Manipulation, Just Late," *New York Times*, April 11, 2017, https://www.nytimes.com/2017/04/11/business /economy/trump-china-currency-manipulation-trade.html.

53. Quoted in Jacob Pramuk, "Trump: I Don't Give a Specific ISIS Plan Because I Don't Want Enemies to Know It," CNBC, September 7, 2016, https://www.cnbc .com/2016/09/07/trump-i-dont-give-a-specific-isis-plan-because-i-dont-want-enemies -to-know-it.html.

54. "Transcript: Donald Trump's Foreign Policy Speech."

55. "Here's Donald Trump's Presidential Announcement Speech."

56. "Transcript: Republican Presidential Debate."

57. "Here's Donald Trump's Presidential Announcement Speech"; and "Transcript of the First Debate."

58. Hugh Hewitt, "Donald Trump on the Day He Took the Pledge," HughHewitt.com, September 3, 2015, http://www.hughhewitt.com/donald-trump-on-the-day-he-took -the-pledge/.

59. Quoted in Dan Balz, "Bush Takes Soft Line on Abortion Stance of Running Mate," *Washington Post*, June 24, 1999, p. A7, https://www.washingtonpost.com/archive /politics/1999/06/24/bush-takes-soft-line-on-abortion-stance-of-running-mate /58e84a42-db03-4257-9290-bb72523b393d/?utm_term=.e429b25606b1.

60. Quoted in Eric Zorn, "Nobody Is More Skeptical of Donald Trump's Boasts than I Am," *Chicago Tribune*, October 18, 2016, http://www.chicagotribune.com/news /opinion/zorn/ct-donald-trump-ignorant-policy-perspec-zorn-1019-20161018 -column.html; Chris Cillizza, "The Dangerous Anger of Donald Trump," *Washington Post*, November 13, 2015, https://www.washingtonpost.com/news/the-fix/wp/2015/11/13

/the-remarkably-unappealling-anger-of-donald-trump/?utm_term=.896fa7ed07aa;
Tim Hains, "Trump: I Own a Store in Manhattan Worth More than Mitt Romney,"
RealClearPolitics.com, March 3, 2016, https://www.realclearpolitics.com/video/2016/03
/03/trump_i_own_a_store_in_manhattan_worth_more_than_mitt_romney.html;
Donald J. Trump, "Remarks at the AIPAC Policy Conference in Washington, DC," March
21, 2016, http://www.presidency.ucsb.edu/ws/?pid=116597; and "Trump Explains Why
He Thinks the Primary Process Is 'Unfair,'" FoxNews.com, April 13, 2016, http://www
.foxnews.com/transcript/2016/04/13/trump-explains-why-feels-primary-process-is-unfair.html.

61. Hewitt, "Donald Trump on the Day He Took the Pledge."

62. "Transcript: Donald Trump's Foreign Policy Speech."

63. Hugh Hewitt, "Donald Trump Returns," HughHewitt.com, September 21, 2015,
http://www.hughhewitt.com/donald-trump-returns/.

64. See Missy Ryan and Steve Mufson, "One of Trump's Foreign Policy Advisers Is
a 2009 College Grad Who Lists Model UN as a Credential," *Washington Post*, March
22, 2016, https://www.washingtonpost.com/news/checkpoint/wp/2016/03/21/meet
-the-men-shaping-donald-trumps-foreign-policy-views/?utm_term=.3c274c9cbb3f.

65. Quoted in Eliza Collins, "Trump: I Consult Myself on Foreign Policy," Politico,
March 16, 2016, https://www.politico.com/blogs/2016-gop-primary-live-updates-and
-results/2016/03/trump-foreign-policy-adviser-220853.

66. Quoted in Ashley Killough, "Lindsey Graham: Donald Trump Is a 'Jackass,'" CNN, July 21 2015, http://www.cnn.com/2015/07/20/politics/jeb-bush-john
-mccain-donald-trump/index.html; Jesse Burns, "Graham: GOP Will Get 'Slaughtered'
If Trump Nominee," The Hill, February 17, 2016, http://thehill.com/blogs/ballot-box
/presidential-races/269675-graham-republicans-will-get-slaughtered-if-trump
-nominee; Colin Campbell, "Republican Rival Goes Nuclear: 'Trump's a Race-Baiting,
Xenophobic, Religious Bigot," *Business Insider*, December 8, 2015, http://www
.businessinsider.com/lindsey-graham-donald-trump-bigot-muslim-plan-cnn-2015-12;
Daniel White, "Jeb Bush: 'Donald Trump Is a Jerk,'" *Time*, December 19, 2015, http://time
.com/4156094/jeb-bush-donald-trump-jerk/; David Sherfinski, "The Gloves Are Off:
Rubio Slams Trump as 'Con Artist' in Wake of Nasty Debate," *Washington Times*, February 26, 2016, https://www.washingtontimes.com/news/2016/feb/26/marco-rubio
-donald-trump-con-artist-who-sticks-it-/; Pema Levy, "Five Times Rubio Slammed
Trump—Before Promising to Vote for Him," *Mother Jones*, May 27, 2016, http://www
.motherjones.com/politics/2016/05/marco-rubio-will-vote-donald-trump/; and Melanie
Mason, "Ted Cruz Lobs Searing Attack at Donald Trump, Calls Him 'Amoral'
and 'a Pathological Liar,'" *Los Angeles Times*, May 3, 2016, http://www.latimes.com
/politics/la-na-live-updates-indian-ted-cruz-lobs-searing-attack-on-donald-trump
-call-1462295410-htmlstory.html.

67. "Open Letter on Donald Trump from GOP National Security Leaders," *War on
the Rocks*, March 2, 2016, https://warontherocks.com/2016/03/open-letter-on-donald
-trump-from-gop-national-security-leaders/.

68. "A Letter from G.O.P. National Security Officials Opposing Donald Trump,"
New York Times, August 8, 2016, https://www.nytimes.com/interactive/2016/08/08/us
/politics/national-security-letter-trump.html.

Chapter 4—A Very Organized Process

1. Corey R. Lewandowski and David N. Bossie, *Let Trump Be Trump: The Inside Story of His Rise to the Presidency* (New York: Center Street, 2017), p. 245.

2. Donald J. Trump, Facebook, November 16, 2016, https://www.facebook.com /DonaldTrump/posts/10158138791990725.

3. Quoted in Julie Pace, "Trump Son-in-Law Kushner Expected to Stay a Power Center," *Boston Globe*, November 14, 2016, https://www.bostonglobe.com/news /politics/2016/11/14/trump-orbit-son-law-jared-kushner-expected-stay-power-center /NXX8jsbgZNOMLaSEgIFdEL/story.html.

4. Louis Nelson, "Trump Says He's Consulted Obama on Cabinet Picks," Politico, December 7, 2016, https://www.politico.com/story/2016/12/trump-obama-consultation -cabinet-232304.

5. Nancy Cook, "How Flynn—and the Russia Scandal—Landed in the West Wing," Politico, November 11, 2017, https://www.politico.com/story/2017/11/11/how-michael -flynn-got-west-wing-job-244790.

6. Quoted in Matthew Rosenberg, Mark Mazzetti, and Adam Goldman, "Trump's National Security Pick Sees Ally in Fight Against Islamists: Russia," *New York Times*, January 10, 2017, https://www.nytimes.com/2017/01/10/us/politics/trumps-national -security-pick-sees-ally-in-fight-against-islamists-russia.html.

7. Eric Mack, "Retired Gen. Keane Declines Trump's Defense Secretary Offer," Newsmax, November 20, 2016, https://www.newsmax.com/headline/gen-jack-keane -declines-defense-secretary-trump-administration/2016/11/20/id/759862/.

8. Donald J. Trump (@realDonaldTrump), Twitter, November 20, 2016, https:// twitter.com/realDonaldTrump/status/800332639844659201.

9. Quoted in Michael D. Shear, Julie Hirschfeld Davis, and Maggie Haberman, "Trump, in Interview, Moderates Views but Defies Conventions," *New York Times*, November 22, 2016, https://www.nytimes.com/2016/11/22/us/politics/donald-trump -visit.html.

10. "Transcript: The Middle East at an Inflection Point with Gen. Mattis," Center for Strategic and International Studies, April 22, 2016, https://www.csis.org/analysis /middle-east-inflection-point-gen-mattis.

11. Quoted in Michael R. Gordon and Eric Schmitt, "James Mattis, Outspoken Retired Marine, Is Trump's Choice as Defense Secretary," *New York Times*, December 1, 2016, https://www.nytimes.com/2016/12/01/us/politics/james-mattis-secrtary-of-defense -trump.html.

12. Quoted in Dexter Filkins, "James Mattis, a Warrior in Washington," *New Yorker*, May 29, 2017, http://www.newyorker.com/magazine/2017/05/29/james-mattis-a-warrior -in-washington.

13. Quoted in Gordon and Schmitt, "James Mattis, Outspoken Retired Marine, Is Trump's Choice as Defense Secretary."

14. Quoted in ibid.

15. Quoted in Filkins, "James Mattis, a Warrior in Washington."

16. Quoted in ibid.

17. Quoted in Elise Labott, "Donald Trump Told Nikki Haley She Could Speak Her Mind. She's Doing Just That," CNN, September 2017, http://www.cnn.com /interactive/2017/politics/state/nikki-haley-donald-trump-united-nations/.

18. Quoted in Jeremy W. Peters and Maggie Haberman, "Republicans Divided Between Romney and Giuliani for Secretary of State," *New York Times*, November 24, 2016, https://www.nytimes.com/2016/11/24/us/politics/donald-trump-mitt-romney -rudy-giuliani-state.html.

19. Quoted in Michael Kranish, Anne Gearan, Dan Balz, and Philip Rucker, "Trump Wasn't Happy with His State Department Finalists. Then He Heard a New Name," *Washington Post*, December 13, 2016, https://www.washingtonpost.com/politics /trump-wasnt-happy-with-his-state-department-finalists-then-he-heard-a-new -name/2016/12/13/0727658e-c161-11e6-8422-eac61c0ef74d_story.html?utm_term =.a6d337ffa225.

20. Peter Nicholas, Michael C. Bender, and Carol E. Lee, "How Rex Tillerson, a Late Entry to Be Secretary of State, Got Donald Trump's Nod," *Wall Street Journal*, December 14, 2016, https://www.wsj.com/articles/how-rex-tillerson-a-late-entry-to-be-secretary -of-state-got-donald-trumps-nod-1481676709.

21. Quoted in Jason Zengerle, "Rex Tillerson and the Unraveling of the State Department," *New York Times Magazine*, October 17, 2017, https://mobile.nytimes .com/2017/10/17/magazine/rex-tillerson-and-the-unraveling-of-the-state-department .html?_r=1&referer=.

22. "Trump: Tillerson Is 'Much More than a Business Executive,'" Fox News, December 10, 2016, http://video.foxnews.com/v/5242979174001/#sp=show-clips.

23. "Transcript: Remarks at Town Hall: Rex W. Tillerson, Secretary of State; Steven (Steve) Goldstein, Under Secretary for Public Diplomacy and Public Affairs," US Department of State, December 12, 2017, https://www.state.gov/secretary /20172018tillerson/remarks/2017/12/276563.htm.

24. Quoted in Erin McPike, "Trump's Diplomat," IJR.com, March 21, 2017, https:// ijr.com/2017/03/814687-trumps-diplomat/.

25. Quoted in Neil MacFarquhar and Andrew E. Kramer, "How Rex Tillerson Changed His Tune on Russia and Came to Court Its Rulers," *New York Times*, December 20, 2016, https://www.nytimes.com/2016/12/20/world/europe/russia-rex-tillerson -donald-trump-secretary-of-state.html?_r=0.

26. Quoted in David E. Sanger, Maggie Haberman, and Clifford Krauss, "Rex Tillerson, Exxon Chief, Is Expected to Be Pick for Secretary of State," *New York Times*, December 10, 2016, https://www.nytimes.com/2016/12/10/us/politics/rex-tillerson -secretary-of-state-trump.html.

27. Marco Rubio (@marcorubio), Twitter, December 11, 2016, https://twitter.com /marcorubio/status/807962818272235521?ref_src=twsrc%5Etfw.

28. Quoted in Peter Nicholas, Paul Vieira, and José de Córdoba, "Why Donald Trump Decided to Back Off NAFTA Threat," *Wall Street Journal*, April 27, 2017, https://www.wsj.com/articles/trump-says-nafta-partners-persuaded-him-to-keep-u-s -in-trade-pact-1493320127.

29. Zengerle, "Rex Tillerson and the Unraveling of the State Department."

30. "Transcript of Clinton's Remarks on White House Transition," *New York Times*, November 5, 1992, http://www.nytimes.com/1992/11/05/nyregion/transcript -of-clinton-s-remarks-on-white-house-transition.html.

31. Adam Entous and Evan Osnos, "Jared Kushner Is China's Trump Card," *New Yorker*, January 29, 2018, https://www.newyorker.com/magazine/2018/01/29/jared -kushner-is-chinas-trump-card.

32. Lauren Said-Moorhouse, "Golf Legend Greg Norman Hooks Up Australian PM's Call with Donald Trump," CNN, November 17, 2016, http://www.cnn .com/2016/11/17/politics/greg-norman-malcolm-turnbull-call-donald-trump /index.html.

33. Lauren Said-Moorhouse, "What's Different About Donald Trump's Phone Calls with World Leaders?" CNN, December 2, 2016, http://www.cnn.com/2016/11/18 /politics/donald-trump-world-leaders-calls/index.html.

34. Quoted in Lucy Fisher, "Trump's Special Relationship . . . with the Queen," *The Times*, November 17, 2016, https://www.thetimes.co.uk/article/trumps-special -relationship-with-the-queen-fkwfqnx9m.

35. Official Site of the President of the Republic of Kazakhstan, "Telephone Conversation with the United States President-elect Donald Trump," akorda.kz, November 30, 2016, http://www.akorda.kz/en/events/international_community/phone_calls /telephone-conversation-with-the-united-states-president-elect-donald-trump.

36. Press Information Department: Ministry of Information Broadcasting, National History, and Literary Heritage, "PR No. 298 PM Telephones President-Elect USA Islamabad," Government of Pakistan, November 30, 2016, http://pid.gov.pk/site/press _detail/5886.

37. Quoted in Felipe Villamor, "Rodrigo Duterte Says Donald Trump Endorses His Violent Antidrug Campaign," *New York Times*, December 3, 2016, https://www.nytimes .com/2016/12/03/world/asia/philippines-rodrigo-duterte-donald-trump.html.

38. Donald J. Trump (@realDonaldTrump), Twitter, December 2, 2016, https:// twitter.com/realDonaldTrump/status/804848711599882240.

39. "Transcript: Exclusive: Donald Trump on Cabinet Picks, Transition Process," Fox News, December 11, 2016, http://www.foxnews.com/transcript/2016/12/11/exclusive -donald-trump-on-cabinet-picks-transition-process.html.

40. Te-Ping Chen and Carol E. Lee, "Donald Trump Commits to 'One China' Policy in Call with Xi Jinping," *Wall Street Journal*, February 10, 2017, https://www.wsj.com /articles/donald-trump-affirms-commitment-to-one-china-policy-in-call-with -xi-jinping-1486699771.

41. "Full Transcript: President Obama's Final End-of-Year Press Conference," Politico, December 16, 2016, https://www.politico.com/story/2016/12/obama-press-conference -transcript-232763.

42. Carol D. Leonnig, Adam Entous, Devlin Barrett, and Matt Zapotosky, "Michael Flynn Pleads Guilty to Lying to FBI on Contacts with Russian Ambassador," *Washington Post*, December 1, 2017, https://www.washingtonpost.com/politics/ michael-flynn-charged-with-making-false-statement-to-the-fbi/2017/12/01/e03a6c48 -d6a2-11e7-9461-ba77d604373d_story.html?utm_term=.64b758520cf4.

43. Kate O'Keeffe and Farnaz Fassihi, "Inside the Trump Team's Push on Israel Vote That Mike Flynn Lied About," *Wall Street Journal*, January 5, 2018, https://www.wsj.com/articles/inside-the-trump-teams-lobbying-blitz-on-2016-u-n-israel-vote-1515153600.

44. Donald J. Trump (@realDonaldTrump), Twitter, December 22, 2016, https://twitter.com/realDonaldTrump/status/811928543366148096.

45. Colum Lynch, "Flynn Pressured U.N. on Israel Vote before Taking Office," *Foreign Policy*, February 17, 2017, https://foreignpolicy.com/2017/02/17/logan-trump-israel-flynn-pressured-u-n-on-israel-vote-before-taking-office/; and Barak Ravid, "Britain Pulled the Strings and Netanyahu Warned New Zealand It Was Declaring War: New Details on Israel's Battle Against the UN Vote," *Haaretz*, December 28, 2016, https://www.haaretz.com/israel-news/.premium-1.761706.

46. Colum Lynch, "Jared Kushner Struck Out in His First Foray into Middle East Diplomacy," *Foreign Policy*, March 21, 2017, https://foreignpolicy.com/2017/03/21/jared-kushner-struck-out-in-his-first-foray-into-middle-east-diplomacy/.

47. "Joint Statement from the Department of Homeland Security and Office of the Director of National Intelligence on Election Security," US Department of Homeland Security, October 7, 2016, https://www.dhs.gov/news/2016/10/07/joint-statement-department-homeland-security-and-office-director-national.

48. Barack Obama, "Statement by the President on Actions in Response to Russian Malicious Cyber Activity and Harassment," obamawhitehouse.archives.gov, December 29, 2016, https://obamawhitehouse.archives.gov/the-press-office/2016/12/29/statement-president-actions-response-russian-malicious-cyber-activity.

49. "Transcript: Exclusive: Donald Trump on Cabinet Picks, Transition Process."

50. Ellen Nakashima, Adam Entous, and Greg Miller, "Russian Ambassador Told Moscow That Kushner Wanted Secret Communications Channel with Kremlin," *Washington Post*, May 26, 2017, https://www.washingtonpost.com/world/national-security/russian-ambassador-told-moscow-that-kushner-wanted-secret-communications-channel-with-kremlin/2017/05/26/520a14b4-422d-11e7-9869-bac8b446820a_story.html?utm_term=.9f2d7a918aa3.

51. Michael S. Schmidt, Sharon LaFraniere, and Scott Shane, "Emails Dispute White House Claims That Flynn Acted Independently on Russia," *New York Times*, December 2, 2017, https://www.nytimes.com/2017/12/02/us/russia-mcfarland-flynn-trump-emails.html.

52. Andrew Roth, "Putin Says He Won't Deport U.S. Diplomats as He Looks to Cultivate Relations with Trump," *Washington Post*, December 30, 2016, https://www.washingtonpost.com/world/russia-plans-retaliation-and-serious-discomfortoverus-hacking-sanctions/2016/12/30/4efd3650-ce12-11e6-85cd-e66532e35a44_story.html?tid=a_inl&utm_term=.5a1d15621d87.

53. Donald J. Trump (@realDonaldTrump), Twitter, December 30, 2016, https://twitter.com/realDonaldTrump/status/814919370711461890.

Chapter 5—A Fine-Tuned Machine

1. Trump, "Transcript: The Inaugural Address," January 20, 2017, https://www.whitehouse.gov/briefings-statements/the-inaugural-address/.

2. Quoted in Yasha Ali, "What George W. Bush Really Thought of Donald Trump's Inauguration," *New York Magazine*, March 29, 2017, http://nymag.com/daily/intelligencer/2017/03/what-george-w-bush-really-thought-of-trumps-inauguration.html.

3. Quoted in "Trump Era Signals Dramatic Changes," *Global Times*, January 20, 2017, http://www.globaltimes.cn//content/1029958.shtml.

4. Quoted in Sofia Fischer, "How the World Reacted to Trump's Inauguration as US President," *The Guardian*, January 21, 2017, https://www.theguardian.com/world/2017/jan/21/how-world-reacted-donald-trump-inauguration-us-president.

5. Trump, "Transcript: The Inaugural Address."

6. Quoted in Glenn Thrush and Maggie Haberman, "Trump and Staff Rethink Tactics After Stumbles," *New York Times*, February 5, 2017, https://www.nytimes.com/2017/02/05/us/politics/trump-white-house-aides-strategy.html.

7. Jim VandeHei and Mike Allen, "The Committee to Save America," Axios, August 10, 2017, https://www.axios.com/the-committee-to-save-america-1513304754-2e4002e8-5720-422a-a668-8db4210785fb.html.

8. *The Public Papers of the President of the United States: Ronald Reagan, 1988–1989* (Washington DC: US Government Printing Office, 1991), p. 1722.

9. Quoted in Michael Finnegan, "'It's going to be a big, fat, beautiful wall!': Trump's words make his California climb an even steeper trek," *Los Angeles Times*, June 3, 2016, http://www.latimes.com/politics/la-na-pol-trump-california-campaign-20160602-snap-story.html; Quoted in Katie Zezima, "Donald Trump calls for 'extreme vetting' of people looking to come to the United States," *Washington Post*, August 15, 2016, https://www.washingtonpost.com/news/post-politics/wp/2016/08/15/donald-trump-calls-for-extreme-vetting-of-people-looking-to-come-to-the-united-states/?utm_term=.95efdcb9eb65; Quoted in Tom LoBianco, "Donald Trump promises 'deportation force' to remove 11 million," CNN.com, November 12, 2015, https://www.cnn.com/2015/11/11/politics/donald-trump-deportation-force-debate-immigration/index.html; Quoted in Jenna Johnson, "Donald Trump calls for a 'total and complete shutdown of Muslims entering the United States," *Washington Post*, December 7, 2015, https://www.washingtonpost.com/news/post-politics/wp/2015/12/07/donald-trump-calls-for-total-and-complete-shutdown-of-muslims-entering-the-united-states/?utm_term=.bcfa310a5be2.

10. Quoted in Michael D. Shear and Helene Cooper, "Trump Bars Refugees and Citizens of 7 Muslim Countries," *New York Times*, January 27, 2017, https://www.nytimes.com/2017/01/27/us/politics/trump-syrian-refugees.html.

11. Quoted in Michael D. Shear and Julie Hirschfeld Davis, "Stoking Fears, Trump Defied Bureaucracy to Advance Immigration Agenda," *New York Times*, December 23, 2017, https://www.nytimes.com/2017/12/23/us/politics/trump-immigration.html.

12. Quoted in Gabriel Sherman, "'I Have Power': Is Steve Bannon Running For President?" *Vanity Fair*, December 21, 2017, https://www.vanityfair.com/news/2017/12/bannon-for-president-trump-kushner-ivanka.

13. Donald J. Trump (@realDonaldTrump), Twitter, February 4, 2017, https://twitter.com/realDonaldTrump/status/827981079042805761.

14. Quoted in "Chancellor Rejects Immigration Ban," bundesregierung.de, January 30, 2017, https://www.bundesregierung.de/Content/EN/Artikel/2017/01_en/2017 -01-30-einreiseverbot-usa_en.html?nn=709674.

15. Quoted in Joanna Plucinska, "Theresa May, Angela Merkel among European Leaders Bashing Trump's Refugee Move," Politico, January 28, 2017, https://www.politico .eu/article/leaders-react-to-us-president-donald-trump-refugee-and-muslim-restrictions/.

16. Justin Trudeau (@JustinTrudeau), Twitter, January 28, 2017, https://twitter.com /JustinTrudeau/status/825438460265762816.

17. Donald J. Trump, "Presidential Memorandum regarding Withdrawal of the United States from the Trans-Pacific Partnership Negotiations and Agreement," January 23, 2017, https://www.whitehouse.gov/presidential-actions/presidential-memorandum-regarding -withdrawal-united-states-trans-pacific-partnership-negotiations-agreement/.

18. Ibid.

19. "Full Transcript: Donald Trump's Jobs Plan Speech," Politico, June 28, 2016, https:// www.politico.com/story/2016/06/full-transcript-trump-job-plan-speech-224891.

20. Quoted in Maggie Severns, "Trump Pins NAFTA, 'Worst Trade Deal Ever,' on Clinton," Politico, September 26, 2016, https://www.politico.com/story/2016/09 /trump-clinton-come-out-swinging-over-nafta-228712.

21. Quoted in Ashley Parker, Philip Rucker, Damian Paletta, and Karen DeYoung, "'I Was All Set to Terminate': Inside Trump's Sudden Shift on NAFTA," *Washington Post*, April 27, 2017, https://www.washingtonpost.com/politics/i-was-all-set-to-terminate -inside-trumps-sudden-shift-on-nafta/2017/04/27/0452a3fa-2b65-11e7-b605-33413 c691853_story.html.

22. Quoted in Kai Diekmann, Michael Gove, and Daniel Biskup, "Es Wird Extreme Sicherheits-Checks Geben," Bild, January 15, 2017, http://www.bild.de/bild-plus/politik /ausland/donald-trump/das-grosse-bild-interview-49790140,jsRedirectFrom =conversionToLogin.bild.html.

23. Michael Gove, "Donald Trump: 'Brexit Will Be a Great Thing . . . You Were So Smart,'" *Times*, January 16, 2017, https://www.thetimes.co.uk/article/brexit-will-be-a -great-thing-you-were-so-smart-to-get-out-09gp9z357.

24. Ibid.

25. Quoted in Landler, "Trump, the Insurgent, Breaks with 70 Years of American Foreign Policy."

26. Donald J. Trump (@realDonaldTrump), Twitter, January 26, 2017, https://twitter .com/realDonaldTrump/status/824616644370714627.

27. Quoted in Tracy Wilkinson and Brian Bennet, "Trump, in Meeting with Mexican President, Again Insists Mexico Will Pay for the Wall," *Los Angeles Times*, July 7, 2017, http://beta.latimes.com/nation/la-fg-trump-mexico-20170707-story.html.

28. Greg Miller, Julie Vitkovskaya, and Reuben Fischer-Baum, "'This Deal Will Make Me Look Terrible': Full Transcripts of Trump's Calls with Mexico and Australia," *Washington Post*, August 3, 2017, https://www.washingtonpost.com/graphics/2017 /politics/australia-mexico-transcripts/.

29. Quoted in Michael C. Bender, "Trump on Tough Phone Calls with Foreign Leaders: 'Don't Worry About It,'" *Wall Street Journal*, February 2, 2017, https://www

.wsj.com/articles/trump-on-tough-phone-calls-with-foreign-leaders-dont-worry -about-it-1486047568.

30. Interview with a senior British diplomat, Washington, DC, March 30, 2017.

31. "Joint Statement from President Donald J. Trump and Prime Minister Shinzo Abe," February 10, 2017, https://www.whitehouse.gov/briefings-statements /joint-statement-president-donald-j-trump-prime-minister-shinzo-abe/.

32. Gove, "Donald Trump: 'Brexit Will Be a Great Thing . . . You Were So Smart.'"

33. Greg Miller, Greg Jaffe, and Philip Rucker, "Doubting the Intelligence, Trump Pursues Putin and Leaves a Russian Threat Unchecked," *Washington Post*, December 14, 2017, https://www.washingtonpost.com/graphics/2017/world/national-security/donald-trump -pursues-vladimir-putin-russian-election-hacking/?tid=a_inl&utm_term=.b73aa0528c0c.

34. Ivo Daalder, "The Value of NATO Goes beyond Defence Spending," *Financial Times*, May 23, 2017, https://www.ft.com/content/a68bf372-3Bd6-11e7-82b6 -896b95f30f58.

35. Interview with a senior German diplomat, Berlin, March 23, 2017. See also Roger Cohen, "The Offender of the Free World," *New York Times*, March 28, 2017, https://www.nytimes.com/2017/03/28/opinion/the-offender-of-the-free-world.html; and Bojan Pancevski, "Germany Slams 'Intimidating' £300bn White House Bill," *Times*, March 26, 2017, http://www.thetimes.co.uk/article/germany-dismisses-white-houses -intimidating-300bn-bill-for-defence-dl7dk629k.

36. Donald J. Trump (@realDonaldTrump), Twitter, March 18, 2017, https://twitter .com/realDonaldTrump/status/843088518339612673; https://twitter.com/realDonaldTrump /status/843090516283723776.

37. Interview, April 5, 2018.

38. Gove, "Donald Trump: 'Brexit Will Be a Great Thing . . . You Were So Smart.'"

39. Donald J. Trump (@realDonaldTrump), Twitter, November 21, 2016, https:// twitter.com/realDonaldTrump/status/800887087780294656.

40. Interview with a senior European diplomat, Chicago, January 10, 2017.

41. Interview, Berlin, March 23, 2017.

42. Quoted in Susan B. Glasser, "Donald Trump's Year of Living Dangerously," *Politico Magazine*, January–February 2018, https://www.politico.com/magazine /story/2018/01/02/donald-trump-foreign-policy-analysis-dangerous-216202.

43. "'United We Stand, Divided We Fall': Letter by President Donald Tusk to the 27 EU Heads of State or Government on the Future of the EU before the Malta Summit," Council of the European Union, January 31, 2017, http://www.consilium.europa.eu /en/press/press-releases/2017/01/31/tusk-letter-future-europe/.

44. Quoted in Gardiner Harris, "As Ties with U.S. Cool, Europeans Look to Forge Other Alliances," *New York Times*, February 10, 2017, https://www.nytimes.com/2017/02/10 /world/europe/as-ties-with-us-cool-europeans-look-to-forge-other-alliances.html.

45. Quoted in Susan B. Glasser, "Trump Takes On the Blob," *Politico Magazine*, March/April 2017, http://politi.co/2m9L3Ox.

46. Julie Pace and Eric Tucker, "Trump Fires Justice Dept. Head over Executive Order Defiance," *AP News*, January 31, 2017, https://apnews.com/98c2a8cac3b74bd e803f03af4e53af47/Trump-faces-blowback-from-Cabinet,-diplomats-for-refugee-ban.

47. Donald J. Trump, "Remarks by President Trump in Press Conference," February 16, 2017, https://www.whitehouse.gov/briefings-statements/remarks-president-trump-press-conference/.

48. See Ivo Daalder and I. M. Destler, *In the Shadow of the Oval Office* (New York: Simon and Schuster, 2009).

49. "National Security Presidential Memorandum—2," January 28, 2017, https://fas.org/irp/offdocs/nspm/nspm-2.pdf; see also John Bellinger, "National Security Presidential Memorandum 2—President Trump's NSC and HSC," Lawfare, January 28, 2017, https://www.lawfareblog.com/national-security-presidential-memorandum-2—president-trumps-nsc-and-hsc; and I. M. Destler, "How to Read Trump's National Security Council Reboot," *Politico Magazine*, January 29, 2017, https://www.politico.com/magazine/story/2017/01/how-to-read-trumps-national-security-council-reboot-214709.

50. Kimberly Dozier, "Steve Bannon Builds a New Node of Power in the Trump White House," *Daily Beast*, January 31, 2017, https://www.thedailybeast.com/steve-bannon-builds-a-new-node-of-power-in-the-trump-white-house.

51. Trump, "Transcript: The Inaugural Address."

52. Quoted in Philip Rucker and Robert Costa, "Bannon Vows a Daily Fight for 'Deconstruction of the Administrative State,'" *Washington Post*, February 23, 2017, https://www.washingtonpost.com/politics/top-wh-strategist-vows-a-daily-fight-for-deconstruction-of-the-administrative-state/2017/02/23/03f6b8da-f9ea-11e6-bf01-d47f8cf9b643_story.html?utm_term=.f43af7ad1584.

53. Quoted in Mark Landler, "State Dept. Officials Should Quit If They Disagree with Trump, White House Warns," *New York Times*, January 31, 2017, https://www.nytimes.com/2017/01/31/us/politics/sean-spicer-state-dept-travel-ban.html.

54. Kimberly Dozier, "New Power Center in Trumpland: The 'Axis of Adults,'" *Daily Beast*, April 16, 2017, https://www.thedailybeast.com/new-power-center-in-trumpland-the-axis-of-adults; and "Steve Bannon Is Removed from the NSC," *Economist*, April 6, 2017, https://www.economist.com/news/united-states/21720301-donald-trumps-government-turns-slightly-more-ordinary-steve-bannon-removed-nsc.

55. Quoted in Chris Cillizza, "Bob Corker Just Told the World What He Really Thinks of Donald Trump," CNN.com, October 5, 2017, https://www.cnn.com/2017/10/04/politics/bob-corker-trump/index.html.

56. Michael D. Shear and Ron Nixon, "How Trump's Rush to Enact an Immigration Ban Unleashed Global Chaos," *New York Times*, January 30, 2017, p. A1, https://www.nytimes.com/2017/01/29/us/politics/donald-trump-rush-immigration-order-chaos.html.

57. Quoted in Shear and Davis, "Stoking Fears, Trump Defied Bureaucracy to Advance Immigration Agenda."

58. Quoted in Michael R. Gordon and Helene Cooper, "James Mattis Strikes Far Harsher Tone than Trump on Russia," *New York Times*, January 12, 2017, https://www.nytimes.com/2017/01/12/us/politics/james-mattis-defense-secretary-nominee.html.

59. Quoted in David Lawler, "Rex Tillerson Talks Tough on Russia in Confirmation Hearing but Will Not Call Vladimir Putin a War Criminal," *Telegraph*, January 11,

2017, http://www.telegraph.co.uk/news/2017/01/11/rex-tillerson-talks-tough-russia -confirmation-hearing-will-not/.

60. "Transcript: Remarks by Secretary Mattis and Prime Minister Abe in Tokyo, Japan," US Department of Defense, February 3, 2017, https://www.defense.gov /News/Transcripts/Transcript-View/Article/1070919/remarks-by-secretary-mattis-and -prime-minister-abe-in-tokyo-japan/.

61. "Transcript: Press Conference by Secretary Mattis at NATO Headquarters, Brussels, Belgium," US Department of Defense, February 16, 2017, https://www.defense.gov /News/Transcripts/Transcript-View/Article/1085679/press-conference-by-secretary -mattis-at-nato-headquarters-brussels-belgium/.

62. Mike Pence, "Remarks by Vice President Pence at the Munich Security Conference February 18," US Embassy and Consulate in the Netherlands, February 18, 2017, https://nl.usembassy.gov/remarks-vice-president-pence-munich-security-conference -february-18/.

63. In a memorandum recording a January 27, 2017, dinner conversation with Trump, then FBI Director James Comey records the president as saying of Flynn, "The guy has serious judgment issues." See "Read: James Comey's Memos," CNN.com, April 19, 2018, https://www.cnn.com/2018/04/19/politics/comey-memo-release/index.html.

64. Quoted in James Hohmann, "The Daily 202: Trump's New National Security Adviser Literally Wrote the Book on Vietnam," *Washington Post*, February 21, 2017, https://www.washingtonpost.com/news/powerpost/paloma/daily-202/2017/02/21 /daily-202-trump-s-new-national-security-adviser-literally-wrote-the-book-on-vietnam /58ab8a21e9b69b1406c75cd2/.

65. Quoted in Mark Landler and Eric Schmitt, "H.R. McMaster Breaks with Administration on Views of Islam," *New York Times*, February 24, 2017, https://www .nytimes.com/2017/02/24/us/politics/hr-mcmaster-trump-islam.html.

66. Jordan Brunner, "NSPM-4: 'Organization of the National Security Council, the Homeland Security Council, and Subcommittees': A Summary," Lawfare, April 5, 2017, https://www.lawfareblog.com/nspm-4-organization-national-security-council-homeland -security-council-and-subcommittees-summary.

67. Quoted in Michael D. Shear and Michael R. Gordon, "63 Hours: From Chemical Attack to Trump's Strike in Syria," *New York Times*, April 7, 2017, https://www.nytimes .com/2017/04/07/us/politics/syria-strike-trump-timeline.html.

68. Dan Merica, "Trump, Xi Talked Syria Strike over 'Beautiful' Chocolate Cake," CNN, April 12, 2017, http://www.cnn.com/2017/04/12/politics/donald-trump-xi -jingping-syria-chocolate-cake/index.html.

69. Quoted in Theodore Schleifer and Dan Merica, "Trump: 'I Now Have Responsibility' When It Comes to Syria," CNN, April 6, 2017, http://www.cnn.com/2017/04/05 /politics/trump-syria-comments-response/index.html.

70. David Ignatius, "Trump Gets a Taste of Success," *Washington Post*, April 13, 2017, https://www.washingtonpost.com/opinions/trump-gets-a-taste-of-success/2017 /04/13/1aeb8f3a-2090-11e7-a0a7-8b2a45e3dc84_story.html?utm_term =.32f94c3108b1.

Chapter 6—Peace through Strength

1. Donald J. Trump (@realDonaldTrump), Twitter, April 8, 2018, https://twitter
.com/realDonaldTrump/status/982966315467116544 and https://twitter.com/real
DonaldTrump/status/982967389028569088; and Donald J. Trump (@realDonald
Trump), Twitter, April 11, 2018, https://twitter.com/realDonaldTrump/status/984022
625440747520.

2. Donald J. Trump, "Statement on Syria," White House, April 13, 2018, https://
www.whitehouse.gov/briefings-statements/statement-president-trump-syria/.

3. "Remarks by President Trump at the Conservative Political Action Conference,"
February 24, 2017, https://www.whitehouse.gov/briefings-statements/remarks-president
-trump-conservative-political-action-conference/.

4. US Office of Management and Budget, "America First: A Budget Blueprint to
Make America Great Again, Budget of the United States Government, Fiscal Year
2018," March 16, 2017, whitehouse.gov, https://www.whitehouse.gov/wp-content
/uploads/2017/11/2018_blueprint.pdf.

5. Quoted in Russell Berman, "President Trump's 'Hard Power' Budget," *Atlantic*, March 16, 2017, https://www.theatlantic.com/politics/archive/2017/03/president
-trumps-hard-power-budget/519702/.

6. Quoted in Julian Borger, David Smith, Spencer Ackerman, and Saeed Kamali
Dehghan, "Trump Administration 'Officially Putting Iran on Notice,' Says Michael
Flynn," *Guardian*, February 2, 2017, https://www.theguardian.com/world/2017/feb/01
/iran-trump-michael-flynn-on-notice.

7. Quoted in James Kitfield, "Trump's Generals Are Trying to Save the World. Starting with the White House," *Politico Magazine*, August 4, 2017, https://www.politico
.com/magazine/story/2017/08/04/donald-trump-generals-mattis-mcmaster-kelly
-flynn-215455.

8. Quoted in Filkins, "James Mattis, a Warrior in Washington."

9. Quoted in Linda Qiu, "Can Trump Claim Credit for a Waning Islamic State?"
New York Times, October 17, 2017, https://www.nytimes.com/2017/10/17/us/politics
/trump-islamic-state-raqqa-fact-check.html.

10. Quoted in Melissa Chan, "Donald Trump Wants Military to Hatch Plan to Stop
ISIS in 30 Days,"Time.com, September 7, 2016, http://time.com/4481791/donald-trump
-isis-30-days/.

11. "President Obama: 'We Will Degrade and Ultimately Destroy ISIL,'" September
10, 2014, https://obamawhitehouse.archives.gov/blog/2014/09/10/president-obama-we
-will-degrade-and-ultimately-destroy-isil.

12. "Transcript: Department of Defense Press Briefing by Secretary Mattis, General
Dunford and Special Envoy McGurk on the Campaign to Defeat ISIS in the Pentagon Press Briefing Room," May 19, 2017, https://www.defense.gov/News/Transcripts
/Transcript-View/Article/1188225/department-of-defense-press-briefing-by
-secretary-mattis-general-dunford-and-sp/.

13. Calculated from data in Haley Britzkey, "3 Years of US Air Strikes in Syria," Axios,
April 20, 2018, https://www.axios.com/us-airstrikes-in-syria-over-time-5bee8960

-09e6-475d-b69b-685e108ad60d.html?utm_source=newsletter&utm_medium= email&utm_campaign=newsletter_axiospm&stream=top-stories.

14. Charlie Savage and Eric Schmitt, "Trump Poised to Drop Some Limits on Drone Strikes and Commando Raids," *New York Times*, September 21, 2017, https://www .nytimes.com/2017/09/21/us/politics/trump-drone-strikes-commando-raids-rules.html.

15. Eric Schmitt, "A Shadow War's Newest Front: A Drone Base Rising from Saharan Dust," *New York Times*, April 22, 2017, p. A1, https://www.nytimes.com/2018/04/22/us /politics/drone-base-niger.html.

16. "Transcript: Department of Defense Press Briefing by Secretary Mattis, General Dunford and Special Envoy McGurk on the Campaign to Defeat ISIS in the Pentagon Press Briefing Room."

17. CJTF-OIR PAO, "CJTF-OIR Reflects on 2017 and Looks Forward to 2018," Operation Inherent Resolve, January 1, 2018, http://www.inherentresolve.mil/News /News-Releases/Article/1406595/cjtf-oir-reflects-on-2017-and-looks-forward -to-2018/.

18. Quoted in Zachary Cohen and Dan Merica, "Trump Takes Credit for ISIS 'Giving Up,'" CNN.com, October 17, 2017, http://www.cnn.com/2017/10/17/politics /trump-isis-raqqa/index.html.

19. Karen DeYoung and Liz Sly, "After Raqqa, the U.S. Sees Russia, Assad Looming Over Remaining Syrian Battlefield," *Washington Post*, October 19, 2017, https://www .washingtonpost.com/world/national-security/after-raqqa-the-us-sees-russia-assad -looming-over-remaining-syrian-battlefield/2017/10/19/0281c7da-b41e-11e7-be94 -fabb0f1e9ffb_story.html?utm_term=.0a98e354d68c&wpisrc=nl_daily202&wpmm=1.

20. David Ignatius, "The Rubble in Raqqa Reminds Us of Our Military Might. But What's Next?" *Washington Post*, https://www.washingtonpost.com/opinions/the -rubble-in-raqqa-reminds-us-of-our-military-might-but-whats-next/2017/10/19 /98fac87a-b503-11e7-a908-a3470754bbb9_story.html?utm_term=.c5e1d51ff2a6& wpisrc=nl_daily202&wpmm=1.

21. "Transcript: Department of Defense Press Briefing by Secretary Mattis, General Dunford and Special Envoy McGurk on the Campaign to Defeat ISIS in the Pentagon Press Briefing Room."

22. Quoted in James Kitfield, "How James Mattis Tried to Explain Trump to the World," *Atlantic*, August 26, 2017, https://www.theatlantic.com/international/archive /2017/08/mattis-trump-turkey-jordan-iraq-ukraine-isis/538086/.

23. Rex W. Tillerson, "Remarks on the Way Forward for the United States regard- ing Syria," January 17, 2018, https://www.state.gov/secretary/20172018tillerson /remarks/2018/01/277493.htm.

24. Donald J. Trump, "Remarks in a Joint Press Conference with Heads of the Baltic States," April 3, 2018, https://www.whitehouse.gov/briefings-statements/remarks -president-trump-heads-baltic-states-joint-press-conference/.

25. Karen DeYoung and Shane Harris, "Trump Instructs Military to Begin Plan- ning for Withdrawal from Syria," *Washington Post*, April 4, 2018, https://www .washingtonpost.com/world/national-security/trump-instructs-military-to-begin -planning-for-withdrawal-from-syria/2018/04/04/1039f420-3811-11e8-8fd2-49fe3c

675a89_story.html?utm_term=.85ba535edf1a&wpisrc=al_news__alert-world--alert-national&wpmk=1.

26. Quoted in Mark Landler and Maggie Haberman, "Angry Trump Grilled His Generals About Troop Increase, Then Gave In," *New York Times*, August 21, 2017, https://www.nytimes.com/2017/08/21/world/asia/trump-afghanistan.html.

27. Daalder and Lindsay, *America Unbound*, pp. 110ff.

28. Quoted in Ann Scott Tyson, "Top Military Officer Urges Major Change in Afghanistan Strategy," *Washington Post*, September 11, 2008, http://www.washingtonpost.com/wp-dyn/content/article/2008/09/10/AR2008091001396.html.

29. Quoted in Paul McLeary, "U.S. General Wants More Troops, More Time, in Afghanistan," *Foreign Policy*, February 9, 2017, http://foreignpolicy.com/2017/02/09/u-s-general-wants-more-troops-time-in-afghanistan-russia-iran/.

30. Susan B. Glasser, "The Trump White House's War Within," *Politico Magazine*, July 24, 2017, https://www.politico.com/magazine/story/2017/07/24/donald-trump-afghanistan-215412.

31. Donald J. Trump (@realDonaldTrump), Twitter, January 14, 2013, https://twitter.com/realDonaldTrump/status/290926188787036161.

32. Mark Landler, Eric Schmitt, and Michael R. Gordon, "Trump Aides Recruited Businessmen to Devise Options for Afghanistan," *New York Times*, July 10, 2017, https://www.nytimes.com/2017/07/10/world/asia/trump-afghanistan-policy-erik-prince-stephen-feinberg.html.

33. Carol E. Lee and Courtney Kube, "Trump Says U.S. 'Losing' Afghan War in Tense Meeting with Generals," NBC News, August 2, 2017, http://www.nbcnews.com/news/us-news/amp/trump-says-u-s-losing-afghan-war-tense-meeting-generals-n789006.

34. Donald J. Trump, "Remarks by President Trump on the Strategy in Afghanistan and South Asia," August 21, 2017, https://www.whitehouse.gov/briefings-statements/remarks-president-trump-strategy-afghanistan-south-asia/.

35. Ibid.

36. Quoted in "Admiral: Troops Alone Will Not Yield Victory in Afghanistan," CNN, September 2008, http://www.cnn.com/2008/POLITICS/09/10/mullen.afghanistan/.

37. Rex W. Tillerson, "Secretary of State Rex Tillerson Press Availability," August 22, 2017, https://www.state.gov/secretary/20172018tillerson/remarks/2017/08/273577.htm.

38. Quoted in Roberta Rampton and Jonathan Landlay, "Trump Rejects Peace Talks with Taliban in Departure from Afghan Strategy," Reuters, January 29, 2018, https://www.reuters.com/article/us-afghanistan-blast-trump/trump-rejects-peace-talks-with-taliban-in-departure-from-afghan-strategy-idUSKBN1FI2BU.

39. George P. Shultz, *Turmoil and Triumph: Diplomacy, Power, and the Victory of the American Deal* (New York: Charles Scribners, 1993), p. 128.

40. Quoted in Carol Morello, "Tillerson Tells State Department Employees That Budget Cut Reflects New Priorities," *Washington Post*, March 16, 2017, https://www.washingtonpost.com/world/national-security/tillerson-tells-state-department-employees-that-budget-cut-reflects-new-priorities/2017/03/16/1880475e-0a4c-11e7-a15f-a58d4a988474_story.html.

41. Rex W. Tillerson, "Press Availability with Japanese Foreign Minister Fumio Kishida," March 16, 2017, https://www.state.gov/secretary/20172018tillerson/remarks/2017/03/268476.htm.

42. Rex W. Tillerson, "The U.S. and Europe: Strengthening Western Alliances," November 28, 2017, https://www.state.gov/secretary/20172018tillerson/remarks/2017/11/276002.htm.

43. Rex W. Tillerson, "Remarks to the Staff and Families of U.S. Embassy London," September 14, 2017, https://www.state.gov/secretary/20172018tillerson/remarks/2017/09/274098.htm.

44. Rex W. Tillerson, "Remarks at Town Hall," December 12, 2017, https://www.state.gov/secretary/20172018tillerson/remarks/2017/12/276563.htm, and Nahal Toosi, "Rex Tillerson's $12 Million Army of Consultants," Politico, April 5, 2018, https://www.politico.com/story/2018/04/05/tillerson-state-department-consultants-503557.

45. Quoted in Patricia Zengerle, "Senate Panel Rejects Trump's Doctrine of Defeat," Reuters, September 8, 2017, https://www.reuters.com/article/us-usa-trump-diplomacy/senate-panel-rejects-trumps-doctrine-of-retreat-on-foreign-policy-idUSKCN1BJ2PQ.

46. Gardiner Harris, "Diplomats Question Tactics of Tillerson, the Executive Turned Secretary of State," New York Times, August 6, 2017, https://www.nytimes.com/2017/08/06/us/politics/rex-tillerson-state-department.html.

47. Quoted in Gardiner Harris, "Trying to Defend President Trump's Derision, Diplomatically," New York Times, January 19, 2018, https://www.nytimes.com/2018/01/19/world/trump-diplomats-tillerson-embassy.html.

48. Quoted in Roger Cohen, "The Desperation of Diplomats," New York Times, July 29, 2017, p. SR1, https://www.nytimes.com/2017/07/28/opinion/sunday/trump-tillerson-state-department-diplomats.html.

49. Numbers calculated as of March 31, 2018, from "Tracking How Many Key Positions Trump Has Filled So Far," Washington Post, https://www.washingtonpost.com/graphics/politics/trump-administration-appointee-tracker/database/?utm_term=.1139f9182a9a.

50. Quoted in Nick Wadhams, "How Rex Tillerson Is Remaking the State Department," Bloomberg Businessweek, October 26, 2017, https://www.bloomberg.com/news/articles/2017-10-26/how-rex-tillerson-is-remaking-the-state-department.

51. Josh Rogin, "State Department Considers Scrubbing Democracy Promotion from Its Mission," Washington Post, August 1, 2017, https://www.washingtonpost.com/amphtml/news/josh-rogin/wp/2017/08/01/state-department-considers-scrubbing-democracy-promotion-from-its-mission/.

52. Quoted in Connor Finnegan: "Tillerson: Pushing Human Rights 'Creates Obstacles' to US Interests," ABC News, May 3, 2017, http://abcnews.go.com/Politics/tillerson-pushing-human-rights-abroad-creates-obstacles/story?id=47190743.

53. Brian Hook, "Note for the Secretary: Balancing Interests and Values," Washington, DC, Department of State, May 17, 2017, https://www.politico.com/f/?id=00000160-6c37-da3c-a371-ec3f13380001.

54. John McCain, "Why We Must Support Human Rights," *New York Times*, May 7, 2017, p. A21, https://www.nytimes.com/2017/05/08/opinion/john-mccain-rex-tillerson -human-rights.html.

55. Mehul Srivastava and Jim Brundsen, "Trump Congratulates Erdogan on Controversial Referendum Victory," *Financial Times*, April 18, 2017, https://www.ft.com /content/aa8a2222-2401-11e7-8691-d5f7e0cd0a16.

56. Quoted in Kevin Liptak, "Trump on Xi's Consolidating Power: 'Maybe We'll Give That a Shot One Day,'" CNN, March 3, 2018, https://www.cnn.com/2018/03/03 /politics/trump-maralago-remarks/index.html.

57. Carole D. Leonnig, David Nakamura, and Josh Dawsey, "Trump's National Security Advisers Warned Him Not to Congratulate Putin. He Did It Anyway," *Washington Post*, March 20, 2018, https://www.washingtonpost.com/politics/trumps -national-security-advisers-warned-him-not-to-congratulate-putin-he-did-it-anyway /2018/03/20/22738ebc-2c68-11e8-8ad6-fbc50284fce8_story.html.

58. "Transcript of Call between President Trump and Philippine President Duterte," May 2, 2017, http://apps.washingtonpost.com/g/documents/politics/transcript-of-call -between-president-trump-and-philippine-president-duterte/2446/.

59. Quoted in Philip Bump, "The Commerce Secretary Praises Lack of Protests Where It Is Punishable by Death," *Washington Post*, May 22, 2017, https://www.washingtonpost .com/news/politics/wp/2017/05/22/the-commerce-secretary-praises-the-lack-of -protest-in-a-country-where-its-punishable-by-death/?utm_term=.4b9dedceb799.

60. Quoted in Zengerle, "Rex Tillerson and the Unraveling of the State Department."

61. Quoted in Anne Gearan, Philip Rucker, and Ashley Parker, "'Death Spiral': Tillerson Makes Nice but May Not Last Long with Trump," *Washington Post*, October 4, 2017, https://www.washingtonpost.com/politics/a-death-spiral-tillerson-makes-nice-but-may -not-last-long-with-trump/2017/10/04/7ad19894-a921-11e7-850e-2bdd1236be5d _story.html.

62. Quoted in Karen DeYoung and Greg Jaffe, "For Some Foreign Diplomats, the Trump White House Is a Troubling Enigma," *Washington Post*, October 9, 2017, https://www.washingtonpost.com/amphtml/world/national-security/for-some-foreign -diplomats-the-trump-white-house-is-a-troubling-enigma/2017/10/09/50323152 -a534-11e7-ade1-76d061d56efa_story.html.

Chapter 7—America Alone

1. H. R. McMaster and Gary D. Cohn, "America First Doesn't Mean America Alone," *Wall Street Journal*, May 30, 2017, https://www.wsj.com/articles/america-first-doesnt -mean-america-alone-1496187426.

2. Donald J. Trump, "President Trump's Speech to the Arab Islamic American Summit," Riyadh, May 21, 2017, https://www.whitehouse.gov/briefings-statements /president-trumps-speech-arab-islamic-american-summit/.

3. Quoted in Philip Rucker and Karen DeYoung, "Trump Signs 'Tremendous' Deals with Saudi Arabia on His First Day Overseas," *Washington Post*, May 20, 2017, https://www .washingtonpost.com/politics/trump-gets-elaborate-welcome-in-saudi-arabia-embarking

-on-first-foreign-trip/2017/05/20/679f2766-3d1d-11e7-a058-ddbb23c75d82_story.html?utm_term=.b37c1773c639.

4. "Remarks with Saudi Foreign Minister Adel al-Jubeir at a Press Availability," Riyadh, May 20, 2017, https://www.state.gov/secretary/20172018tillerson/remarks/2017/05/271005.htm.

5. Trump, "President Trump's Speech to the Arab Islamic American Summit."

6. Declan Walsh, "Tiny, Wealthy Qatar Goes Its Own Way, and Pays for It," *New York Times*, January 22, 2018, https://www.nytimes.com/2018/01/22/world/middleeast/qatar-saudi-emir-boycott.html.

7. Donald J. Trump (@realDonaldTrump), Twitter, June 6, 2017, https://twitter.com/realDonaldTrump/status/872084870620520448; Donald J. Trump (@realDonaldTrump), Twitter, June 6, 2017, https://twitter.com/realDonaldTrump/status/872086906804240384.

8. Rex W. Tillerson, "Remarks on the Middle East," June 9, 2017, https://www.state.gov/secretary/20172018tillerson/remarks/2017/06/271672.htm.

9. "Remarks by President Trump and President Iohannis of Romania in a Joint Press Conference," Washington, DC, June 9, 2017, https://www.whitehouse.gov/briefings-statements/remarks-president-trump-president-iohannis-romania-joint-press-conference/.

10. Donald J. Trump (@realDonaldTrump), Twitter, November 6, 2017, https://twitter.com/realDonaldTrump/status/927672843504177152.

11. Quoted in Greg Jaffe, "In Speech to Jewish Group, McMaster Celebrates Trump's First Foreign Trip," *Washington Post*, June 4, 2017, https://www.washingtonpost.com/world/national-security/in-speech-to-jewish-group-mcmaster-celebrates-trumps-first-foreign-trip/2017/06/04/2cd527de-497a-11e7-a186-60c031eab644_story.html?tid=sm_tw&utm_term=.2ff5d742263a.

12. Monica Langley and Gerard Baker, "Donald Trump, in Exclusive Interview, Tells WSJ He Is Willing to Keep Parts of Obama Health Law," *Wall Street Journal*, November 11, 2016, https://www.wsj.com/articles/donald-trump-willing-to-keep-parts-of-health-law-1478895339.

13. Quoted in Peter Baker and Ian Fisher, "Trump Comes to Israel Citing a Palestinian Deal as Crucial," *New York Times*, May 22, 2017, https://www.nytimes.com/2017/05/22/world/middleeast/trump-israel-visit.html.

14. Interview with a European diplomat, Washington, DC, October 4, 2017.

15. Quoted in Ashley Feinberg, "Kushner on Middle East Peace: 'What Do We Offer That's Unique? I Don't Know,'" *Wired*, August 1, 2017, https://www.wired.com/story/jared-kushner-middle-east/.

16. Quoted in Jack Khoury, "Abbas Rips Into Trump: Palestinians Are Original Canaanites, Were in Jerusalem Before the Jews," *Haaretz*, January 17, 2018, https://www.haaretz.com/middle-east-news/palestinians/abbas-palestinians-are-canaanites-were-in-jerusalem-before-jews-1.5743576.

17. "Remarks by President Trump and Prime Minister Netanyahu of Israel before Bilateral Meeting," Davos, January 25, 2018, https://www.whitehouse.gov/briefings-statements/remarks-president-trump-prime-minister-netanyahu-israel-bilateral-meeting-davos-switzerland/.

18. "President Trump and Prime Minister May's Opening Remarks," Washington, DC, January 27, 2017, https://www.whitehouse.gov/briefings-statements/president-trump-prime-minister-mays-opening-remarks/; "Joint Press Conference with President Trump and German Chancellor Merkel," Washington, DC, March 17, 2017, https://www.whitehouse.gov/briefings-statements/joint-press-conference-president-trump-german-chancellor-merkel/; and "Joint Press Conference of President Trump and NATO Secretary General Stoltenberg," Washington, DC, April 12, 2017, https://www.whitehouse.gov/briefings-statements/joint-press-conference-president-trump-nato-secretary-general-stoltenberg/. See also Greg Miller, Greg Jaffe, and Philip Rucker, "Doubting the Intelligence, Trump Pursues Putin and Leaves a Russian Threat Unchecked," *Washington Post*, December 14, 2017, https://www.washingtonpost.com/graphics/2017/world/national-security/donald-trump-pursues-vladimir-putin-russian-election-hacking/?utm_term=.f7e3e42e677d.

19. "Merkel: 'It Is Not Isolation and the Building of Walls That Make Us Successful,'" *Grabien*, May 25, 2017, https://grabien.com/story.php?id=106945.

20. Michael D. Shear and Mark Landler, "Trump Is Expected to Endorse NATO's Mutual Aid Pledge, Ending Silence," *New York Times*, May 24, 2017, https://www.nytimes.com/2017/05/24/world/trump-nato.html; and interview with a NATO diplomat, Chicago, October 19, 2017.

21. "Remarks by President Trump at NATO Unveiling of the Article 5 and Berlin Wall Memorials," Brussels, May 25, 2017, https://www.whitehouse.gov/briefings-statements/remarks-president-trump-nato-unveiling-article-5-berlin-wall-memorials-brussels-belgium/.

22. Interviews with European diplomats, Chicago, October 19, 2017, and Munich, February 16, 2018. See also Robbie Gramer, "Trump Discovers Article 5 After Disastrous NATO Visit," *Foreign Policy*, June 9, 2017, https://foreignpolicy.com/2017/06/09/trump-discovers-article-5-after-disastrous-nato-visit-brussels-visit-transatlantic-relationship-europe/.

23. White House spokesperson Sean Spicer quoted in Susan B. Glasser, "The 27 Words Trump Wouldn't Say," *Politico Magazine*, June 6, 2017, https://www.politico.com/magazine/story/2017/06/06/trump-nato-speech-27-words-commitment-215231.

24. Susan B. Glasser, "Trump National Security Team Blindsided by NATO Speech," *Politico Magazine*, June 5, 2017, https://www.politico.com/magazine/story/2017/06/05/trump-nato-speech-national-security-team-215227.

25. "Remarks by President Trump and President Iohannis of Romania in a Joint Press Conference."

26. NATO Press Release, "Defence Expenditure of NATO Countries (2010–2017)," June 29, 2017, https://www.nato.int/nato_static_fl2014/assets/pdf/pdf_2017_06/20170629_170629-pr2017-111-en.pdf.

27. NATO, "Wales Summit Declaration," September 5, 2014, https://www.nato.int/cps/ic/natohq/official_texts_112964.htm.

28. Interview with a European diplomat, Washington, DC, January 11, 2018.

29. Quoted in Peter Müller, "Trump in Brussels: 'The Germans Are Bad, Very Bad,'" *Spiegel Online*, May 26, 2017, http://www.spiegel.de/international/world/trump-in-brussels-the-germans-are-bad-very-bad-a-1149330.html.

30. Quoted in "G7 Taormina Leaders' Communiqué," May 2017, http://www.mofa.go.jp/files/000260041.pdf.

31. Quoted in "Donald Trump Would 'Cancel' Paris Climate Deal," BBC News, May 27, 2016, http://www.bbc.com/news/election-us-2016-36401174.

32. Quoted in Anne-Sylvaine Chassany and George Parker, "Trump in G7 Clashes over Trade and Climate," *Financial Times*, May 26, 2017, https://www.ft.com/content/efec8ef8-41fd-11e7-9d56-25f963e998b2.

33. "G7 Taormina Leaders' Communiqué."

34. Quoted in Ashley Parker, Philip Rucker, and Michael Birnbaum, "Inside Trump's Climate Decision: After Fiery Debate, He 'Stayed Where He's Always Been,'" *Washington Post*, June 1, 2017, https://www.washingtonpost.com/politics/inside-trumps-climate-decision-after-fiery-debate-he-stayed-where-hes-always-been/2017/06/01/e4acb27e-46db-11e7-bcde-624ad94170ab_story.html?hpid=hp_hp-top-table-main_parisreconstruct-850pm:homepage/story&utm_term=.b47afa2b6d03&wpisrc=al_alert-COMBO-politics%252Bnation&wpmk=1.

35. Quoted in Spiegel Staff, "Paris Disagreement: Donald Trump's Triumph of Stupidity," *Spiegel Online*, June 2, 2017, http://www.spiegel.de/international/world/trump-pulls-out-of-climate-deal-western-rift-deepens-a-1150486.html.

36. Quoted in Parker, Rucker, and Birnbaum, "Inside Trump's Climate Decision: After Fiery Debate, He 'Stayed Where He's Always Been.'"

37. Donald J. Trump, "Statement by President Trump on the Paris Climate Accord," Washington, DC, June 1, 2017, https://www.whitehouse.gov/briefings-statements/statement-president-trump-paris-climate-accord/.

38. Michael Birnbaum, "Trump's Tangle with Europe Leads the Continent to Find Partners Elsewhere," *Washington Post*, June 2, 2017, https://www.washingtonpost.com/world/europe/trumps-tangle-with-europe-leads-the-continent-to-find-partners-elsewhere/2017/06/02/429b1c0c-4599-11e7-8de1-cec59a9bf4b1_story.html?stream=top-stories&utm_campaign=newsletter_axiosam&utm_medium=email&utm_source=newsletter&utm_term=.521c5cb95474.

39. The Star Online, "Macron: Make Our Planet Great Again," YouTube, June 2, 2017, https://www.youtube.com/watch?v=03NMa4X0dyQ.

40. Quoted in Melissa Eddy, "Angela Merkel Sets Collision Course with Trump Ahead of G-20," *New York Times*, June 29, 2017, https://www.nytimes.com/2017/06/29/world/europe/angela-merkel-trump-group-of-20.html?smid=tw-nytimesworld&smtyp=cur&_r=0.

41. Quoted in Peter Nicholas, "Trump's 'America First' Policy Proves to Be an Immovable Object at G-20," *Wall Street Journal*, July 9, 2017, https://www.wsj.com/articles/trumps-america-first-policy-proves-to-be-an-immovable-object-at-g-20-1499616791.

42. Quoted in Nick Gass, "Trump: Putin's Compliments Are a 'Great Honor,'" Politico, December 17, 2015, https://www.politico.com/story/2015/12/trump-vladimir-putin-praise-216892.

43. David Filipov and Andrew Roth, "'Yes We Did': Russia's Establishment Basks in Trump's Victory," *Washington Post*, February 28, 2018, https://www.washingtonpost.com/news/worldviews/wp/2016/11/09/yes-we-did-russias-establishment-basks-in-trumps-victory/?utm_term=.715fdeba1ea5.

44. Quoted in Politico Staff, "Trump Releases Letter from Putin Asking to 'Restore' U.S.-Russia Relationship," Politico, December 23, 2016, https://www.politico.com /story/2016/12/putin-christmas-letter-to-trump-232952.

45. Peter Nicholas, Paul Beckett, and Gerald F. Seib, "Trump Open to Shift on Russia Sanctions, 'One China' Policy," *Wall Street Journal*, January 13, 2017, https://www.wsj.com /articles/donald-trump-sets-a-bar-for-russia-and-china-1484360380.

46. "'Background to Assessing Russian Activities and Intentions in Recent US Elections': The Analytic Process and Cyber Incident Attribution," Intelligence Community Assessment, January 6, 2017, https://www.dni.gov/files/documents/ICA_2017_01.pdf.

47. Interview with a British diplomat, Washington, DC, March 30, 2017.

48. Quoted in Susan B. Glasser, "Trump, Putin and the New Cold War," *Politico Magazine*, December 22, 2017, http://politi.co/2kCCKcD.

49. "Remarks by President Trump in Press Conference."

50. "Excerpts from Trump's Conversation with Journalists on Air Force One," *New York Times*, July 13, 2017, https://www.nytimes.com/2017/07/13/us/politics/trump-air-force -one-excerpt-transcript.html.

51. "Transcript: Secretary of State Tillerson on Trump's Meeting with Putin," NPR, July 7, 2017, https://www.npr.org/2017/07/07/536035953/transcript-secretary-of-state -tillerson-on-trumps-meeting-with-putin.

52. Julie Hirschfeld Davis, "Trump and Putin Held a Second, Undisclosed, Private Conversation," *New York Times*, July 18, 2017, https://www.nytimes.com/2017/07/18 /world/europe/trump-putin-undisclosed-meeting.html.

53. "Transcript: Secretary of State Tillerson on Trump's Meeting with Putin."

54. Quoted in "Germany Fears Donald Trump Will Divide Europe," *Economist*, July 15, 2017, https://www.economist.com/news/europe/21725025-angela-merkel-troubled -presidents-chumminess-putin-and-poland-germany-fears-donald.

55. Quoted in Kailani Koenig, "Graham Slams 'Disastrous Meeting' with Putin, Calls Russia Trump's 'Blind Spot,'" NBC News, July 9, 2017, https://www.nbcnews.com /politics/national-security/graham-slams-disastrous-meeting-putin-calls-russia-trump -s-blind-n781096.

56. Donald J. Trump, "Statement by President Donald J. Trump on Signing the 'Countering America's Adversaries through Sanctions Act,'" Washington, DC, August 2, 2017, https://www.whitehouse.gov/briefings-statements/statement-president-donald -j-trump-signing-countering-americas-adversaries-sanctions-act/.

57. Quoted in Oleg Matsnev, "Trump Is 'Not My Bride,' Putin Says," *New York Times*, September 5, 2017, https://www.nytimes.com/2017/09/05/world/europe/vladimir-putin -donald-trump.html?mcubz=1.

58. "National Security Strategy of the United States of America," December 2017, https://www.whitehouse.gov/wp-content/uploads/2017/12/NSS-Final-12-18-2017 -0905.pdf, pp. 25, 27.

59. Donald J. Trump, "Remarks by President Trump on the Administration's National Security Strategy," Washington, DC, December 18, 2017, https://www.whitehouse .gov/briefings-statements/remarks-president-trump-administrations-national-security -strategy/.

60. McMaster and Cohn, "America First Doesn't Mean America Alone."

61. "READ: Trump's speech to the World Economic Forum," CNN, January 26, 2018, https://www.cnn.com/2018/01/26/politics/read-trump-davos-speech/index .html.

Chapter 8—Fire and Fury

1. Donald J. Trump (@realDonaldTrump), Twitter, October 12, 2012, https://twitter .com/realdonaldtrump/status/253488938264715264?lang=en.

2. Trump, "Remarks at the AIPAC Policy Conference in Washington, DC."

3. "Remarks by President Trump to the 72nd Session of the United Nations General Assembly," September 19, 2017, https://www.whitehouse.gov/the-press-office /2017/09/19/remarks-president-trump-72nd-session-united-nations-general -assembly.

4. Quoted in David Jackson, "At United Nations, Trump Threatens to 'Totally Destroy North Korea' If It Continues on Nuclear Path," *USA Today*, September 19, 2017, https://www.usatoday.com/story/news/politics/2017/09/19/trump-we-have-no-choice -but-totally-destroy-north-korea-if-continues-nuclear-path/680329001/.

5. Quoted in Anna Fifield and Simon Denyer, "Jitters and Surprise in South Korea and Japan over Trump's Speech to the U.N.," *Washington Post*, September 19, 2017, https:// www.washingtonpost.com/world/russia-calls-trumps-korea-remarks-a-dangerous -step-toward-instability/2017/09/19/1a6d9b56-9d69-11e7-b2a7-bc70b6f98089_story .html?utm_term=.593c13dd2251.

6. Quoted in Max de Haldevang, "Being the Anti-Trump Is the Must-Have Look at This Week's General Assembly," Quartz.com, September 20, 2017, https://qz.com /1082972/unga-2017-federica-mogherini-outlined-the-european-unions-values-to-set -it-apart-from-the-us-under-trump/.

7. Quoted in "Reaction to Trump's UN General Assembly Speech," Associated Press, September 20, 2017, https://apnews.com/83c48ade898f4fe58644912af4288eec.

8. "Full Text: Iran's Hassan Rouhani's Speech to the General Assembly," *Haaretz*, September 20, 2017, https://www.haaretz.com/middle-east-news/full-text-iran-s-rohani -addresses-un-general-assembly-1.5452552.

9. Quoted in Choe Sang-Hun, "Kim's Rejoinder to Trump's Rocket Man: 'Mentally Deranged U.S. Dotard,'" *New York Times*, September 21, 2017, https://www.nytimes .com/2017/09/21/world/asia/kim-trump-rocketman-dotard.html?hp&action=click &pgtype=Homepage&clickSource=story-heading&module=first-column-region&region =top-news&WT.nav=top-news.

10. Quoted in Steve Holland, "Exclusive: Trump Wants to Make Sure the U.S. Nuclear Arsenal at 'Top of the Pack,'" Reuters, February 23, 2017, https://in.reuters .com/article/usa-trump/exclusive-trump-wants-to-make-sure-u-s-nuclear-arsenal-at -top-of-the-pack-idINKBN1622IM.

11. See David E. Sanger and William J. Broad, "Trump Inherits a Secret Cyber War Against North Korean Missiles," *New York Times*, March 4, 2017, https://www.nytimes .com/2017/03/04/world/asia/north-korea-missile-program-sabotage.html?_r=0.

12. "A Conversation with James Clapper," Council on Foreign Relations, October 25, 2016, https://www.cfr.org/event/conversation-james-clapper.

13. "Transcript of Republican Debate in Miami, Full Text," CNN, March 15, 2016, https://www.cnn.com/2016/03/10/politics/republican-debate-transcript-full-text /index.html; and "Transcript of the New Hampshire GOP Debate, Annotated," *Washington Post*, February 6, 2016, https://www.washingtonpost.com/news/the-fix/wp/2016/02/06 /transcript-of-the-feb-6-gop-debate-annotated/?utm_term=.cb51e4361f7c.

14. Donald J. Trump (@realDonaldTrump), Twitter, January 2, 2017, https://twitter .com/realdonaldtrump/status/816057920223846400?lang=en.

15. Secretary of State Rex Tillerson quoted in David E. Sanger, "Rex Tillerson Rejects Talks with North Korea on Nuclear Program," *New York Times*, March 17, 2017, https://www.nytimes.com/2017/03/17/world/asia/rex-tillerson-north-korea-nuclear .html?smprod=nytcore-ipad&smid=nytcore-ipad-share&_r=0.

16. Quoted in Stephen J. Adler, Steve Holland, and Jeff Mason, "Exclusive: Trump Says 'Major, Major' Conflict with North Korea Possible, but Seeks Diplomacy," Reuters, April 27, 2017, https://www.reuters.com/article/us-usa-trump-exclusive /exclusive-trump-says-major-major-conflict-with-north-korea-possible-but-seeks -diplomacy-idUSKBN17U04E.

17. Quoted in Peter Baker and Choe Sang-Hun, "Trump Threatens 'Fire and Fury' Against North Korea If It Endangers U.S.," *New York Times*, August 8, 2017, https:// www.nytimes.com/2017/08/08/world/asia/north-korea-un-sanctions-nuclear-missile -united-nations.html.

18. Donald J. Trump (@realDonaldTrump), Twitter, August 11, 2017, https://twitter .com/realDonaldTrump/status/895970429734711298.

19. Donald J. Trump (@realDonaldTrump), Twitter, April 11, 2017, https://twitter .com/realDonaldTrump/status/851766546825347076.

20. Donald J. Trump (@realDonaldTrump), Twitter, September 3, 2017, https://twitter .com/realDonaldTrump/status/904377075049656322.

21. "Remarks by President Obama at G-20 Press Conference in Toronto, Can-ada," June 27, 2010, https://obamawhitehouse.archives.gov/the-press-office/remarks -president-obama-g-20-press-conference-toronto-canada.

22. Quoted in Daniella Silva, "Trump on North Korea's Kim Jong Un: 'He's a Pretty Smart Cookie,'" NBC News, April 30, 2017, https://www.nbcnews.com/politics/donald -trump/trump-north-korea-s-kim-jong-un-he-s-pretty-n753006.

23. Jim Mattis and Rex Tillerson, "We're Holding Pyongyang to Account," *Wall Street Journal*, August 13, 2017, https://www.wsj.com/articles/were-holding-pyongyang-to -account-1502660253.

24. Donald J. Trump (@realDonaldTrump), Twitter, October 1, 2017, https:// twitter.com/realDonaldTrump/status/914497877543735296; and Donald J. Trump (@realDonaldTrump), Twitter, October 1, 2017, https://twitter.com/realDonaldTrump /status/914497947517227008.

25. See Adam Taylor, "3 Big Questions About North Korea and No-Precondition Talks," *Washington Post*, December 13, 2017, https://www.washingtonpost.com/news /worldviews/wp/2017/12/13/3-big-questions-about-north-korea-and-no-precondition -talks/?utm_term=.85efcdab2107.

26. On China's evasion of sanctions, see, for example, Donald J. Trump (@real-DonaldTrump), Twitter, December 28, 2017, https://twitter.com/realDonaldTrump/status/946416486054285314. On Russia's unwillingness to help, see Steve Holland, Roberta Rampton, and Jeff Mason, "Exclusive: Trump Accuses Russia of Helping North Korea Evade Sanctions; Says U.S. Needs More Missile Defense," Reuters, January 17, 2018, https://www.reuters.com/article/us-usa-trump-exclusive/exclusive-trump-accuses-russia-of-helping-north-korea-evade-sanctions-says-u-s-needs-more-missile-defense-idUSKBN1F62KO.

27. "Kim Jong Un's 2018 New Year's Address," National Committee on North Korea, https://www.ncnk.org/node/1427.

28. Quoted in Rick Gladstone and David E. Sanger, "Security Council Tightens Economic Vise on North Korea, Blocking Fuel, Ships and Workers," *New York Times*, December 22, 2017, https://www.nytimes.com/2017/12/22/world/asia/north-korea-security-council-nuclear-missile-sanctions.html.

29. Quoted in Euan McKirdy, "North Korea State Media Celebrate 'Gift' to 'American Bastards,'" CNN.com, July 5, 2017, http://www.cnn.com/2017/07/05/asia/north-korea-missile-nuclear-gift/index.html.

30. Quoted in Mark Landler and Choe Sang-Hun, "North Korea Says It's Now a Nuclear State. Could That Mean It's Ready to Talk?" *New York Times*, November 29, 2017, https://www.nytimes.com/2017/11/29/world/asia/north-korea-nuclear-missile-.html.

31. "Gen. H.R. McMaster on Trump's New Iran Strategy," Fox News Sunday, October 15, 2017, http://www.foxnews.com/transcript/2017/10/15/gen-h-r-mcmaster-on-president-trumps-new-iran-strategy.html.

32. Ben Riley-Smith, "US Making Plans for 'Bloody Nose' Military Attack on North Korea," *The Daily Telegraph*, December 20, 2017, http://www.telegraph.co.uk/news/2017/12/20/exclusive-us-making-plans-bloody-nose-military-attack-north/.

33. Quoted in Erik Ortiz and Arata Yamamoto, "Sen. Lindsey Graham: Trump Says War with North Korea an Option," Nbcnews.com, August 1, 2017, https://www.nbcnews.com/news/north-korea/sen-lindsey-graham-trump-says-war-north-korea-option-n788396?icid=today_hp_NBCtopheadlines.

34. Interview, Tokyo, Japan, October 24, 2017.

35. Interview, Tokyo, Japan, October 24, 2017.

36. Moon Jae-in, *Republic of Korea Asks* (대한민국이 묻는다), published January 20, 2017, p. 342.

37. Quoted in Anna Fifield, "South Korea's Likely Next President Asks the U.S. to Respect Its Democracy," *Washington Post*, May 2, 2017, https://www.washingtonpost.com/world/south-koreas-likely-next-president-warns-the-us-not-to-meddle-in-its-democracy/2017/05/02/2295255e-29c1-11e7-9081-f5405f56d3e4_story.html?utm_term=.f759b040727c.

38. Quoted in Bryan Harris, "South Korean Presidential Hopeful Rejects U.S. Sabre-Rattling," *Financial Times*, April 11, 2017, https://www.ft.com/content/7a52b8ac-1e62-11e7-a454-ab04428977f9.

39. Quoted in Jeremy Diamond, "Trump: US Patience with the North Korean Regime 'Is Over,'" CNN.com, June 30, 2017, https://www.cnn.com/2017/06/30/politics/trump-moon-jae-in-rose-garden/index.html.

40. Interview, Seoul, South Korea, October 26, 2017.

41. Interview, Seoul, South Korea, October 26, 2017.

42. Interview, Seoul, South Korea, October 25, 2017.

43. Donald J. Trump (@realDonaldTrump), Twitter, September 3, 2017, https://twitter .com/realDonaldTrump/status/904309527381716992.

44. Quoted in Andrew Jeong, "Kim Jong Un Says He Has a Nuclear Launch Button on His Office Desk," *Wall Street Journal*, January 2, 2018, https://www.wsj.com/articles /kim-jong-un-says-he-has-a-nuclear-launch-button-on-his-office-desk-1514770845.

45. Donald J. Trump (@realDonaldTrump), Twitter, January 2, 2018, https://twitter .com/realDonaldTrump/status/948355557022420992.

46. Choe Sang-Hun and Mark Landler, "North Korea Signals Willingness to 'Denuclearize,' South Says," *New York Times*, March 6, 2018, https://www.nytimes .com/2018/03/06/world/asia/north-korea-south-nuclear-weapons.html.

47. Donald J. Trump (@realDonaldTrump), Twitter, January 4, 2018, https://twitter .com/realDonaldTrump/status/948879774277128197.

48. Quoted in Choe Sang-Hun, "South Korea's Leader Credits Trump for North Korea Talks," *New York Times*, January 10, 2018, https://www.nytimes.com/2018/01/10 /world/asia/moon-jae-in-trump-north-korea.html?rref=collection%2Fsectioncollection %2Fworld.

49. Peter Baker and Choe Sang-Hun, "With a Snap 'Yes' in Oval Office, Trump Gambles on North Korea," *New York Times*, March 10, 2018, p. A1, https://www.nytimes .com/2018/03/10/world/asia/trump-north-korea.html.

50. Donald J. Trump (@realDonaldTrump), Twitter, March 9, 2018, https://twitter .com/realDonaldTrump/status/972271520847466498.

51. Rep. Michael McCaul, "North Korea Might Negotiate in Good Faith This Time but It Would Be the First Time," Daily Caller, March 6, 2018, http://dailycaller .com/2018/03/06/north-korea-might-negotiate-in-good-faith-this-time-but-it-would -be-the-first-time/.

52. Quoted in Jonathan Cheng, "North Korea Threatens to Call off Summit, Calls Pence a 'Political Dummy,'" *Wall Street Journal*, May 22, 2018, https://www.wsj.com/articles /north-korea-threatens-to-call-off-summit-calls-pence-a-political-dummy-1527122683.

53. Quoted in Kim Jaewon, "South Korean President Moon 'Embarrassed' by Summit's Collapse," *Nikkei Asian Review*, May 25, 2018, https://asia.nikkei.com/Spotlight/North -Korea-crisis-2/South-Korean-President-Moon-embarrassed-by-summit-s-collapse.

54. Quoted in David E. Sanger, "Trump's Letter to Kim Canceling North Korea Summit Meeting, Annotated," *New York Times*, May 24, 2018, https://www.nytimes .com/2018/05/24/world/asia/read-trumps-letter-to-kim-jong-un.html.

55. Quoted in Peter Baker, "Trump Announces Summit Meeting with Kim Jong-un Is Back On," *New York Times*, June 1, 2018, https://www.nytimes.com/2018/06/01 /world/asia/trump-north-korea-summit-kim.html.

56. "Joint Statement of President Donald J. Trump of the United States of America and Chairman Kim Jong Un of the Democratic People's Republic of Korea at the Singapore Summit," Singapore, June 12, 2018, https://www.whitehouse.gov /briefings-statements/joint-statement-president-donald-j-trump-united-states-america -chairman-kim-jong-un-democratic-peoples-republic-korea-singapore-summit/.

57. Quoted in Mark Landler, "Trump and Kim See New Chapter for Nations after Summit," *New York Times*, June 11, 2018, https://www.nytimes.com/2018/06/11/world /asia/trump-kim-summitmeeting.html.

58. Donald J. Trump. "Press Conference," Singapore, June 12, 2018, https://www .whitehouse.gov/briefings-statements/press-conference-president-trump/.

59. Donald J. Trump (@realDonaldTrump), Twitter, June 13, 2018, https://twitter .com/realDonaldTrump/status/1006837823469735936.

60. Donald J. Trump (@realDonaldTrump), Twitter, June 13, 2018, https://twitter .com/realDonaldTrump/status/1006839007492308992.

61. "Transcript of the Second Debate," *New York Times*, October 10, 2016, https:// www.nytimes.com/2016/10/10/us/politics/transcript-second-debate.html.

62. "Trump: Iran Deal Horrible, but I Can Make It Good," MSNBC, September 4, 2015, http://www.msnbc.com/morning-joe/watch/trump--iran-deal-horrible--but-i -can-make-it-good-519415363853?playlist=associated.

63. Trump, "Remarks at the AIPAC Policy Conference in Washington, DC."

64. Borger, Smith, Ackerman, and Dehghan, "Trump Administration 'Officially Putting Iran on Notice,' Says Michael Flynn."

65. United Nations Security Council Resolution 2231, July 14, 2015, http://www .un.org/en/sc/2231/restrictions-ballistic.shtml.

66. Lesley Wroughton, "U.S. Says Iran Complies with Nuke Deal but Orders Review on Lifting Sanctions," Reuters, April 18, 2017, https://www.reuters.com/article/us-iran -nuclear-usa-tillerson/u-s-says-iran-complies-with-nuke-deal-but-orders-review-on -lifting-sanctions-idUSKBN17L08I?wpisrc=nl_daily202&wpmm=1.

67. Peter Baker, "Trump Recertifies Iran Nuclear Deal, but Only Reluctantly," *New York Times*, July 17, 2017, https://www.nytimes.com/2017/07/17/us/politics /trump-iran-nuclear-deal-recertify.html.

68. Press Statement, "U.S. Announces New Iran-Related Sanctions," US Department of State, Washington, DC, July 18, 2017, https://www.state.gov/r/pa/prs/ps /2017/07/272635.htm.

69. Jana Winter, Robbie Gramer, and Dan De Luce, "Trump Assigns White House Team to Target Iran Nuclear Deal, Sidelining State Department," ForeignPolicy .com, July 21, 2017, http://foreignpolicy.com/2017/07/21/trump-assigns-white-house -team-to-target-iran-nuclear-deal-sidelining-state-department/.

70. "Excerpts: Donald Trump's Interview with the *Wall Street Journal*," *Wall Street Journal*, July 25, 2017, https://blogs.wsj.com/washwire/2017/07/25/donald-trumps -interview-with-the-wall-street-journal-edited-transcript/.

71. "United Nations General Assembly–Speech by M. Emmanuel Macron, President of the Republic," New York, September 19, 2017, https://www.diplomatie.gouv.fr /en/french-foreign-policy/united-nations/united-nations-general-assembly-sessions /unga-s-72nd-session/article/united-nations-general-assembly-speech-by-m -emmanuel-macron-president-of-the.

72. Quoted in Emily Ashton, "Donald Trump Apparently Snubbed Theresa May When She Asked Him About the Iran Nuclear Deal," BuzzFeed, September 21, 2017, https://www.buzzfeed.com/emilyashton/donald-trump-apparently-snubbed-theresa -may-when-she-asked?utm_term=.jeDjWRzmm#.kjajWJr77.

73. David Nakamura and Anne Gearan, "Rex Tillerson Was Startled That Trump Told Reporters He Had Made Up His Mind on Iran Deal," *Washington Post*, September 20, 2017, https://www.washingtonpost.com/news/post-politics/wp/2017/09/20/rex-tillerson-was-startled-that-trump-told-reporters-he-had-made-up-his-mind-on-iran-deal/?utm_term=.d2303ce757f0.

74. Interview, London, February 15, 2018.

75. "Remarks at a Press Availability," US Department of State, Washington, DC, August 1, 2017, https://www.state.gov/secretary/20172018tillerson/remarks/2017/08/272979.htm.

76. Quoted in Thomas Gibbons-Neff and David E. Sanger, "Mattis Contradicts Trump on Iran Deal Ahead of Crucial Deadline," *New York Times*, October 3, 2107, https://www.nytimes.com/2017/10/03/world/middleeast/mattis-iran-deal-trump.html?smprod=nytcore-ipad&smid=nytcore-ipad-share&_r=0.

77. Quoted in Rebecca Kheel, "House Foreign Affairs Chairman: US Should Stay in Iran Deal, but 'Enforce the Hell' out of It," The Hill, October 11, 2017, http://thehill.com/policy/defense/354898-foreign-affairs-chairman-us-should-stay-in-iran-deal-but-enforce-the-hell-out.

78. Donald J. Trump, "Remarks by President Trump on Iran Strategy," White House, Washington, DC, October 13, 2017, https://www.whitehouse.gov/briefings-statements/remarks-president-trump-iran-strategy/.

79. Quoted in "Rouhani Hits Back at Trump After Nuclear Deal Speech," Al Jazeera, October 13, 2017, http://www.aljazeera.com/news/2017/10/rouhani-hits-trump-nuclear-deal-speech-171013190257102.html.

80. "Foreign Ministry Spokesperson Lu Kang's Regular Press Conference," October 17, 2017, http://www.fmprc.gov.cn/mfa_eng/xwfw_665399/s2510_665401/2511_665403/t1502395.shtml.

81. Quoted in "Russia Says Trump's 'Aggressive' Stance on Iran Doomed to Fail," Reuters, October 13, 2017, https://www.reuters.com/article/us-iran-nuclear-russia-ministry/russia-says-trumps-aggressive-stance-on-iran-doomed-to-fail-idUSKBN1CI2OH.

82. "Declaration by the Heads of State and Government of France, Germany and the United Kingdom," Prime Minister's Office, 10 Downing Street, October 13, 2017, https://www.gov.uk/government/news/declaration-by-the-heads-of-state-and-government-of-france-germany-and-the-united-kingdom.

83. Donald J. Trump, "Statement by the President on the Iran Nuclear Deal," White House, January 12, 2018, https://www.whitehouse.gov/briefings-statements/statement-president-iran-nuclear-deal/.

84. "PM Calls with President Macron and Chancellor Merkel: April 29," Statement by a Downing Street Spokesman, London, April 29, 2018, https://www.gov.uk/government/news/pm-calls-with-president-macron-and-chancellor-merkel-29-april-2018.

85. Donald J. Trump, "Remarks by President Trump on the Joint Comprehensive Plan of Action," White House, May 8, 2018, https://www.whitehouse.gov/briefings-statements/remarks-president-trump-joint-comprehensive-plan-action/.

86. Quoted in "Trump Withdrew from the Iran Deal. Here's How Republicans, Democrats, and the World Reacted," *New York Times*, May 8, 2018, https://www.nytimes

.com/2018/05/08/world/middleeast/trump-iran-deal-republicans-democrats-world
-reactions.html.

87. Indian Foreign Minister Sushma Swaraj, quoted in Nidhi Verma, "India Says It Only Follows U.N. Sanctions, Not U.S. Sanctions on Iran," May 28, 2018, Reuters, https://www.reuters.com/article/us-india-iran/india-says-it-only-follows-u-n-sanctions -not-unilateral-us-sanctions-on-iran-idUSKCN1IT0WJ.

88. Mark Landler, "Clashing Views on Iran Reflect a New Balance of Power in the Cabinet," *New York Times*, May 12, 2018, https://www.nytimes.com/2018/05/12/us/politics /trump-iran-bolton-mattis-pompeo.html?hp&action=click&pgtype=Homepage& clickSource=story-heading&module=first-column-region&region=top-news&WT.nav =top-news.

89. Quoted in Barbara Plett Usher, "Trumplomacy over Iran Leaves Europe Scrambling for Answers," BBC News, May 15, http://www.bbc.com/news/world-us-canada -44114625.

90. Quoted in "The Latest: Macron Calls US Exit from Iran Deal a 'Mistake,'" Associated Press, May 9, 2018, https://www.apnews.com/bb6dd8120b824d529132 bcd9ba9e612b.

91. "Time for Europe to Join the Resistance," Der Spiegel Online, May 11, 2018, http://www.spiegel.de/international/world/editorial-trump-deals-painful-blow-to -trans-atlantic-ties-a-1207260.html.

Chapter 9—Trade Wars Are Good, and Easy to Win

1. James Mattis, "Memorandum for the Secretary of Commerce," Undated, https://www.commerce.gov/sites/commerce.gov/files/department_of_defense_memo _response_to_steel_and_aluminum_policy_recommendations.pdf.

2. Donald J. Trump, "Remarks by President Trump in Listening Session with Representatives from the Steel and Aluminum Industry," White House, March 1, 2018, https://www.whitehouse.gov/briefings-statements/remarks-president-trump-listening -session-representatives-steel-aluminum-industry/.

3. Steven Mufson and Andrew Van Dam, "How American Steelmakers Have Survived—Without Trump's Help," *Washington Post*, March 2018, https://www .washingtonpost.com/news/wonk/wp/2018/03/06/how-american-steelmakers-have -survived-without-trumps-help/?utm_term=.3ca35f6fe494.

4. Donald J. Trump, "Remarks by President Trump in Listening Session with Representatives from the Steel and Aluminum Industry."

5. Quoted in Amanda Connolly, "Steel Tariffs: Justin Trudeau Says Move by Trump 'Makes No Sense,' Adds He Spoke with President," *Global News*, March 2, 2018, https://globalnews.ca/news/4058176/steel-tariffs-bill-morneau-donald-trump/.

6. "PM Call with President Trump: 4 March 2018," London, March 4, 2018, https://www.gov.uk/government/news/pm-call-with-president-trump-4-march-2018.

7. Quoted in Reuters Staff, "France's Macron Urges WTO Action over U.S. Steel Tariffs," Reuters, March 5, 2018, https://www.reuters.com/article/usa-trade-macron /frances-macron-urges-wto-action-over-us-steel-tariffs-idUSP6N1HS00D.

8. Quoted in Jack Ewing, "E.C.B. Shifts Guidance, as Europe Moves toward Normalcy," *New York Times*, March 7, 2018, https://www.nytimes.com/2018/03/07/business /economy/ecb-euro-italy.html.

9. Quoted in Tom Miles, "WTO Chief Makes Rare Warning of Trade War over U.S. Tariff Plan," Reuters, March 2, 2018, https://www.reuters.com/article/us-usa-trade-wto /wto-chief-makes-rare-warning-of-trade-war-over-u-s-tariff-plan-idUSKCN1GE28P.

10. Quoted in "Donald Trump Threatens Tax on European Cars in Tariff Row," DW, March 2, 2018, http://www.dw.com/en/donald-trump-threatens-tax-on-european-cars -in-tariff-row/a-42816187.

11. Donald J. Trump, *The Art of the Deal* (New York: Random House, 1987), p. 59.

12. Donald J. Trump (@realDonaldTrump), Twitter, March 2, 2018, https://twitter .com/realdonaldtrump/status/969525362580484098?lang=en.

13. Donald J. Trump (@realDonaldTrump), Twitter, March 3, 2018, https://twitter .com/realdonaldtrump/status/969994273121820672?lang=en.

14. Donald J. Trump (@realDonaldTrump), Twitter, March 5, 2018, https://twitter .com/realDonaldTrump/status/970626966004162560.

15. Donald J. Trump, "Presidential Proclamation on Adjusting Imports of Steel into the United States," White House, March 8, 2018, https://www.whitehouse.gov /presidential-actions/presidential-proclamation-adjusting-imports-steel-united-states/.

16. Quoted in "Germany Panics: Angela Merkel Admits 'Concern' over Trump Tariffs as Trump Takes Aim," Internationally News, March 9, 2018, http://www .internationallynews.com/world-news/germany-panics-angela-merkel-admits-concern -over-trump-tariffs-as-us-takes-aim/.

17. Quoted in Chieko Tsuneoka, "TPP Members Reach Agreement on Major Trade Pact," *Wall Street Journal*, January 23, 2018, https://www.wsj.com/articles/tpp-members -reach-agreement-a-year-after-u-s-exit-1516709064.

18. "Full Transcript: Donald Trump's Jobs Plan Speech."

19. David Leonhardt, "Trump Tries to Destroy the West," *New York Times*, June 10, 2018, https://www.nytimes.com/2018/06/11/opinion/trump-g7-north-korea.html.

20. "The Ten Vehicles in the Donald Trump Car Collection," RMAutobuzz.com, April 7, 2016, http://rmautobuzz.com/many-vehicles-donald-trump-car-collection/.

21. See Zeeshan Aleem, "'Another Kick in the Teeth': A Top Economist on How Trade with China Helped Elect Trump," *Vox*, March 29, 2017, https://www.vox .com/new-money/2017/3/29/15035498/autor-trump-china-trade-election; Daron Acemoglu, David Autor, David Corn, Gordon H. Hanson, and Brendan Price, "Import Competition and the Great US Employment Sag of the 2000s," *Journal of Labor Economics* 34, no. 1, pt. 2 (2016): S141–198, https://economics.mit.edu/ files/9811; and David H. Autor, David Dorn, and Gordon H. Hanson, "The China Syndrome: Local Labor Market Effects of Import Competition in the United States," *American Economic Review* 103, no. 6 (October 2013), 2121–2168, http:// economics.mit.edu/files/6613. For accessible discussions of the limits to quantify the China Shock, see Phil Levy, "Did China Trade Cost the United States 2.4 Million Jobs?" Foreign Policy, May 8, 2016, http://foreignpolicy.com/2016/05/08/did-china -trade-cost-the-united-states-2-4-million-jobs/; and Alan Reynolds, "Did the U.S.

Lose 2.4 Million Jobs from China Imports?" Cato Institute, September 15, 2016, https://www.cato.org/blog/did-china-trade-lose-24-million-factory-jobs?utm_source =Cato.

22. See Eduardo Porter, "Trade Wars Can Be a Game of Chicken. Sometimes, Literally," *New York Times*, March 13, 2018, https://www.nytimes.com/2018/03/13 /business/economy/trade-chicken.html.

23. See Edward Alden, *Failure to Adjust: How Americans Got Left Behind in the Global Economy* (Lanham, MD: Rowman and Littlefield, 2016), chap. 8.

24. Quoted in Gregory Korte, "Trump Wields His Presidential Pen, Signing Memos on Trade, Hiring, Abortion," *USA Today*, January 23, 2017, https://www.usatoday.com /story/news/politics/2017/01/23/trump-wields-his-presidential-pen-signing-orders -trade-hiring-abortion/96945308/.

25. Quoted in Charlotte Greenfield, "After U.S. Exit, Asian Nations Try to Save TPP Trade Deal," Reuters, January 23, 2017, https://www.reuters.com/article/us-usa-trump -asia/after-u-s-exit-asian-nations-try-to-save-tpp-trade-deal-idUSKBN15800V.

26. Quoted in "Chile Eyes New Deals with Pacific Trade Pact Members: Minister," Reuters, January 23, 2017, https://www.reuters.com/article/us-usa-trump-chile/chile -eyes-new-deals-with-pacific-trade-pact-members-minister-idUSKBN1572T6?il=0.

27. Quoted in Jane Patterson, "PM's Focus Still on TPP Deal," RNZ, January 24, 2017, https://www.radionz.co.nz/news/political/323021/pm's-focus-still-on-tpp-deal.

28. Quoted in Klaus Stratmann and Thomas Sigmund, "Sigmar Gabriel: Now Is the Time to Strengthen Europe," Handelsblatt Global, January 24, 2017, https:// global.handelsblatt.com/politics/sigmar-gabriel-now-is-the-time-to-strengthen -europe-688500.

29. Quoted in Josh Chin, "China Says Prepared to Lead Global Economy If Necessary," *Wall Street Journal*, January 23, 2017, https://www.wsj.com/articles/china -says-prepared-to-lead-global-economy-if-necessary-1485178890.

30. "Full Text of Xi Jinping Keynote at the World Economic Forum," CGTN, January 17, 2017, https://america.cgtn.com/2017/01/17/full-text-of-xi-jinping-keynote-at-the -world-economic-forum.

31. Quoted in Noah Barkin and Elizabeth Piper, "In Davos, Xi Makes Case for Chinese Leadership Role," Reuters, January 17, 2017, https://www.reuters.com /article/us-davos-meeting-china/in-davos-xi-makes-case-for-chinese-leadership-role -idUSKBN15118V.

32. Quoted in Matthew J. Belvedere, "Start a Trade War? Commerce's Wilbur Ross Says the U.S. Is Already in One," CNBC, March 31, 2017, https://www.cnbc .com/2017/03/31/commerces-wilbur-ross-us-is-already-in-a-trade-war.html.

33. Donald J. Trump (@realDonaldTrump), Twitter, April 16, 2017, https://twitter .com/realDonaldTrump/status/853583417916755968.

34. Quoted in Jeff Mason and David Lawder, "Trump Says He Was 'Psyched to Terminate NAFTA' but Reconsidered," Reuters, April 26, 2017, https://ca.reuters.com /article/topNews/idCAKBN17S2DG-OCATP.

35. Quoted in Parker, Rucker, Paletta, and De Young, "'I Was All Set to Terminate.'"

36. Trump, *Art of the Deal*, p. 45.

37. Neil Irwin, "Most Americans Produce Services, Not Stuff," *New York Times*, March 16, 2018, p. B1, https://www.nytimes.com/2018/03/16/upshot/most-americans -produce-services-not-stuff-trump-ignores-that-in-talking-about-trade.html.

38. "Economic Report of the President, Together with the Annual Report of the Council of Economic Advisers," White House, February 2018, p. 231, https:// www.whitehouse.gov/wp-content/uploads/2018/02/ERP_2018_Final-FINAL.pdf #page=236.

39. "Canada: U.S.-Canada Trade Facts," Office of the US Trade Representative, undated, https://ustr.gov/countries-regions/americas/canada.

40. "NAFTA and the Future of U.S.-Canadian Relations," Council on Foreign Relations, January 31, 2018, https://www.cfr.org/event/nafta-and-future-us-canada -relations; and interviews with former Mexican trade officials, Mexico City, Mexico, January 15, 2018.

41. Quoted in Binyamin Appelbaum, "U.S. Begins NAFTA Renegotiations with Harsh Words," *New York Times*, August 16, 2017, https://www.nytimes.com/2017/08/16 /business/economy/nafta-negotiations-canada-mexico.html; and Doug Palmer, Adam Behsudi, and Megan Casella, "U.S. Sets Tough Tone with Canada and Mexico as NAFTA Talks Begin," Politico, August 16, 2017, https://www.politico.com/story/2017/08/16 /us-nafta-rewrite-trade-deficits-241702.

42. Quoted in Palmer, Behsudi, and Casella, "U.S. Sets Tough Tone with Canada and Mexico as NAFTA Talks Begin."

43. "Opening Statement of USTR Robert Lighthizer at the First Round of NAFTA Renegotiations," Office of the US Trade Representative, August 16, 2017, https:// ustr.gov/about-us/policy-offices/press-office/press-releases/2017/august/opening -statement-ustr-robert-0.

44. Quoted in Joel Baglole, "NAFTA Talks Go Into Their Seventh Round. Canada Isn't Optimistic," *Washington Post*, February 25, 2018, https://www.washingtonpost.com /world/the_americas/nafta-talks-are-going-into-their-seventh-round-canada-isnt- optimistic/2018/02/24/59cb7140-1732-11e8-930c-45838ad0d77a_story.html?utm _term=.a47209fb671f.

45. Quoted in Josh Wingrove, Eric Martin, and Andrew Mayeda, "Trump's 'Poison Pill' NAFTA Proposals Threaten to Derail Talks," Bloomberg, October 11, 2017, https://www.bloomberg.com/news/articles/2017-10-11/u-s-partners-ponder-life -after-nafta-as-talks-hail-chapter-deal.

46. "CNBC Transcript: United States Secretary of Commerce Wilbur Ross Speaks with CNBC's Becky Quick on 'Closing Bell' Today," CNBC.com, October 25, 2017, https:// www.cnbc.com/2017/10/25/cnbc-exclusive-cnbc-transcript-united-states-secretary-of -commerce-wilbur-ross-speaks-with-cnbcs-becky-quick-on-closing-bell-today.html.

47. Quoted in Glen Plaskin, "Playboy Interview: Donald Trump (1990), *Playboy*, March 14, 2016, http://www.playboy.com/articles/playboy-interview-donald-trump-1990.

48. Quoted in Philip Rucker, "Trump: 'We May Terminate' U.S.-South Korea Trade Agreement," *Washington Post*, April 28, 2017, https://www.washingtonpost.com/politics /trump-we-may-terminate-us-south-korea-trade-agreement/2017/04/27/75ad1218 -2bad-11e7-a616-d7c8a68c1a66_story.html?utm_term=.8334b0bfcfe1.

49. Andrew Restuccia, "Promotion Would Give Navarro Deeper Influence over Trade Policy," Politico, February 25, 2018, https://www.politico.com/story/2018/02/25/navarro-trump-trade-tariffs-423462.

50. Quoted in Jonathan Swan, "Exclusive: Trump Vents in Oval Office, 'I Want Tariffs. Bring Me Some Tariffs!'" Axios, August 2017, https://www.axios.com/exclusive-trump-vents-in-oval-office-i-want-tariffs-bring-me-some-tariffs-1513305111-5cba21a2-6438-429a-9377-30f6c4cf2e9e.html.

51. Quoted in Julie Hirschfeld Davis, "Trump Opens Asia Trip Talking Tough in Campaign-Style Rally," *New York Times*, November 5, 2017, https://www.nytimes.com/2017/11/05/world/asia/trump-asia-japan-korea.html?rref=collection%2Fsectioncollection%2Fworld&_r=0.

52. Interview, Tokyo, October 24, 2017; and Justin Sink and Jennifer Jacobs, "Trump Pushes Japan to Buy Military Equipment, Hits Out on Trade," Bloomberg, November 5, 2017, https://www.bloomberg.com/news/articles/2017-11-06/trump-complains-of-unfair-trade-with-japan-defends-tpp-pullout.

53. Donald J. Trump (@realDonaldTrump), Twitter, November 6, 2017, https://twitter.com/realDonaldTrump/status/927645648685551616.

54. "Remarks by President Trump and President Moon of the Republic of Korea in Joint Press Conference," Seoul, Republic of Korea, White House, November 7, 2017, https://www.whitehouse.gov/briefings-statements/remarks-president-trump-president-moon-republic-korea-joint-press-conference-seoul-republic-korea/.

55. Donald J. Trump, "Remarks by President Trump at Business Event with President Xi of China, Beijing, China," White House, November 9, 2017, https://www.whitehouse.gov/briefings-statements/remarks-president-trump-business-event-president-xi-china-beijing-china/.

56. Mark Landler, Julie Hirschfield Davis, and Jane Perlez, "Trump, Aiming to Coax Xi Jinping, Bets on Flattery," *New York Times*, November 9, 2017, https://www.nytimes.com/2017/11/09/world/asia/trump-xi-jinping-north-korea.html.

57. Quoted in David Nakamura and Ashley Parker, "In Beijing, Trump Declines to Hit President Xi Jinping on Trade: 'I Don't Blame China,'" *Washington Post*, November 9, 2017, https://www.washingtonpost.com/news/post-politics/wp/2017/11/08/in-beijing-trump-lavishes-praise-on-chinese-leader-touts-great-chemistry-between-them/?utm_term=.e43b3a6fc84e.

58. Donald J. Trump, "Remarks by President Trump at APEC CEO Summit in Da Nang, Vietnam," White House, November 10, 2017, https://www.whitehouse.gov/briefings-statements/remarks-president-trump-apec-ceo-summit-da-nang-vietnam/.

59. Interview, Washington, DC, December 8, 2017.

60. Asia-Pacific Economic Cooperation, "2017 Leaders Declaration," Da Nang, Vietnam, November 11, 2017, https://www.apec.org/Meeting-Papers/Leaders-Declarations/2017/2017_aelm.

61. Donald J. Trump, "Remarks by President Trump in Press Gaggle Aboard Air Force One en Route Honolulu, Hawaii," White House, November 14, 2017, https://www.whitehouse.gov/briefings-statements/remarks-president-trump-press-gaggle-aboard-air-force-one-en-route-honolulu-hawaii/.

62. Donald J. Trump (@realDonaldTrump), Twitter, November 15, 2017, https://twitter.com/realDonaldTrump/status/930744931609694208.

63. Quoted in Landler, "Trump, the Insurgent, Breaks with 70 Years of American Foreign Policy."

64. Ian Schwartz, "Full Lou Dobbs Interview: Trump Asks What Could Be More Fake than CBS, NBC, ABC and CNN," Real Clear Politics, October 25, 2017, https://www.realclearpolitics.com/video/2017/10/25/full_lou_dobbs_interview_trump_asks_what_could_be_more_fake_than_cbs_nbc_abc_and_cnn.html.

65. Robert Farley, "Trump Wrong About WTO Record," FactCheck.org, October 27, 2017, https://www.factcheck.org/2017/10/trump-wrong-wto-record/.

66. Jacob M. Schlesinger, "Globalization in Retreat: How China Swallowed the WTO," *Wall Street Journal*, November 1, 2017, https://www.wsj.com/articles/how-china-swallowed-the-wto-1509551308.

67. Edward Alden, "Trump, China, and Steel Tariffs: The Day the WTO Died," CFR.org, March 9, 2018, https://www.cfr.org/blog/trump-china-and-steel-tariffs-day-wto-died.

68. See, for example, Doug Palmer, "Why Steel Tariffs Failed When Bush Was President," Politico, March 7, 2018, https://www.politico.com/story/2018/03/07/steel-tariffs-trump-bush-391426.

69. David J. Lynch and Damian Paletta, "Trump Announces Steel and Aluminum Tariffs Thursday over Objections from Advisers and Republicans," *Washington Post*, March 1, 2018, https://www.washingtonpost.com/news/business/wp/2018/03/01/white-house-planning-major-announcement-thursday-on-steel-and-aluminum-imports/?utm_term=.b04e96d3bfe4.

70. Aaron Sheldrick, "Asia's Biggest Exporters Bristle over U.S. Tariffs, Fanning Trade War Fears," Reuters, March 8, 2018, https://www.reuters.com/article/us-usa-trade-china/asias-biggest-exporters-bristle-over-u-s-tariffs-fanning-trade-war-fears-idUSKCN1GL03Q.

71. Quoted in Anne Gearan and Karoun Demirjian, "Trump Trade Adviser Says No Exceptions for Allies on New Aluminum and Steel Tariffs," *Washington Post*, March 4, 2018, https://www.washingtonpost.com/news/post-politics/wp/2018/03/04/trump-trade-adviser-says-no-exceptions-for-allies-on-new-aluminum-and-steel-tariffs/?utm_term=.6eecd736727b.

72. Donald J. Trump, "Remarks by President Trump at Signing of a Presidential Memorandum Targeting China's Economic Aggression," White House, March 22, 2018, https://www.whitehouse.gov/briefings-statements/remarks-president-trump-signing-presidential-memorandum-targeting-chinas-economic-aggression/.

73. "President Donald J. Trump's Summit Meeting with Prime Minister Shinzo Abe," White House, April 18, 2018, https://www.whitehouse.gov/briefings-statements/president-donald-j-trumps-summit-meeting-prime-minister-shinzo-abe/.

74. Donald J. Trump, "Remarks by President Trump on the Infrastructure Initiative," Richfield, OH, March 30, 2018, https://www.whitehouse.gov/briefings-statements/remarks-president-trump-infrastructure-initiative/.

75. Ana Swanson, "Trump Initiates Trade Inquiry that Could Lead to Tariffs on Foreign Cars," *New York Times*, May 23, 2018, https://www.nytimes.com/2018/05/23

/business/trump-tariffs-foreign-autos.html?rref=collection%2Fbyline%2Fana-swanson &action=click&contentCollection=undefined&region=stream&module=stream _unit&version=latest&contentPlacement=4&pgtype=collection.

76. "Meet the Press—June 3, 2018," https://www.nbcnews.com/meet-the-press /meet-press-june-3-2018-n879611.

77. Quoted in Ana Swanson, "White House to Impose Metals Tariffs on E.U., Canada and Mexico," *New York Times*, May 31, 2018, https://www.nytimes.com/2018/05/31/us /politics/trump-aluminum-steel-tariffs.html.

78. Quoted in David Reid, "'Protectionism, Pure and Simple:' Europe Promises WTO Action over US Tariffs," CNBC, May 31, 2018, https://www.cnbc.com/2018/05/31 /europe-reacts-angrily-to-us-tariff-protectionism-promises-wto-action.html.

79. Quoted in Michael D. Shear, "Anger Flares as G-7 Heads to Quebec," *New York Times*, June 7, 2018, https://www.nytimes.com/2018/06/07/us/politics/trump-allies-g7 -summit-meeting.html.

80. Donald J. Trump (@RealDonaldTrump), Twitter, June 8, 2018, https://twitter .com/realDonaldTrump/status/1005033088202756097.

81. Donald J. Trump, "Press Conference by Donald J. Trump after G7 Summit," White House, June 9, 2018, https://www.whitehouse.gov/briefings-statements /press-conference-president-trump-g7-summit/.

82. Michael D. Shear and Catherine Porter, "Trump Refuses to Sign G-7 Statement and Calls Trudeau 'Weak,'" *New York Times*, June 10, 2018, https://www.nytimes .com/2018/06/09/world/americas/donald-trump-g7-nafta.html.

83. Quoted in Louis Nelson, "White House Sees 'Short-Term Pain' as Trump Stokes China Trade War," *Politico*, April 4, 2018, https://www.politico.com/story/2018/04/04 /china-tariffs-us-imports-trump-500163.

84. Donald J. Trump (@RealDonaldTrump), Twitter, April 4, 2018, https://twitter .com/realDonaldTrump/status/981521901079146499.

85. Quoted in David J. Lynch and Emily Ruahala, "Trump Pushes Back on Fears of a Trade War with China," *Washington Post*, April 4, 2018, https://www.washingtonpost .com/world/asia_pacific/china-fires-back-at-trump-with-tariffs-on-106-us-products -including-soybeans-cars/2018/04/04/338134f4-37d8-11e8-b57c-9445cc4dfa5e_story .html?utm_term=.d2878950047b.

86. Quoted in Julie Pace and Josh Boak, "Analysis: Wall Street's Patience with Trump Has Its Limits," AP News, April 5, 2018, https://www.apnews.com/b25184 1f52ff4281834b3884064e7663/Analysis:-Wall-Street's-patience-with-Trump-has-its -limits.

87. Gabriel Wildau and Shawn Donnan, "US Demands China Cut Trade Deficit by \$200 Billion," *Financial Times*, May 4, 2018, https://www.ft.com/content/d0eb3e4a -4f77-11e8-a7a9-37318e776bab.

88. "Joint Statement of the United States and China regarding Trade Consulta- tions," White House, May 19, 2018, https://www.whitehouse.gov/briefings-statements /joint-statement-united-states-china-regarding-trade-consultations/.

89. Quoted in Ana Swanson and Alan Rappeport, "U.S. Suspends Tariffs on China, Stoking Fears of a Loss of Leverage," *New York Times*, May 20, 2108, https://www .nytimes.com/2018/05/20/us/politics/mnuchin-kudlow-china-trade.html.

90. Donald J. Trump (@RealDonaldTrump), Twitter, May 21, 2018, https://twitter.com/realDonaldTrump/status/998526637657546753.

91. Ana Swanson and James Tankersley, "China Pledges $200 Billion in U.S. Purchases by Overhauling Trade Rules," *New York Times*, May 18, 2108, https://www.nytimes.com/2018/05/18/us/politics/trump-china-trade-talks.html.

92. Natasha Turak, "China Says It Hasn't Offered to Cut Its Trade Surplus with the US by $200 Billion," CNBC, May 18, 2019, https://www.cnbc.com/2018/05/18/china-did-not-offer-trump-a-200-billion-trade-surplus-cut-ministry.html.

93. "President Donald J. Trump is Confronting China's Unfair Trade Policies," White House, May 29, https://www.whitehouse.gov/briefings-statements/president-donald-j-trump-confronting-chinas-unfair-trade-policies/.

94. Quoted in Ana Swanson, "U.S. Moves ahead with Trade Measures on China," *Austin-American Statesman*, May 30, 2018, https://www.pressreader.com/usa/austin-american-statesman/20180530/282084867481494.

95. Quoted in Jacob Pramuk, "Trump to Slap 25% Tariffs on Up to $50 Billion of Chinese Goods; China Retaliates," CNBC, June 15, 2018, https://www.cnbc.com/2018/06/15/trump-administration-to-slap-a-25-percent-tariff-on-50-billion-of-chinese-goods-threatens-more.html.

96. Quoted in Jen Kirby, "Trump Says He'll Impose Tariffs in a 'Loving Way,'" *Vox*, March 6, 2017, https://www.vox.com/2018/3/6/17087714/trump-tariffs-sweden-steel-aluminum.

97. David J. Lynch, "Trump Said He'd Shrink the Trade Deficit with China. It Just Hit a Record High," *Washington Post*, February 6, 2018, https://www.washingtonpost.com/news/wonk/wp/2018/02/06/trump-said-hed-shrink-the-trade-deficit-with-china-it-just-hit-a-record-high/?utm_term=.a32fd1eabe06.

98. See, for example, Binyamin Appelbaum, "Trump's Tax Cuts Are Likely to Increase Trade Deficit," *New York Times*, November 17, 2017, https://www.nytimes.com/2017/11/17/us/politics/tax-cuts-trade-deficit-trump.html.

99. Trump, *Art of the Deal*, p. 335.

Chapter 10—Winning Again

1. Donald J. Trump, "Remarks by President Trump and President Putin of the Russian Federation in Joint Press Conference," July 16, 2018, https://www.whitehouse.gov/briefings-statements/remarks-president-trump-president-putin-russian-federation-joint-press-conference/.

2. Trump, "Transcript: The Inaugural Address," January 20, 2017, https://www.whitehouse.gov/briefings-statements/the-inaugural-a

3. "Read John McCain's Statement on Trump's Meeting with Putin," *Boston Globe*, July 16, 2018, https://www.bostonglobe.com/news/politics/2018/07/16/read-john-mccain-statement-trump-meeting-with-putin/U88mUGY32Yilx3F4OlibNM/story.html.

4. John O. Brennan (@JohnBrennan), Twitter, July 16, 2018, https://twitter.com/JohnBrennan/status/1018885971104985093.

5. Quoted in Connor O'Brien, "'I Was Just Doing My Job,' Coats Says, Defending Russian Election Meddling Findings," Politico, July 19, 2018, https://www.politico.com /story/2018/07/19/coats-russia-election-meddling-trump-7

6. Quoted in Jonathan Lemire and Jill Colvin, "President Trump Kicks Off NATO Summit by Claiming Germany Is `Controlled' by Russia," *Time*, July 11, 2018, http:// time.com/5335412/trump-nato-summit-germany-controlled-russia/.

7. Quoted in Michael Birnbaum and Philip Rucker, "At NATO, Trump Claims Allies Make New Defense Spending Commitments After He Upends Summit," *Washington Post*, July 12, 2018, https://www.washingtonpost.com/world/europe/trump-upends -nato-summit-demanding-immediate-spending-increases-or-he-willdo-his-own -thing/2018/07/12/a3818cc6-7f0a-11e8-a63f-7b5d2aba7ac5_story.html?utm_term =.d5d407b3ae24.

8. Donald J. Trump, "Remarks by President Trump at Press Conference After NATO Summit," July 12, 2018, https://www.whitehouse.gov/briefings-statements/remarks -president-trump-press-conference-nato-summit-brussels-belgium/; and NATO, "Brussels Summit Declaration," July 11, 2018, https://www.nato.int/cps/en/natohq /official_texts_156624.

9. Quoted in Tom Newton Dunn, "Trump's Brexit Blast: Donald Trump Told Theresa May How to Do Brexit `But She Wrecked It'—and Says That the US Trade Deal Is Off," Sun, July 13, 2018, https://www.thesun.co.uk/news/6766531/trump-may-brexit -us-deal-off/.

10. "'I Think the European Union Is a Foe,' Trump Says ahead of Putin Meeting in Helsinki," CBS News, July 15, 2018, https://www.cbsnews.com/news/donald-trump -interview-cbs-news-european-union-is-a-foe-ahead-of-putin-meeting-in-helsinki -jeff-glor/.

11. "Remarks by President Trump and President Putin of the Russian Federation in Joint Press Conference."

12. Donald J. Trump, "Remarks by President Trump in Meeting with Members of Congress," White House, July 17, 2018, https://www.whitehouse.gov/briefings-state ments/remarks-president-trump-meeting-members-congress/.

13. Quoted in Scott Neuman, "In Interview, Trump Appears to Question NATO's 'Collective Defense' Clause," NPR, July 19, 2018, https://www.npr.org/2018/07/19 /630361006/in-interview-trump-appears-to-question-natos-collective-defense-clause.

14. Salena Zito, "Taking Trump Seriously, Not Literally," *The Atlantic*, September 23, 2016, https://www.theatlantic.com/politics/archive/2016/09/trump-makes-his-case -in-pittsburgh/501335/.

15. Quoted in Nash Jenkins, "President Trump Gives Himself 'A+' Grade for his First Year in Office in Rambling Fox Interview," *Time*, April 26, 2018, http://time .com/5255631/donald-trump-gives-himself-a-fox-interview/.

16. Quoted in Julie Hirshfeld Davis, "Trump Drops Push for Immediate Withdrawal of Troops from Syria," *New York Times*, April 4, 2018, https://www.nytimes .com/2018/04/04/world/middleeast/trump-syria-troops.html.

17. Trump, "Remarks by the President on the Strategy in Afghanistan and South Asia."

18. Jeff Stein, "Deficit to Top $1 Trillion Per Year by 2020, CBO Says," *Washington Post*, April 9, 2018, https://www.washingtonpost.com/business/economy/deficit-to-top -1-trillion-per-year-by-2020-cbo-says/2018/04/09/93c331d4-3c0e-11e8-a7d1 -e4efec6389f0_story.html?utm_term=.bea849097672.

19. Damian Paletta and Erica Werner, "How Congress's and Trump's Latest Deficit Binge Paved the Way for the Next One," *Washington Post*, April 16, 2018, https:// www.washingtonpost.com/business/economy/how-congress-and-trumps-latest-deficit -binge-paved-the-way-for-the-next-one/2018/04/15/2d198608-3f2f-11e8-8d53 -eba0ed2371cc_story.html?utm_term=.4fc5f2e12194.

20. CBO, *The Budget and Economic Outlook* (Washington: Congressional Budget Office, April 2018), p. 87, https://www.cbo.gov/system/files/115th-congress-2017-2018/reports /53651-outlook.pdf.

21. American Association for the Advancement of Sciences, *FY2018 R&D Appropriations Dashboard*, https://www.aaas.org/page/fy-2018-rd-appropriations-dashboard.

22. Quoted in Brianna Gurciullo, "Trump Promises to Build the Infrastructure 'of Tomorrow,'" Politico, July 22, 2016, https://www.politico.com/tipsheets/morning -transportation/2016/07/trump-promises-to-build-the-infrastructure-of-tomorrow -215475; and Harry Cheadle, "Remember When Trump Made All Those Promises about Infrastructure?" Vice, May 10, 2018, https://www.vice.com/en_us/article/ywez3v/trump -broke-one-of-his-biggest-campaign-pledges-and-no-one-cares.

23. Dan Merica and Brandon Miller, "Trump's False Claims about the Polar Ice Caps," CNN, January 29, 2018, https://www.cnn.com/2018/01/29/politics/trump-false -claim-polar-ice-caps/index.html.

24. David E. Sanger, "Trump Grappling with Risks of Proceeding with North Korea Meeting," *New York Times*, May 21, 2018, p. A1, https://www.nytimes.com/2018/05/20 /us/politics/trump-north-korea-nuclear.html.

25. Quoted in John Wagner, "'It's about the Attitude': Trump Says He Doesn't Have to Prepare Much for His Summit with North Korea's Leader," *Washington Post*, June 7, 2018, https://www.washingtonpost.com/politics/its-about-the-attitude -trump-says-he-doesnt-have-to-prepare-much-for-his-summit-with-north-koreas -leader/2018/06/07/2af3ec7e-6a6d-11e8-9e38-24e693b38637_story.html?utm _term=.30ee03ebe7ce.

26. Quoted in Bill Chapell, "'I'm the Only One That Matters,' Trump Says of State Dept. Job Vacancies," NPR, November 3, 2017, https://www.npr.org/sections/thetwo -way/2017/11/03/561797675/im-the-only-one-that-matters-trump-says-of-state -dept-job-vacancies.

27. *National Security Strategy of the United States of America*, December 2017, p. 2, https://www.whitehouse.gov/wp-content/uploads/2017/12/NSS-Final-12-18-2017 -0905.pdf.

28. "Remarks of President Trump and President Juncker of the European Commission in Joint Press Statements," White House, July 25, 2018, https://www.whitehouse .gov/briefings-statements/remarks-president-trump-president-juncker-european -commission-joint-press-statements/.

29. Interview with a European Ambassador, Washington DC, April 2018.

30. See for example, "Remarks by the President and Secretary General Stolten-berg of NATO before Bilateral Meeting," White House, May 17, 2018, https://www.whitehouse.gov/briefings-statements/remarks-president-trump-secretary-general-stoltenberg-nato-bilateral-meeting/.

31. Quoted in Robert Fife and Michelle Zilio, "Freeland Questions U.S. Leader-ship, Says Canada Must Set Own Course," *Globe and Mail*, June 6, 2017, https://www.theglobeandmail.com/news/politics/canada-must-re-invest-in-military-as-us-withdraws-from-world-freeland-says/article35212024/.

32. Quoted in Madeleine Albright, *Madam Secretary: A Memoir* (New York: Harper Perennial, 2003), p. 186.

33. Quoted in Glasser, "Trump's Year of Living Dangerously: It's Worse Than You Think."

34. Quoted in Steve Erlanger, "Feeling that Trump Will 'Say Anything,' Europe Is Less Restrained, Too," *New York Times*, July 9, 2017, https://www.nytimes.com/2017/07/09/world/europe/donald-trump-europe.html?hp&action=click&pgtype=Homepage&clickSource=story-heading&module=first-column-region&region=top-news&WT.nav=top-news&_r=0.

35. Quoted in Chris Giles and Michael Hunter, "Mnuchin Backs Weaker Dollar in Break with Tradition," *Financial Times*, January 24, 2018, https://www.ft.com/content/84c19cd8-00eb-11e8-9650-9c0ad2d7c5b5.

36. Quoted in Jacob Heilbrunn, "Trump Isn't Fighting American Decline. He's Speeding It Up," *Washington Post*, May 25, 2018, https://www.washingtonpost.com/news/global-opinions/wp/2018/05/25/trump-isnt-fighting-american-decline-hes-speeding-it-up/?utm_term=.734cddd2280b.

37. Quoted in Michael Birnbaum, "E.U. Leader Lights into Trump: 'With Friends Like That, Who Needs Enemies?' *Washington Post*, May 16, https://www.washingtonpost.com/news/worldviews/wp/2018/05/16/e-u-leader-lights-into-trump-with-friends-like-that-who-needs-enemies/?utm_term=.04f483a28dc5.

38. Quoted in Steven Erlanger, "Europe, Again Humiliated by Trump, Strug-gles to Defend Its Interests," *New York Times*, May 9, 2018, https://www.nytimes.com/2018/05/09/world/europe/europe-iran-trump.html.

39. Quoted in ibid.

40. Richard Wike, Bruce Stokes, Jacob Poushter, and Janell Fetterole, "U.S. Image Suffers as Publics Around World Question Trump's Leadership," Pew Research Cen-ter, June 26, 2017, http://www.pewglobal.org/2017/06/26/u-s-image-suffers-as-publics-around-world-question-trumps-leadership/.

41. *Rating World Leaders 2018: The U.S. Versus Germany, China and Russia*, Gallup, 2018, https://www.politico.com/f/?id=00000161-0647-da3c-a371-867f6acc0001.

42. The phrase is Charles Kupchan's.

43. Quoted in Ben Smith, "Macron Says Trump Will Likely Kill the Iran deal," BuzzFeed, April 25, 2018, https://www.buzzfeed.com/bensmith/macron-says-trump-will-likely-kill-the-iran-deal?utm_term=.yhGagnGnd#.lf9BPJGJw.

44. Heiko Maas, "Courage to Stand Up for Europe--#EuropeUnited," June 13, 2018, https://www.auswaertiges-amt.de/en/newsroom/news/maas-europeunited/2106528.

45. International Trade Administration, *Jobs Supported by State Exports*, December 2017, https://www.trade.gov/mas/ian/build/groups/public/@tg_ian/documents/webcontent/tg_ian_005558.pdf.

46. Komal Sri-Kumar, "Trump's Trade Swagger Leaves Markets Unimpressed," Bloomberg, November 13, 2017, https://www.bloomberg.com/view/articles/2017-11-14/trump-s-trade-swagger-leaves-markets-unimpressed.

47. See Adam Behsudi, "Trump's Trade Pullout Roils Rural America," Politico, August 7, 2017, https://www.politico.com/magazine/story/2017/08/07/trump-tpp-deal-withdrawal-trade-effects-215459.

48. Quoted in Peter Landers, "Strange Bedfellows: Trump Trade Fight Brings Japan and China Together," *Wall Street Journal*, June 18, 2018, https://www.wsj.com/articles/japan-views-china-as-ally-in-trump-trade-fight-1529336612.

49. Jason Schwartz, "Trump's 'Fake News' Mantra a Hit with Despots," Politico, December 8, 2017, https://www.politico.com/story/2017/12/08/trump-fake-news-despots-287129.

50. Quoted in Jon Lee Anderson, "Behind the Wall," *New Yorker*, May 28, 2018, p. 30, https://www.newyorker.com/magazine/2018/05/28/the-diplomat-who-quit-the-trump-administration.

51. See Niall Ferguson, "Donald Trump's New World Order," *American Interest*, vol. 12, no. 4, March–April 2017, https://www.the-american-interest.com/2016/11/21/donald-trumps-new-world-order/; and Arthur Herman, "The New Era of Global Stability," *Wall Street Journal*, December 19, 2017, https://www.wsj.com/articles/the-new-era-of-global-stability-1513728226.

52. See Haass, *A World in Disarray.*

53. Sergey Lavrov, "Address at the 53rd Munich Security Conference," Munich, February 18, 2017, http://www.mid.ru/en/press_service/minister_speeches/-/asset_publisher/7OvQR5KJWVmR/content/id/2648249.

54. Xi Jinping, "Secure a Decisive Victory in Building a Moderately Prosperous Society in All Respects and Strive for the Great Success of Socialism with Chinese Characteristics for a New Era," Address to the 19th National Congress of the Communist Party of China, Beijing, October 18, 2017, http://www.xinhuanet.com/english/download/Xi_Jinping's_report_at_19th_CPC_National_Congress.pdf.

55. Quoted in Osnos, "Making China Great Again."

56. Interview, October 24, 2017.

57. Quoted in Hannah Beech, "Vietnam, in a Bind, Tries to Chart a Course between U.S. and China," *New York Times*, November 11, 2017, https://www.nytimes.com/2017/11/11/world/asia/vietnam-china-us.html.

58. Quoted in "Latin America Should Not Rely on China: U.S. Secretary of State Tillerson," *Reuters*, February 1, 2018, https://www.reuters.com/article/us-usa-diplomacy-latam-china/latin-america-should-not-rely-on-china-u-s-secretary-of-state-tillerson-idUSKBN1FL6D5.

59. Quoted in Ernest Londoño, Shasta Darlington, and Daniel Politi, "'World Upside Down': As Trump Pushes Tariffs, Latin America Links Up," *New York Times*,

March 19, 2018, p. A5, https://www.nytimes.com/2018/03/18/world/americas/trump
-trade-latin-america.html.

60. Quoted in Gardiner Harris, "Tillerson, in Africa, Dodges Questions on Vulgarity
and Trolling," *New York Times*, March 8, 2018, https://www.nytimes.com/2018/03/08
/world/africa/tillerson-africa-shithole-russia.html.

61. Quoted in Osnos, "Making China Great Again," p. 39.

62. "Chapter Two: Comparative Defence Statistics," *The Military Balance* 118, no. 1
(2018): 19, doi:10.1080/04597222.2017.1271208.

63. Quoted in Washington Post Staff, "Tillerson Emphasizes Allies in in First
Remarks Since Firing but Doesn't Mention Trump," *Washington Post*, March 13, 2018,
https://www.washingtonpost.com/news/post-politics/wp/2018/03/13/tillerson-glosses
-over-trump-in-first-remarks-since-firing-emphasizing-allies-and-partners/?utm_term
=.315d090b2c0d.

64. Alex Gray, "The World's 10 Biggest Economies," World Economic Forum,
May 9, 2017, https://www.weforum.org/agenda/2017/03/worlds-biggest-economies
-in-2017/.

65. "Chapter Two: Comparative Defence Statistics," p. 19.

66. Quoted in Alissa J. Rubin and Adam Nossiter, "Macron Takes a Risk in Courting
Trump, but Has Little to Show for It," *New York Times*, April 22, 2018, https://www
.nytimes.com/2018/04/22/world/europe/donald-trump-emmanuel-macron.html.

67. *What Americans Think About America First.*

68. Interview, October 23, 2017.

69. Transcript, "Trump: Witch Hunt Drove a Phony Wedge between US, Russia,"
Fox News, July 16, 2018, http://www.foxnews.com/transcript/2018/07/16/trump
-witch-hunt-drove-phony-wedge-between-us-russia.html.

70. Lena Felton, "Read President Trump's U.S. Naval Academy Commencement
Address," *The Atlantic*, May 25, 2018, https://www.theatlantic.com/politics
/archive/2018/05/read-president-trumps-us-naval-academy-commencement-address
/561206/.

Index

Credit: Courtesy of the author

Ivo H. Daalder is president of the Chicago Council on Global Affairs. Prior to joining the council, Daalder served as the ambassador to the North Atlantic Treaty Organization under President Obama and on the National Security Council staff of President Clinton. His previous book with James Lindsay, *America Unbound: The Bush Revolution in Foreign Policy*, was selected as a top book of 2003 by *The Economist*. Daalder is a frequent contributor to the opinion pages of the world's leading newspapers and a regular commentator on international affairs on television and radio.

Credit: Kaveh Sardari

James M. Lindsay is senior vice president, director of studies, and Maurice R. Greenberg chair at the Council on Foreign Relations. He served on the National Security Council Staff of President Clinton and has written widely on American foreign policy and international relations. His previous book with Ivo Daalder, *America Unbound: The Bush Revolution in Foreign Policy*, was awarded the 2003 Lionel Gelber Prize for the best nonfiction book in English on foreign affairs. He blogs at *The Water's Edge*, hosts *The President's Inbox* podcast, and cohosts *The World Next Week* podcast.

PublicAffairs is a publishing house founded in 1997. It is a tribute to the standards, values, and flair of three persons who have served as mentors to countless reporters, writers, editors, and book people of all kinds, including me.

I. F. STONE, proprietor of *I. F. Stone's Weekly*, combined a commitment to the First Amendment with entrepreneurial zeal and reporting skill and became one of the great independent journalists in American history. At the age of eighty, Izzy published *The Trial of Socrates*, which was a national bestseller. He wrote the book after he taught himself ancient Greek.

BENJAMIN C. BRADLEE was for nearly thirty years the charismatic editorial leader of *The Washington Post*. It was Ben who gave the *Post* the range and courage to pursue such historic issues as Watergate. He supported his reporters with a tenacity that made them fearless and it is no accident that so many became authors of influential, best-selling books.

ROBERT L. BERNSTEIN, the chief executive of Random House for more than a quarter century, guided one of the nation's premier publishing houses. Bob was personally responsible for many books of political dissent and argument that challenged tyranny around the globe. He is also the founder and longtime chair of Human Rights Watch, one of the most respected human rights organizations in the world.

·   ·   ·

For fifty years, the banner of Public Affairs Press was carried by its owner Morris B. Schnapper, who published Gandhi, Nasser, Toynbee, Truman, and about 1,500 other authors. In 1983, Schnapper was described by *The Washington Post* as "a redoubtable gadfly." His legacy will endure in the books to come.

Peter Osnos, *Founder*